American Accent Training

A guide to speaking and pronouncing
American English for everyone who speaks
English as a second language

THIRD EDITION • ANN COOK

Illustrated by Holly Forsyth, Nathalie Jean-Barth, Randy Gossman,
Erik Scott, and Nelson Afian

Audio by Voice Trax Studios with Marcus Harwell

BARRON'S

This book is dedicated to Nate Cook and Benjamin Ferguson.

Also, my special thanks for their extensive contributions to Benjamin Ferguson, Nate Cook, Bob Freud, Kathryn Reed, Dr. Hani Al Sharif, Nazeeh Melhem, Dr. Lauren Enzie, and Deborah Pless.

All inquiries should be addressed to:
Barron's Educational Series, Inc.
250 Wireless Boulevard
Hauppauge, NY 11788
www.barronseduc.com

ISBN: 978-1-4380-7165-7 (book and CD package)

Library of Congress Control Number: 2011945147

PRINTED IN THE UNITED STATES OF AMERICA
9 8

Table of Contents

Read This First

Welcome to *American Accent Training*. This book and CD set is designed to get you started on your American accent. We'll follow the book and go through the 25 lessons and all the exercises step-by-step. Everything is explained and a complete Answer Key is in the back of the text.

What Is Accent?

Accent is a combination of four main components: *voice quality*, *intonation* (speech music), *liaisons* (word connections), and *pronunciation* (the spoken sounds of vowels, consonants, and combinations). As you go along, you'll notice that you're being asked to look at accent in a different way. You'll also realize that the grammar you studied before and this accent you're studying now are completely different.

Part of the difference is that grammar and vocabulary are systematic and structured—the *letter* of the language. Accent, on the other hand, is free form, intuitive, and creative—more the *spirit* of the language. So, thinking of music, feeling, and flow, let your mouth relax into the American accent.

Can I Learn a New Accent?

Can a person actually learn a new accent? Many people feel that after a certain age, it's just not possible. Can classical musicians play jazz? If they practice, of course they can! For your American accent, it's just a matter of learning and practicing techniques this book and CD set will teach you. It is up to you to use them or not. How well you do depends mainly on how open and willing you are to sounding different from the way you have sounded all your life.

A very important thing you need to remember is that you can use your accent to say *what* you mean and *how* you mean it. Word stress conveys meaning through tone or feeling, which can be much more important than the actual words that you use. We'll cover the expression of these feelings through intonation in the first lesson.

You may have noticed that I talk fast and often run my words together. You've probably heard enough "English-teacher English"—where ... everything ... is ... pronounced without having to listen too carefully. That's why on the CDs we're going to talk just like the native speakers that we are, in a normal conversational tone.

Native speakers often tell people who are learning English to "slow down" and to "speak clearly." This is meant with the best of intentions, but it is exactly the opposite of what a student really needs to do. If you speak fairly quickly, with strong intonation and good voice quality, you will be understood more easily. To illustrate this point, you will hear a Chinese gentleman first trying to speak slowly and carefully and then repeating the same two sentences quickly and with clear intonation. The difference makes him sound like a completely different person.

Hello, my name is Raymond Choon.

You may have to listen to this CD a couple of times to catch everything. To help you, every word on the CD is also written in the book. By seeing and hearing simultaneously, you'll learn to reconcile the differences between the *appearance* of English (spelling) and the *sound* of English (pronunciation and the other aspects of accent).

The CD leaves a rather short pause for you to repeat into. The point of this is to get you responding quickly and without spending too much time thinking about your response.

Accent Versus Pronunciation

Many people equate *accent* with *pronunciation*. I don't feel this to be true at all. America is a big country, and while the pronunciation varies from the East Coast to the West Coast, from the southern to the northern states, two components that are uniquely American stay basically the same—the speech music, or *intonation*, and the word connections, or *liaisons*. Throughout this program, we will focus on them. In the latter part of the book we will work on pronunciation concepts, such as Cat? Caught? Cut? and Betty Bought a Bit of Better Butter; we also will work our way through some of the difficult sounds, such as **TH**, the American **R**, the **L**, **V**, and **Z**.

"Which Accent Is Correct?"

American Accent Training was created to help people "sound American" for lectures, interviews, teaching, business situations, and general daily communication. Although America has many regional pronunciation differences, the accent you will learn is that of standard American English as spoken and understood by the majority of educated native speakers in the United States. Don't worry that you will sound slangy or too casual because you most definitely won't. This is the way a professor lectures to a class, the way a national newscaster broadcasts, the way that is most comfortable and familiar to the majority of native speakers.

"Why Is My Accent So Bad?"

Learners can be seriously hampered by a negative outlook, so I'll address this very important point early. First, your accent is *not* bad; it is nonstandard to the American ear. There is a joke that goes: What do you call a person who can speak three languages? *Trilingual.* What do you call a person who can speak two languages? *Bilingual.* What do you call a person who can only speak one language? *American.*

Every language is equally valid or good, so every accent is *good.* The average American, however, truly does have a hard time understanding a nonstandard accent. George Bernard Shaw said that the English and Americans are two people *divided* by the same language!

Some students learn to overpronounce English because they naturally want to say the word as it is written. Too often an English teacher may allow this, perhaps thinking that colloquial American English is unsophisticated, unrefined, or even incorrect. Not so at all! Just as you don't say the **T** in *listen*, the **TT** in *better* is pronounced **D**, *bedder.* Any other pronunciation will sound foreign, strange, wrong, or different to a native speaker.

Less than It Appears ... More than It Appears

As you will see in Exercise 4-23, "Squeezed-Out Syllables," on page 41, some words appear to have three or more syllables, but all of them are not actually spoken. For example, *business* is not (*bi•zi•*ness), but rather (*biz•*ness).

Just when you get used to eliminating whole syllables from words, you're going to come across other words that look as if they have only one syllable but really need to be said with as many as three! In addition, the inserted syllables are filled with letters that are not in the written word. I'll give you two examples of this strange phenomenon: *Pool* looks like a nice, one-syllable word, but if you say it this way, at best it will sound like *pull* and at worst will be unintelligible to your listener. For clear comprehension, you need to say three syllables (pu/wuh/luh). Where did that **W** come from? It's certainly not written down anywhere, but it is there just as definitely as the **P** is there. The second example is a word like *feel.* If you say just the letters that you see, it will sound more like *fill.* You need to say (fee/yuh/luh). Is that really a **Y**? Yes. These mysterious semivowels are explained under Liaison Rule 3 in Chapter 11. They can appear either inside a word as you have seen or between words as you will learn.

Language Is Fluent and Fluid

Just like your own language, conversational English has a very smooth, fluid sound. Imagine that you are walking along a dry riverbed with your eyes closed. Every time you come to a rock, you trip over it, stop, continue, and trip over the next rock. This is how the average foreigner speaks English. It is slow, awkward, and even painful. Now imagine that you are a great river rushing through that same riverbed—rocks are no problem, are they? You just slide over and around them without ever breaking your smooth flow. It is *this* feeling that I want you to capture in English.

Changing your old speech habits is very similar to changing from a stick shift to an automatic transmission. Yes, you continue to reach for the gearshift for a while, and your foot still tries to find the clutch pedal, but this soon phases itself out. In the same way, you may still say "telephone **call**" (kohl) instead of (kahl) for a while, but this too will soon pass.

You will also have to think about your speech more than you do now. In the same way that you were very aware and self-conscious when you first learned to drive, you will eventually relax and deal with the various components simultaneously.

A new accent is an adventure. Be bold! Exaggerate wildly! You may worry that Americans will laugh at you for putting on an accent, but I guarantee you, they won't even notice. They'll just think that you've finally learned to "talk right." Good luck with your new accent!

A Few Words on Pronunciation

CD 1 Track 2

I'd like to introduce you to the pronunciation guide outlines in the following chart. There aren't too many characters that are different from the standard alphabet, but just so you'll be familiar with them, look at the chart. It shows eight *tense* vowels and six *lax* vowels and semivowels.

Tense Vowels? Lax Vowels?

In some books, tense vowels are called *long* and lax vowels are called *short*. Since you will be learning how to lengthen vowels when they come before a voiced consonant, it would be confusing to say that *hen* has a long, short vowel. It is more descriptive to say that it has a lax vowel that is doubled or lengthened.

Tense Vowels				Lax Vowels			
Symbol	Sound	Spelling	Example	Symbol	Sound	Spelling	Example
ā	ɛi	take	tāk	ɛ	eh	get	gɛt
ē	ee	eat	ēt	i	ih	it	it
ī	äi	ice	īs	ü	ih + uh	took	tük
ō	ou	hope	hōp	ə	uh	some	səm
ū	ooh	smooth	smūth				
ä	ah	caught	kät	**Semivowels**			
æ	ä + ɛ	cat	kæt	ər	er	her	hər
æo	æ + o	down	dæon	ᵊl	ul	dull	dəᵊl

Although this may look like a lot of characters to learn, there are really only four new ones: **æ, ä, ə,** and **ü.** Under Tense Vowels, you'll notice that the vowels that say their own name simply have a line over them: **ā, ē, ī, ō, ū.** There are three other tense vowels. First, **ä,** is pronounced like the sound you make when the doctor wants to see your throat, or when you loosen a tight belt and sit down in a soft chair—*aaaaaaaah!* Next, you'll find **æ,** a combination of the tense vowel **ä** and the lax vowel **ɛ.** It is similar to the noise that a goat or a lamb makes. The last one is **æo,** a combination of **æ** and **o.** This is a very common sound, usually written as *ow* or *ou* in words like *down* or *round*.

A *tense vowel* requires you to use a lot of facial muscles to produce it. If you say **ē,** you must stretch your lips back; for **ū** you must round your lips forward; for **ä** you drop your jaw down; for **æ** you will drop your jaw far down and back; for **ā** bring your lips back and drop your jaw a bit; for **ī** drop your jaw for the *ah* part of the sound and pull it back up for the *ee* part; and for **ō** round the lips, drop the jaw, and pull back up into **ū.** An American **ō** is really **ōū.**

▶ Now you try it. Repeat after me. **ē, ū, ā, æ, ä, ī, ō.**

A *lax vowel,* on the other hand, is very reduced. In fact, you don't need to move your face at all. You only need to move the back of your tongue and your throat. These sounds are very different from most other languages.

Under Lax Vowels, there are four reduced vowel sounds, starting with the Greek letter epsilon **ε**, pronounced *eh*; **i** pronounced *ih*; and **ü** pronounced *ü*, which is a combination of *ih* and *uh*; and the schwa, **ə**, pronounced *uh*—the softest, most reduced, most relaxed sound that we can produce. *It is also the most common sound in English.* The semivowels are the American **R** (pronounced *er*, which is the schwa plus **R**) and the American **L** (which is the schwa plus **L**). Vowels will be covered in greater detail in Chapters 3, 10, 12, 18, and 20.

Voiced Consonants? Unvoiced Consonants?

A consonant is a sound that causes two points of your mouth to come into contact, in three locations—the *lips*, the *tip of the tongue*, and the *throat*. A consonant can either be *unvoiced* (whispered) or *voiced* (spoken), and it can appear at the beginning, middle, or end of a word. You'll notice that for some categories, a particular sound doesn't exist in English.

Beginning		Middle		End	
Whispered	Spoken	Whispered	Spoken	Whispered	Spoken
parry	**b**ury	a**pp**le	a**b**le	mo**p**	mo**b**
ferry	**v**ery	a**f**raid	a**v**oid	of**f**	o**f**
stew	**z**oo	ra**c**es	rai**s**es	fa**c**e	pha**s**e
sheet	■	pre**ss**ure	plea**s**ure	cru**sh**	gara**ge**
two	**d**o	pe**t**al	pe**d**al	no**t**	no**d**
choke	**j**oke	gau**ch**o	gou**g**er	ri**ch**	ri**dge**
think	**th**at	e**th**er	ei**th**er	too**th**	smoo**th**
come	**g**um	bi**ck**er	bi**gg**er	pi**ck**	pi**g**
■	■	a**cc**ent	e**x**it	ta**x**	ta**gs**
■	**y**es	■	pla**y**er	■	da**y**
■	**w**ool	■	sho**w**er	■	no**w**
his	■	a**h**ead	■	■	■
■	**l**ate	■	co**ll**ect	■	towe**l**
■	**r**ate	■	co**rr**ect	■	towe**r**
■	**m**e	■	swi**mm**er	■	sa**m**e
■	**n**ext	■	co**nn**ect	■	ma**n**
■	■	■	fi**n**ger	■	ri**ng**

Pronunciation Points

1. In many dictionaries, you may find a character that looks like an upside-down V (ʌ) and another character that is an upside-down *e* (ə), the *schwa*. There is a linguistic distinction between the two, but they are *pronounced* exactly the same. Since you can't hear the difference between these two sounds, we'll just be using the upside-down *e* to indicate the schwa sound. It is pronounced *uh*.

2. The second point is that we do not differentiate between **ä** and **ɔ**. The **ä** is pronounced *ah*. The backward C (ɔ) is more or less pronounced *aw*. This *aw* sound has a "back East" sound to it, and as it's not common to the entire United States, it won't be included here.

3. **R** can be considered a *semivowel*. One characteristic of a vowel is that nothing in the mouth touches anything else. **R** definitely falls into that category. So in the exercises throughout the book it will be treated not so much as a consonant but as a vowel.

4. The *ow* sound is usually indicated by **äu**, which would be *ah + ooh*. This may have been accurate at some point in some locations, but the sound is now generally **æo**. *Town* is **tæon**, *how* is **hæo**, *loud* is **læod**, and so on.

5. Besides *voiced* and *unvoiced*, there are two words that come up in pronunciation. These are *sibilant* and *plosive*. When you say the **s** sound, you can feel the air *sliding* out over the tip of your tongue—this is a sibilant. When you say the **p** sound, you can feel the air *popping* out from between your lips—this is a plosive. Be aware that there are two sounds that are sometimes mistakenly taught as sibilants but are actually plosives: **th** and **v**.

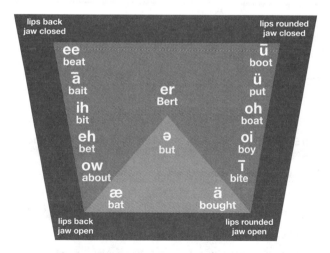

6. For particular points of pronunciation that pertain to your own language, refer to the Nationality Guides in the back of the book.

Throughout this text, we will be using three symbols
to indicate three separate actions:

▶ Indicates a command or a suggestion.

◀ Indicates the beep tone.

✗ Indicates that you need to turn the CD on or off, back up, or pause.

Telephone Tutoring

Preliminary Diagnostic Analysis

CD 1 Track 3

This is a speech analysis to identify the strengths and weaknesses of your American accent. If you are studying American Accent Training on your own, contact toll-free 1 **(800) 457-4255** or **AmericanAccent.com** for a referral to a qualified telephone analyst. The diagnostic analysis is designed to evaluate your current speech patterns to let you know where your accent is standard and nonstandard.

Hello, my name is _____. I'm taking American Accent Training. There's a lot to learn, but I hope to make it as enjoyable as possible. I should pick up on the American intonation pattern pretty easily, although the only way to get it is to practice all of the time.

1. walk, all, long, caught
2. cat, matter, laugh
3. take, say, fail
4. get, any, says, fell
5. ice, I'll, sky
6. tick, fill, will
7. teak, feel, wheel
8. work, first, learn, turn
9. tuck, fun, medicine, indicate
10. too, fool, wooed
11. took, full, would
12. woke, told, so, roll
13. out, house, round
14. loyal, choice, oil

A	B	C	D	E	F
1. pit	1. bit	1. staple	1. stable	1. cap	1. cab
2. fear	2. veer	2. refers	2. reverse	2. half	2. have
3. sue	3. zoo	3. faces	3. phases	3. race	3. raise
4. sheer	▬	4. cashew	4. casual	4. rush	4. rouge
5. tin	5. din	5. metal	5. medal	5. hat	5. had
6. chin	6. gin	6. catcher	6. cadger	6. rich	6. ridge
7. thin	7. then	7. ether	7. either	7. bath	7. bathe
8. cut	8. gut	8. bicker	8. bigger	8. tack	8. tag
9. yellow	9. race	9. million	9. correction	9. say	9. sore
10. would	10. breed	10. coward	10. surprise	10. how	10. peeper
11. him	11. man	11. reheat	11. summer	11. soul	11. palm
12. lace	12. name	12. collection	12. runner	12. people	12. can
13. bleed	▬	13. supplies	13. kingdom	13. sink	13. sing

1. Make him get it.
2. Let her get your keys.
3. You've got to work on it, don't you?
4. Soup or salad?

1. Maykim **ged**dit.
2. Ledder getcher **keez**.
3. Yoov gädda **wr** kä nit, doan choo?
4. Super **salad**?

1. Betty bought a bit of better butter.

2. Beddy bada bida bedder budder.

3. Italian   Italy
4. attack   attic
5. atomic   atom
6. photography   photograph

7. bet   bed

Chapter 1

> Shoulders back, chin up, deepen your voice and project it out!

The American Sound

Voice Quality

CD 1 Track 4

You know how you hear a voice across a crowded room and you can just tell that it's American? What's at play there? To answer that question, let's first define our terms: What *is* voice quality and the American sound? It's a combination of vocal placement and cadence. This means a throaty sound and a stairstep intonation.

Listen to British comedian Eddie Izzard imitate the American accent. Notice how his voice moves back in his throat and down in his chest when he's imitating the American accent. This throaty quality is an essential characteristic. There's even a fancy word to describe it—*rhoticity*—which is that solid **R** as in *hard* and *far*. There are regional dialects that are notable for lacking rhoticity, such as the classic Bostonian *Pahk yah cah in Hahvahd Yahd* for *Park your car in Harvard Yard*, but the overwhelming majority of Americans growl out the **R**.

Intonation, voice quality, and phrasing all contribute to the uniquely American voice, along with a casual, relaxed attitude. This relaxation causes American English to differ from the crisper sounds of British English. Within voice quality, you'll be adjusting your volume (a little louder vs. muted or murmured), pitch (high pitched vs. a deeper register), air flow (popped, hissed, or buzzed), and where the voice is generated (throat and chest vs. head and nose).

Americans tend to be a little louder than you're accustomed to. The stereotypical American is louder, a little brasher, more boisterous, immediately friendly, informal, and slightly jokey. It's important to project your voice with more force than usual and you'll need more breath to push it out. Kids are loud, right? Things stick in their heads because they yell them out. Yell this out! In the privacy of your home, car, or mountaintop, get out and yell some of these sounds and practice sentences so that you can get it really in your head. Don't be afraid to exaggerate and go further than you think the American accent actually is. This will help you embrace the sound.

Music

CD 1 Track 5

Even if you can't sing, you'll recognize the correlation between song and speech music. We're going to listen a range from high to low.

The singer's natural voice is in the middle range, so for him, the highs and lows don't feel natural, just as deepening your voice won't feel natural for you in the beginning. You'll have to practice and get comfortable with it. (See also Chapter 4.)

Pitch / Sound

CD 1 Track 6

Let's transition from song to speech. Interestingly, languages are spoken at different pitches, so it's important to recognize the pitch you're coming from as well as the pitch you're heading toward. Even though there are millions of English speakers, both male and female, there is a general pitch range into which English falls. Listen to this audio clip, ranging from a Japanese woman speaking at a very high pitch, to an Arabic man speaking in a much deeper register. You'll notice that English is in the middle.

Generally speaking, to Americans, a higher pitch indicates stress or tension, and they will respond accordingly, even if you are not stressed. Of course, speaking in a second language can be stressful, so make a conscious effort to match your speaking voice in English to your deepest voice in your own language.

The Daddy Voice
CD 1 Track 7

Americans are culturally programmed to trust the deep voices of authority. In a study from McMaster University in Canada, published in the *Journal of Evolution and Human Behavior*, researchers found that men with lower-pitched voices are found to be more dominant and attractive than are men with higher-pitched voices. They found that lower-pitched voices were associated with favorable personality traits more often than were higher-pitched voices. Listeners were asked to assess the attractiveness, honesty, leadership potential and intelligence—among other qualities—of the speakers. For nearly every attribute they were asked to rate, participants were significantly more likely to prefer the deeper voice.

Think of national broadcasters and the deep mellifluous tones they use. If you deepen your voice, you'll find that Americans become more respectful and attentive. To capture this voice, hark back to when your Dad would call you in for dinner (even if this was never the case). Put your shoulders back, your chest out, take a deep breath and say, *Hey! Get in here!* Notice how that feels physically and mentally. If you come in through the Daddy Voice, you'll probably have a less negative reaction than just by deepening your voice randomly, to which we've had people say, *I sound like a monster! I sound like a gangster!* This is not the direction we want to push you in, but rather the calm, reassuring voice of authority figure. Shoulders back, chin up, chest out, project from your diaphragm, and relax your throat.

Sound/Pronunciation
CD 1 Track 8

In the pronunciation sections, we'll be working on a sound that is produced deep in the throat—the American **R**. In Chapter 12, we study two tense vowels, æ and ä, and the completely neutral schwa, ə (*cat*, *caught*, *cut*). The æ sound has a tendency to sound a little nasal all on its own, and when other vowels are nasalized as well, it puts your whole voice in the wrong place. This is an opportune moment, then, to go into the quality of your voice. In my observation, when people speak a foreign language, they tense up their throat, so their whole communication style sounds forced, pinched, strained, artificial, or nasal. The foreign speaker's voice is also generally higher pitched than would be considered desirable. To practice the difference between high pitch and lower pitch, work on **uh-oh**. In addition to pitch, this exercise will let you discover the difference between a tinny, nasal tone and a deep, rich, mellifluous, basso profundo tone. The tilde (~) is used to indicate a nasal sound. If you try to deepen your voice by expanding your throat, you'll end up with an odd, hollow sound.

Exercise 1-1: Shifting Your Voice Position	CD 1 Track 9

*Pinch your nose closed and say æ. You should feel a high vibration in your nasal passages, as well as in your fingers. Now, continue holding your nose, and completely relax your throat—allow an **ah** sound to flow from deep in your chest. There should be no vibration in your nose at all. Go back and forth several times. Next, we practice flowing from one position to the other, so you can feel exactly when it changes from a nasal sound to a deep, rich schwa. Remember how it was imitating a man's voice when you were little? Do that, pinch your nose, and repeat after me.*

Nose			Throat			Chest
ãæ ▸	ãæ ▸	ãä ▸	ä ▸	ə ▸	ə	

Here, we will practice the same progression, but we will stick with the same sound, æ.

Nose			Throat			Chest
ãæ ▸	ãæ ▸	æ ▸	æ ▸	æ ▸	æ	

As you will see in Chapter 24, there are three nasal consonants, **m**, **n**, and **ng**. These have non-nasal counterparts, **m/b**, **n/d**, **ng/g**. We're going to practice totally denasalizing your voice for a moment, which means turning the nasals into the other consonants. We'll read the same sentence three times. The first will be quite nasal. The second will sound like you have a cold. The third will have appropriate nasal consonants but denasalized vowels. Repeat after me.

Nasal	Hollow	Normal
Mãry might need money.	Berry bite deed buddy.	Mary might need money.

The Underlying Hum
CD 1 Track 10

The underlying hum is quite important and it, too, has to do with your throat. You want to keep the vibration going from one word to the next, gluing the whole phrase together. If words are the train, the hum is the tracks. After applying this technique, a Lebanese doctor was told by his own wife, "Your accent has changed! You're adding extra sounds as if you are filling in the blanks between the words. There's like this background music going on." Exactly! There are no blanks between the words, and there is a continuous hum. (See also Chapter 11.)

I Closed My Eyes and Listened Carefully
CD 1 Track 11

The secret to finally getting the American accent you want is just to *listen*. The most successful speakers say, "I closed my eyes and listened carefully." So while the sentence **Bob and Sam brought a good book** may be hard to pronounce at first as **Bäb an Sæm brädə güd bük**, if you close your eyes and listen to the individual sounds, you will hear the way it actually *is* and not the way it's *spelled*. (See also Chapter 8.)

Listening Comprehension
CD 1 Track 12

We perceive based on past experiences. We're more likely to hear what we *expect* to hear. Everyone thinks that native speakers catch everything when they listen, but actually, they don't. An American listening to the lyric in the classic hymn, **Gladly the cross-eyed bear** might not realize that the actual words are **Gladly the cross I'd bear**, or others like **There's a bathroom on the right** (There's a bad moon on the rise) from *Bad Moon Rising*, and **'Scuze me while I kiss this guy** ('Scuze me while I kiss the sky) from *Purple Haze*. How you hear the language determines how you will speak it. Let's listen for some pure sounds.

Exercise 1-2: The American Sound — CD 1 Track 13

Listen to each of the sounds in **bäbee bädə bäik***. Now, say it quickly and smoothly, and write what you think the standard English spelling is.*

_____

Now when you hear, **Bobby bought a bike**, you'll know that it's spelled one way and pronounced another. **Bäbee bädə bäik** doesn't *look* like English, but if you pronounce the words according to the spelling, it really, really won't *sound* like English!

Go-To Phrase — CD 1 Track 14

Here's a quick trick. When I put on a German accent, I pick out a few sounds that are particular to that language, and a phrase that contains them, such as **Germans will have to work on the V & W**. I then tighten my lips and from the front of my mouth say, **Cheumans vill haff too veuk ohn zee Fee ent Doppel yu**. It may not be perfect, but it certainly gets me in the ballpark.

American English is generated in the back of the mouth and the throat. A couple of go-to phrases in English, to get you in the zone, are *Bob got a water bottle*, *Sam sat back and laughed*, or *Rory ran around*.

Variety Is the Spice of Life — CD 1 Track 15

There's the American sound, and then there's sounding American. An important aspect of the American sound is the heavy use of synonyms. We consider it awkward, both in speech and in writing, for a single word or phrase to be repeated more than twice. Twelve times is disconcerting, as in this writing sample from a Vietnamese physiologist.

*I live in **Dorchester**, Massachusetts which is in the Northeast of the United States. **Dorchester** is just south of Boston. As an urban city, **Dorchester** is very crowded. **Dorchester** is a poor city. It is known for crimes, drugs and gangsters. Most of people living in **Dorchester** are African American, Hispanic, and Asian. There is still a good number of white people living in **Dorchester**. JFK library and University of Massachusetts Boston are located in **Dorchester**. Every year, **Dorchester** residents celebrate **Dorchester** Day on the first Sunday of June. The parade on **Dorchester** Avenue is the main event of the celebration. The Mayor of Boston, Massachusetts Governor and other local political candidates usually attend the event to gain support from **Dorchester** residents. **Dorchester** Day Parade usually lasts until 2PM in the afternoon.*

Rewritten to have an acceptable number of synonyms:

*I live in **Dorchester**, Massachusetts which is in the Northeast of the United States. This urban satellite is just south of Boston. As an urban city, it's very poor and crowded. It is known for crimes, drugs and gangsters. Most of people living here are African American, Hispanic, and Asian, but there is still a good number of white people. JFK library and University of Massachusetts Boston are located here. Every year, the residents celebrate **Dorchester** Day on the first Sunday of June. The parade on **Dorchester** Avenue is the main event of the celebration. The Mayor of Boston, Massachusetts Governor and other local political candidates usually attend the event to gain support from local residents. The parade usually lasts until 2PM in the afternoon.*

Variety also applies to active listening, so instead of having one phrase and overusing it, have at least five to ten different responses that you've practiced.

1. Ah, I see...	6. Really?	11. Is that a fact?
2. Oh, that's interesting!	7. Oh, yeah!	12. You don't say.
3. Hmm, tell me more.	8. Right.	13. Wow, that's weird!
4. Got it!	9. Fair enough.	14. Oh, no!
5. Gotcha!	10. Good point, I can see that.	15. That's too bad.

Intonation and Attitude

CD 1 Track 16

There are certain sounds in any language that are considered nonsense syllables yet impart a large amount of information to the informed listener. Each language has a different set of these sounds, such as **eto ne** in Japanese, **em** in Spanish, **eu** in French, and **um** in English. In this particular case, these are the sounds that a native speaker makes when he is thinking out loud—holding the floor, but not yet committing to actually speaking.

Exercise 1-3: Nonverbal Intonation

CD 1 Track 17

The top eight are the most common nonword communication sounds. They can all be nasalized or not, and said with the mouth open or closed. Intonation is the important factor here. Repeat after me.

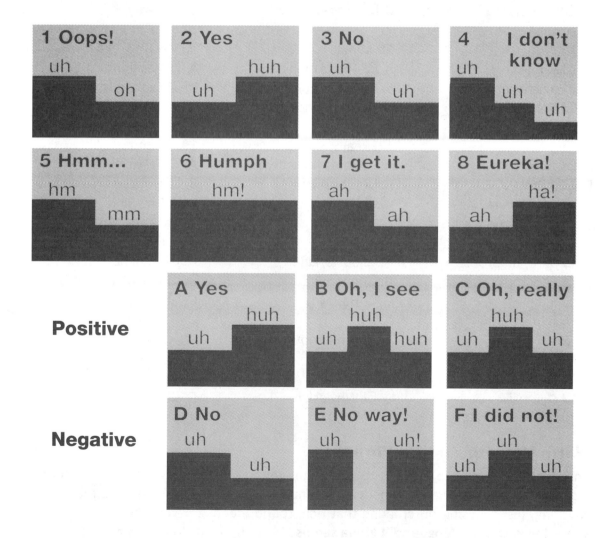

Exercise 1-4: Sounds of Empathy   CD 1 Track 18

Let's see how well you interpret emotionally meaningful words. Check Answer Key beginning on page 210.

1. Okay
A. ❑ Got it!
B. ❑ Uneasy
C. ❑ Depressed

2. Okay
A. ❑ Surprised
B. ❑ Cheerful
C. ❑ Impatient

3. Okay
A. ❑ What a good idea!
B. ❑ Whatever
C. ❑ Doubtful

4. Thanks
A. ❑ Sarcastic
B. ❑ Appreciative
C. ❑ Unsure

5. Fine
A. ❑ Great!
B. ❑ Annoyed
C. ❑ I don't care...

6. Uh-huh
A. ❑ Sure, no problem
B. ❑ I do, too!
C. ❑ Really?

7. No
A. ❑ Absolutely not!
B. ❑ How ridiculous
C. ❑ Defensive

8. Sure
A. ❑ Disbelieving
B. ❑ Worried
C. ❑ Quickly agreeable

9. Yeah
A. ❑ Positive
B. ❑ Unsure
C. ❑ Supportive

10. Sooo
A. ❑ Expecting more info
B. ❑ Impatient
C. ❑ Uneasy

11. What
A. ❑ That's funny
B. ❑ Not caring
C. ❑ Uh-oh, not again

12. Really
A. ❑ Barely attentive
B. ❑ Is that true?
C. ❑ Bored

13. Well
A. ❑ Sorta/kinda
B. ❑ Annoyed
C. ❑ Happy

14. I don't know
A. ❑ Curious
B. ❑ Casual
C. ❑ Why ask me?!

15. Hey
A. ❑ Shy
B. ❑ Canned enthusiasm
C. ❑ Bored

16. Yes
A. ❑ Confused
B. ❑ Go on...
C. ❑ Great joy

17. Sorry
A. ❑ Not sorry at all
B. ❑ Apologetic
C. ❑ Perky

18. Okay
A. ❑ Resigned
B. ❑ Excited
C. ❑ Sure, why not?

19. Hmmm
A. ❑ What?!
B. ❑ Not so sure
C. ❑ Thinking

20. I know
A. ❑ Nonchalant
B. ❑ Knowing
C. ❑ Defensive

21. Oh
A. ❑ Happy
B. ❑ Disappointed
C. ❑ Confused

Warm Up with Run-Up Phrases   CD 1 Track 19

Another trick to oil the joints is to pick some general intro phrases and string them all together with as strong an American accent as possible, without ever actually saying anything, just focusing on creating that rich, round, deep American sound ... **Well, you know, I was just thinking, and it kinda seems like, uhh, what do you think about**...

> Don't overthink it —
> just do it.

Chapter 2

Psycholinguistics

CD 1 Track 20

So You're In a Tough Relationship with English; Let's Talk About That!

Maybe you've tried to pick up an American accent before and it made you uncomfortable. Maybe your family thinks that you shouldn't change. Maybe you've tried and failed, and now you're frustrated. Whatever the reason, you've got an unsatisfying relationship with English. We're here to fix that.

Let's Get Your Head in the Right Place

Learning a whole language is indeed a big deal, but you've already done all the heavy lifting, having learned the grammar and vocabulary. Right now, we're just doing the fine-tuning and working on your accent. Here's what you should expect after the first one to six weeks (depending on your diligence).

CD 1 Track 21

There are two ways to pick up the accent: all at once or step-by-step. CD 1 Track 22 There's the do-it-now people and the people who like to change slowly, thinking that there is no validity to things that happen quickly to them. People don't think it's real if it's fast. But that's the Nike® slogan, "Just do it!" You know you can, and even if it is faster than you expect, it's still valid. It's all about behavior modeling. You don't have to believe it, you just have to do it.

All at Once

Just do it! Listen to the sounds and rhythms. Capture some essential elements, and go!

Step-by-Step

Apply each technique one by one to develop your voice quality, pronunciation, intonation, phrasing, and linking. After you have mastered each of these elements, work on integrating them into speech.

Which method will work best for you? We'll try the all-at-once way first to see if we can jump-start you with this shortcut. This isn't so much about the American accent as much as it's about you doing pure mimicry. Don't think. Don't overanalyze. Just imitate exactly what you hear in every aspect—voice quality, pronunciation, rhythm, phrasing, and word flow.

Exercise 2-1: Pure Mimicry

CD 1 Track 23

Listen to this heavy Australian accent, record yourself, and compare the two. (If you don't have a recorder handy, go to AmericanAccent.com/recorder.)

CD 1 Track 24

Please call Stella.

CD 1 Track 25

When comparing your recording with our Aussie friend, see if you copied his nasality, used *plays* for the pronunciation of *please*, and included the distinctive phrasing as he finishes up the sentence. If your recording matches closely and you were comfortable with the process, go to Chapter 3 and get started. If it wasn't entirely satisfying for you, or your recording didn't sound like him, let's take a moment to think about who you are, and how you learn best.

Exercise 2-2: Are You Steadfast or Freewheeling?　　　**CD 1 Track 26**

Answer the following questions with a check mark in the appropriate box.

1. Would you rather answer...
   - ❑ An essay question
   - ❑ A multiple-choice question

2. Do you...
   - ❑ Start from yes
   - ❑ Start from no

3. Do you prefer solutions that are...
   - ❑ Open-ended, abstract, and subject to interpretation
   - ❑ Clear-cut, precise, and objective

4. Are you...
   - ❑ Comfortable with a flexible time frame with constant updates
   - ❑ More deadline oriented

5. Do you prefer to...
   - ❑ Follow another person's lead
   - ❑ Do things your own way

If you selected the second option two or more times, try this experiment. Just for today, when someone says something to you, practice temporarily suspending judgment. Respond with, "Hmm, that's interesting," "Tell me more," or "You could be right." Not only will this help you listen better, it will also make you a better conversationalist and open your mind to picking up and using this accent.

Exercise 2-3: Mimicry　　　**CD 1 Track 27**

Say the following sentence out loud:

CD 1 Track 28

There was a time when people really had a way with words.

CD 1 Track 29

Did you say it out loud (not to yourself, actually out loud)? If you did, go on to the next exercise. If not, let's talk about why you didn't. As we all know, *stubborn* is a negative word, and nobody wants to attribute a negative word to himself or herself. As the famous curmudgeon Bertrand Russell said, "**I** am firm. **You** are obstinate. **He** is a pig-headed fool." Interestingly, stubbornness has both *positive* (consistent, reliable, persistent) and *negative* (stubborn, inflexible, rigid) aspects.

Think back in your life to a time when persistence paid off. It may have been following through on an idea to successful fruition or overcoming apparently insurmountable odds on something important to you. Own that, it's yours. One of my favorite responses was when I asked a successful businessman if he'd had everything handed to him, if building his business had been easy or if he'd had to fight to succeed. "Fight?!" he barked, "I've had to kill!"

Now, however, we're going to look at how stubbornness can get in your way. Stubbornness isn't necessarily something that just happens later in life, but is often an innate trait. Many of us have a deep-seated feeling of what is *right*, and it's hard to go against this. If you're a visual learner, chances are you did well on spelling tests, and so you have a sense of the *rightness* of spelling. It can be checked and validated. Speech, however, may seem very fluid and free form to you. For this process, however, you need to embrace the *rightness* of phonetic spelling for speech as much as you embrace the *rightness* of spelling for written English and the *rightness* of mathematical notation for numbers.

Sometimes you're not being stubborn—you really *do* forget because you're focusing on **what** you're saying instead of **how** you're saying it. To illustrate this, a researcher had a problem with the door of the lab refrigeration unit, whose tall upright handle had come loose. Not having time to fix it, he decided to open it by pulling on the side. Not five minutes later, he went back to grab some more vials and opened the fridge with the handle. It came completely loose and clonked him on the head! This time, he knew he had to remember, so he put a note right on the handle to remind himself. And again, a few minutes later, when he went back to get another vial, he grabbed the handle and hit himself on the head again. Clearly he needed a more dramatic solution. He took a whole page of newspaper and covered the entire handle of the fridge, so that the next time he mindlessly grabbed the handle, the newspaper crackled, and he realized what he was about to do. It's not like he *wanted* to get hit in the head, he just kept forgetting because he was focused on the **goal** and not the **process**. Sometimes people speaking English are so focused on the end product of using words in conversation, like he was in the end product of getting vials out of the fridge, that they forget to include the accent and pronunciation.

Think, Then Act

CD 1 Track 30

When you have learned the techniques, but forget to apply them in speech, you are **acting** before **thinking**. In order to train yourself to think first, devise a strategy that works for you. For the researcher, it was putting a sheet of newspaper over the fridge handle. For you, it might be taking a deep breath before speaking, counting to three, pulling on a rubber band, or even the old school standby: a string around your finger. The point is, while you are internalizing these new sounds and rhythms, to create a stopgap measure to get you to focus on the process and not so much the goal.

The Four Stages of Learning

Let's look at the transition you will be going through.

1. Unconscious incompetence (you don't even know you're making mistakes).
2. Conscious incompetence (you're aware, but you don't know how to fix them).
3. Conscious competence (when you focus really hard, you're actually pretty good).
4. Unconscious competence (you've internalized the concepts, and it's second nature).

You're most likely edging from **2** to **3**. To get to **4**, the key is consistent practice—a minimum of 15 minutes per day, plus applying the techniques whenever you talk.

Exercise 2-4: Correlating Sounds & Phonetic Transcription CD 1 Track 31

Listen to this sound and correlate it with this phonetic transcription:

CD 1 Track 32

gäddit

Repeat this sound and notice the open **ah** sound of **gä**, the way the tip of your tongue flicks on the bumps on the top of your mouth, and the fact that the air doesn't pop out at the end of the word. Listen to the audio and say this out loud ten times. (See also Chapter 8.)

Exercise 2-5: Correlating Phonetic Transcription & Regular Spelling CD 1 Track 33

Listen to this sound and correlate it with this phonetic transcription:

gäddit Got it!

Using the exact same sounds as before, observe how different the spelling is. Listen to the audio and say this out loud ten times.

Skidiz CD 1 Track 34

Let me tell you a little story about how I came to "get" word connections in French, or as they like to call them, liaisons. I stumbled upon the word **skidiz** and was amazed that it could represent **ce qu'ils disent**. *Wow! That looks different!* I thought to myself. *They'll never understand me if I say it like that.* Fortunately, my empirical side prevailed and I thought, *Okay, fine, I'll try it, even if it's just to prove that it doesn't work.*

 I was in Marseilles, so I combined it with the local pronunciation of **Je ne sais pas** and managed to work **Sheh pah skidiz** in as a conversational response. Whoa! To my huge surprise it worked, and the person started talking to me in real French and not baby language. That led me to part two of the epiphany: *Yikes, if I do this, it'll totally raise their expectations of how well I speak*, and then, *Ahh, I'm talking the way I want them to talk to me, so I can understand them more easily!*

 Once I realized how I'd been sabotaging myself, I started trusting the phonetics and stopped basing my pronunciation on spelling. My confidence went up because thought follows behavior, and my new behavior resulted in more sophisticated, intelligent conversations. People didn't have to talk down to my language level but could actually talk with me at my conversational level. It's my goal that you have that same realization with **gäddit**. My job is to give the epiphany. Your job is to hold on and use it. (See also Chapter 10.)

Exercise 2-6: Gathering that Empirical Evidence CD 1 Track 35

Trusting in this method is an important component of how successful you will be, so we're going to do a short trust exercise. Take this phrase out into the world, and use it exactly the way it's presented here. Try it out on coworkers and friends. Watch how they respond to you now that they can hear you playing with the language a little.

gäddit / Got it!

We tend to think of language primarily as a *tool*,  Instead, start playing around in the English *toy box*.

or as a *weapon*.

Play with the sounds, rhythms, and patterns. Have fun! You'll find that some of the inhibitions fall away, and your linguistic adaptability kicks in.

Phonetic Transcription = Mathematical Notation   CD 1 Track 36

If you accept that **2 x 2** can also be written **2²**, you are comfortable with multiple labels for a single concept. This is the same principle as the word **cat** also being written as **kæt**.

Here is a simple two-part rule for the letter **o**:

> **1.** In a *one-syllable* word, **o** sounds like **ä** (unless the word ends in **e**):
> hot, lost, Tom, Bob, dot com
>
> **2.** In a *stressed* syllable, **o** also sounds like **ä**:
> possible, Holland, philosophy

Here is a two-part rule for the letter **a**:

> **1.** In a *one-syllable* word, **a** sounds like **æ** (unless the word ends in **e**):
> cat, Sam, drab
>
> **2.** In a *stressed* syllable, **a** sounds like **æ**:
> rational, manager, catastrophe

(For more on these two vowels, see Chapter 12.)

Once you have internalized the basic rules of phonetics, you need to diligently, persistently, and *stubbornly* apply them universally. In computing terms, think of doing a global **Search All** and **Replace**.

Some people have an initial aversion to reading phonetics because it's new and confusing. *It doesn't even look like English!* This is where we're going to have you practice some of that open-mindedness and trust. Accept that if you read the phonetics, you *will* have an American accent.

An accountant kept making the same pronunciation errors in English over and over again. Asked why, her response was consistently, "I forgot!" When asked if she forgot arithmetic, the answer was, "Of course not, that would make my life miserable."

Well, not applying the phonetics was making her life miserable!

Over-Confidence

Counterintuitively, it's sometimes overconfidence that gets in a person's way. You're used to the positive rewards of doing things quickly and independently—an algebraic equation, a sales report with a high closing rate, a dissertation. Because you're good at what you do, you can skip over certain details. However, if you try to rush through speaking English you'll end up skipping crucial details. Furthermore, if you only rely on your *own* judgment about your accent, particularly if it's spelling based, you're going to fall far short of the mark.

What to do about it? Start from scratch and make a conscious effort to get rid of your preconceptions. Put yourself in the position of knowing nothing about pronunciation, intonation, voice quality, word connections, etc. Then, lay the foundation with basic sounds and rhythms. Rebuild a new strong structure, using the grammar and vocab you've worked so hard to acquire.

The "What" Factor

Let's do a quick assessment of what other people think of your accent. How often during a day does someone ask you to repeat yourself? How long does it take to give your e-mail address, and how many times do you have to spell your name? That's your "What?" factor. But the real question is, how does this affect you? How does it affect your working situation, your home life, your life as a whole? Does it make you feel discouraged, or does it encourage you to change? Or does it make you feel like everyone else needs to change around you? Let me tell you a story about someone who felt this way. We'll call her Mei Li.

A Chinese professor was studying English in the United States, and her instructor had suggested that, for convenience, she Americanize the pronunciation of her name, and she flew into a rage. She excoriated him in a long e-mail about how disrespectful this was to 5,000 years of her Chinese ancestors. The American instructor was stunned and passed her on upstairs.

The senior instructor set about finding out what was going on. To say Dr. Li was linguistically rigid is a profound understatement. The instructor would ask, "But let's say you're at the DMV. The clerk doesn't know from Chinese ancestors. Don't you just want him to catch your name the first time and to process the transaction?" "No!" she would declare. "It's my *name*!"

The instructor finally told her that they simply had to make a breakthrough, so her entire homework would consist of leaving a voice mail with her name Americanized so it would be easier to understand by any random person. She left eight to ten identical Chinese-sounding attempts. Finally, she left one that started with a deep sigh and a deeper voice, "My name is Mei Li." It was a thing of beauty. Unfortunately, 30 seconds later, she left another *very* nasal one, "My name is Mei Liiiiiiiiiiiiiiii!"

Go On, Change Your Name

CD 1 Track 39

No, not permanently or legally, but get comfortable with saying your own name differently than you have for your entire life. It may feel weird, unreal, surreal, or just plain dumb, but it's an invaluable mental exercise. Every time that I landed in a new country, my first order of business was to find out who I was, or at least how my name was pronounced. I went from Madrid (*Me llamo Anita*) to Paris (*Je m'appelle Annie*) to Tokyo (私はアニーです。).

Drop the Baggage!

For a lot of people, the American accent comes with a lot of emotional baggage. *Americans are loud! Emotionally immature! Unsophisticated!* It may be conflicting for an educated sophisticate such as yourself to work toward actually sounding like this. But you need to fit in and be understood, so drop off the baggage. Just focus on the pure sounds.

Emotional Investment in Particular Sounds

A man with a distinctly Spanish accent had trouble distinguishing *iPod* from *iPad*. He learned the **æ** sound for iPad but didn't extrapolate that sound to other words, such as **cat**, **laugh**, or **dance**. It would be natural to think that he simply didn't know where to use it. But surprisingly, when asked why he didn't use the **æ** sound, he laughingly responded, "Because I hate it."

Some people have a strong identification with their pronunciation, considering it part of their identity or personal brand. They may reject a single sound or the entire accent. Unless the change wells from within, the accent won't take root and become a true part of them.

Motivation

CD 1 Track 40

Sofia Vergara, a Colombian actor in the American sitcom "Modern Family," was doing an interview, explaining that her 21-year-old son had seen a video of her many years earlier and said, "Mom, you're the only person who's come to America and your accent got worse!" Her utterly charming response was, "It's the moh-nee, I don't have to do eet anymore!" In another interview, Oprah Winfrey asked why her accent seems to be getting heavier, even though she'd been living in America for some time. Sofia explained that she actually does it for comedic effect, "I realized that sometimes it was funnier to say **YOOOUHH** rather than **you**." She's very self-aware and has excellent reasons for maintaining her brand.

Over the years, however, we've heard pretty much every excuse from people who have demonstrated that they are able to *create* the sounds in isolation but don't go on to the next step of universally *applying the rules*.

I feel uncomfortable.	It's not possible.	I tried and can't.
I don't understand the rules.	Why should I have to?	It's not "right."
I wasn't thinking about it.	It makes me sound arrogant.	I forgot.
I was focusing on what I was saying.	People will laugh at me.	I was rushing.

Does Pronunciation Really Matter?

People say, *It's just a detail ... does it really matter? Isn't "okay" good enough for what's needed and not worth the effort of going to the next level? We don't have that sound in my language, and we communicate just fine without it.* This may be true, but if you're, let's say, a doctor, don't you want your patients to know the difference between your saying, "He's in urology" and "He's in neurology" or "We did a below-knee amputation" and not "We did a baloney amputation"? So yes: Pronunciation matters!

Go to Extremes

CD 1 Track 41

As an exercise, we have people put on a caricature of an American accent, and generally it's quite accurate. They are reluctant, however, to use it because of the inherent mockery involved. It's okay! I can assure you that Americans won't even notice when you're putting on a superheavy American accent. They'll just think your English got better.

Your family and friends may react negatively and make fun of your nascent attempts to modify your speech. They like you the way you are. They may think your accent is cute. They may think that if you change how you talk you may change who you are. The bottom line is that you will sound different, and they may not like it.

We recommend practicing on strangers. They don't have a baseline and can accept you at face value. At this point, it may be hard for you to conceive how differently you will be treated. A lot of Americans, I regret to say, turn off when they hear a foreign accent, or are less than kind. Since we can't change all of them, we can make a small change in you.

Your Own True Voice

CD 1 Track 42

There is not, of course, just one American voice, even for one person. People associate their voices with themselves but have many different voices throughout their lives. You have a different voice as a child than as an adult, different in business than at a party, and so on.

Stephen Hawking, the British astrophysicist, had an English accent prior to the paralyzation of his vocal cords. After using a robotic voice with an American accent, he came to associate himself with that voice. Several years later, when production of the DECtalk DCT01 voice synthesizer was discontinued, he declined to switch to a model with a British accent. He identified with the American voice and associated it with himself. "I would not want to change, even if I were offered a British-sounding voice. I would feel I had become a different person," he said.

7 Steps to a Perfect Accent

CD 1 Track 43

1. Yep, I have an accent, I want to change it, and I'm sure this program will work for me.
2. I'm making a conscious effort to apply the techniques in an orderly, step-by-step manner.
3. I have taken an inventory of the sounds and rhythm patterns. (See also page x.)
4. I am keeping a daily log of the "**What Factor**." (See also page 12.)
5. I record myself once a week, compare it with my original recording, and take specific and detailed notes of changes.
6. When I talk to people, I consciously and conscientiously apply the techniques.
7. I read aloud for 15 minutes a day with a phonetic transcription or imitate an audio text.

The Pledge

"It's not the duration, it's the consistency. I'm training my mouth, lips, tongue, and mind."

Chapter 3

> Your lips don't move
> much in English.

General Pronunciation

Let's Start at the Beginning

CD 1 Track 44

As the philosophers say, start with yourself and define your terms. What are the parts of your mouth? How do they interact? What is a consonant? What is a vowel? Let's take a tour of the mouth, starting with the most basic sound.

Exercise 3-1: The Starting Point—Mmmm...

*Let's start with the **mmmm** sound. It's super easy to do. All you do is put your lips together and hum. You'll notice a couple things here. Your lips are touching and the air is coming out through your nose in a continuous stream. Put your hand on your throat and say **mmmm**, and observe that you can feel a vibration in your fingertips. This means that the **M** sound is spoken and not whispered.*

Mmmmmm

This exercise tells you four important things about the consonant **M**:

1. Point of contact (*lips*)
2. Where the air comes out of your mouth (*nose*)
3. How the air comes out (*glide*)
4. If the sound is spoken or whispered (*spoken*)

Exercise 3-2: Combining Sounds

CD 1 Track 45

*Now that you know where things are, let's turn it into something. In a deep voice, say the following out loud. We're adding two more consonants at the lip position, **P** & **B**.*

Mmm   Ah

1. mah
2. mah-mah
3. pah
4. pah-pah
5. bah
6. bah-bah

Exercise 3-3: Pronunciation & Cadence

CD 1 Track 46

In your deepest voice, repeat these syllables. To get the physical experience of intonation, either stretch a rubber band, snap your fingers, or tap the table. Repeat this ten times. (See also Chapter 4.)

1. **MAH**-mah   2. mah-**MAH**   3. **PAH**-pah   4. pah-**PAH**   5. **BAH**-bah   6. bah-**BAH**

Exercise 3-4: Pure Sound   CD 1 Track 47

*Let's put this in context. Using the **äh** sound, repeat the following sounds. Don't worry about what it means, just repeat the sounds in a deep, confident voice. That little upside-down **e** sounds like **uh**.*

    1. bä bläs diz jäb   2. skät tädə lät   3. dän bädə bäik

At this point, you may be thinking, *What the heck is this? It's nonsense! It doesn't even look like English! I really need to know what I'm saying, and I don't know what this means! This is gibberish, and I might just sound like a fool here! I need the confidence of understanding what I'm saying. I'm afraid I'll sound completely foolish! I'm not confident with this because it's so different from what I've been taught. I just want to see what it looks like in regular English.*

Exercise 3-5: Regular English   CD 1 Track 48

OK, go ahead and decipher it into regular English as best as you can. Listen to the audio in the previous section to make sure you're getting all the words.

1. _____   2. _____   3. _____

Exercise 3-6: Pure Sound   CD 1 Track 49

*This time, listen and imitate the speaker, while reading the first line. Notice that in the second line, it's spelled out for you, but focus on correlating the sounds with the new letters, including the **T** that turns into a **D**. (This is only a temporary transition, and once you've imprinted the sounds, you'll go back to regular spelling.) The intonation is marked for you, so continue with the physical tapping and snapping. (See also Chapter 8.)*

    1. **bä** bläs diz **jäb**   2. **skät** tädə **lät**   3. **dän** bädə **bäik**
       Bob lost his job.   Scott taught a lot.   Don bought a bike.

You're Visual

If you **see** it, you've **got** it, and it's hard to catch sounds if you can't get a look at them. Now that you've seen the sentences in proper English, you can imprint with the visual representation (a fancy way of saying spelling).

Exercise 3-7: Rhyme Time	CD 1 Track 50

*Let's check your understanding of the differences between the **appearance** of English and the **pronunciation** of spoken American English. Say each pair of words out loud to yourself. If the two words rhyme, check the first box. If they don't rhyme, check the second box. Check Answer Key beginning on page 210. Unless you score 100% on your first try, spend at least an hour on Exercise 3-8.*

Does it rhyme?	Yes	No	Does it rhyme?	Yes	No
1. give – hive	❑	❑	26. goes – does (v)	❑	❑
2. have – save	❑	❑	27. glove – move	❑	❑
3. come – gum	❑	❑	28. oxen – dachshund	❑	❑
4. been – tin	❑	❑	29. beard – heard	❑	❑
5. know – now	❑	❑	30. sew – few	❑	❑
6. use (v) – choose	❑	❑	31. flew – through	❑	❑
7. monkey – donkey	❑	❑	32. little – middle	❑	❑
8. been* – seen	❑	❑	33. would – stood	❑	❑
9. great – heat	❑	❑	34. flood – stood	❑	❑
10. eight – height	❑	❑	35. has – was	❑	❑
11. done – gone	❑	❑	36. food – rude	❑	❑
12. mother – bother	❑	❑	37. enough – though	❑	❑
13. bruise – stews	❑	❑	38. allow – below	❑	❑
14. froze – clothes	❑	❑	39. debt – let	❑	❑
15. her – sure*	❑	❑	40. says – pays	❑	❑
16. where – were	❑	❑	41. dance – pants	❑	❑
17. hour – flower	❑	❑	42. eagle – legal	❑	❑
18. good – food	❑	❑	43. know – though	❑	❑
19. come – dome	❑	❑	44. thought – taught	❑	❑
20. turn – earn	❑	❑	45. laugh – half	❑	❑
21. beard – weird	❑	❑	46. first – worst	❑	❑
22. comb – tomb	❑	❑	47. full – wool	❑	❑
23. taste – waist	❑	❑	48. fool – wool	❑	❑
24. anger – danger	❑	❑	49. drawer – floor	❑	❑
25. cupboard – blubbered	❑	❑	50. maître d' – undersea	❑	❑

been (typically pronounced *bin*) is also pronounced *ben* or *been* in various locales.

sure (typically pronounced *shrr*) is also heard in some places as *shore*, *shoo-er*, or *shoo-wah*.

Vowel & Consonant Mouth Positions

The vowels are in a continuous stream from **e** to **ooh**, and the consonants are in three categories based on the point of contact.

Al A. Gator

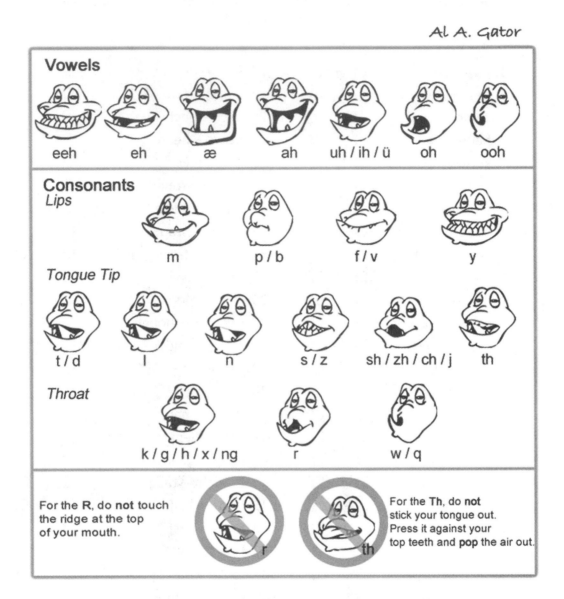

Vowels

eeh eh æ ah uh / ih / ü oh ooh

Consonants

Lips

m p / b f / v y

Tongue Tip

t / d l n s / z sh / zh / ch / j th

Throat

k / g / h / x / ng r w / q

For the R, do **not** touch the ridge at the top of your mouth.

For the Th, do **not** stick your tongue out. Press it against your top teeth and **pop** the air out.

The first step is to reprogram you away from **spelling** to the actual **sounds** of English. Start by mastering these sounds, combining initial consonants and vowels. This will give you a strong leg up on pronunciation.

The first column is **ä** because it's going to be easy for you. I'm going to say that again. Ready? It's going to be **easy** for you. Why? Because as far as I can tell, every language on earth has an "ah" sound. Some of the consonants may be a little tricky (**Th** and **R** spring to mind) but listen and repeat, repeat, repeat...in a deep voice. (Final consonants, diphthongs, and consonant blends such as **BL** and **CR** are covered in later chapters.)

| Exercise 3-8: The Pure Sound Jump-Start | CD 1 Track 52 |

*As you go through this chart, pronouncing all the sounds, deepen your voice and make the vowels a little longer than you are inclined to. Some of these will sound like real words, but most of them are just fragments. Observe that for **ä**, you drop your jaw; for **ē**, you stretch your lips back a bit; for **ū**, you round your lips. There are only five new characters: **ä, æ, ɛ, ə, ü**. Listen carefully, and repeat this whole chart at least five times in columns, and five times across. Record yourself, listen back, and compare.*

	ä	æ	ɛ	i	ə	ü	ē	ō	ū	ā	ī
b	bä	bæ	bɛh	bih	bə	bü	bē	bō	bū	bā	bī
ch	chä	chæ	chɛh	chih	chə	chü	chē	chō	chū	chā	chī
d	dä	dæ	dɛh	dih	də	dü	dē	dō	dū	dā	dī
f	fä	fæ	fɛh	fih	fə	fü	fē	fō	fū	fā	fī
g	gä	gæ	gɛh	gih	gə	gü	gē	gō	gū	gā	gī
h	hä	hæ	hɛh	hih	hə	hü	hē	hō	hū	hā	hī
j	jä	jæ	jɛh	jih	jə	jü	jē	jō	jū	jā	jī
k	kä	kæ	kɛh	kih	kə	kü	kē	kō	kū	kā	kī
l	lä	læ	lɛh	lih	lə	lü	lē	lō	lū	lā	lī
m	mä	mæ	mɛh	mih	mə	mü	mē	mō	mū	mā	mī
n	nä	næ	nɛh	nih	nə	nü	nē	nō	nū	nā	nī
p	pä	pæ	pɛh	pih	pə	pü	pē	pō	pū	pā	pī
r	rä	ræ	rɛh	rih	rə	rü	rē	rō	rū	rā	rī
s	sä	sæ	sɛh	sih	sə	sü	sē	sō	sū	sā	sī
sh	shä	shæ	shɛh	shih	shə	shü	shē	shō	shū	shā	shī
t	tä	tæ	tɛh	tih	tə	tü	tē	tō	tū	tā	tī
th	thä	thæ	thɛh	thih	thə*	thü	thē	thō	thū	thā	thī
v	vä	væ	vɛh	vih	və	vü	vē	vō	vū	vā	vī
w	wä	wæ	wɛh	wih	wə	wü	wē	wō	wū	wā	wī
y	yä	yæ	yɛh	yih	yə	yü	yē	yō	yū	yā	yī
z	zä	zæ	zɛh	zih	zə	zü	zē	zō	zū	zā	zī

*Most commonly used word in English.

CD 1 Track 53

"We don't have some of those sounds in my language..."

This is undoubtedly true, but you can see that you only need to pick up a limited number of new sounds (**ä, æ, ɛ, ə, ü**). Given what you've already accomplished in life, this is not a big deal. A Chinese speaker was once bemoaning how hard it was for him to say the **R**. When asked if he went to college, he said, "Of course, I have a PhD in physics from Caltech." After a beat, he realized that compared to that ... the **R** is not harrrrrrrd.

Exercise 3-9: Other Characters

If you use one of these character sets, compare it with English.

*ва is much softer than the American V

Let me give a quick explanation of why we're using these sounds. When you come in through your own language, you are coming from a place of total and absolute confidence. You *know* that sound. So, we're taking something you know and doing a lateral transference to a set of letters in English. If, on the other hand, you start from scratch, you'll be wondering if you're doing it right, and this will drain your confidence and your energy.

Now that you've worked hard and successfully imitated the sounds, you're going to go on to the next step, which is regular spelling.

Exercise 3-10: Changing to Regular Spelling

*Apply the **phonetic** sound to the entire column, no matter what the **spelling** is. Then, read each row across, making the vowel distinctions.*

	ä	æ	ɛ	i	ü	ə	ē	ō	ū	ā	ī
	ought	at	etch	it		um	eat	oat	oops	ate	I'm
b	Bob	bat	bet	been	book	but	beat	boat	boot	bait	bite
ch	chop	chat	check	chin		chuck	cheat	choke	choose	chase	child
d	Don	Dad	dead	did		done	deal	don't	do	day	die
f	fawn	fat	fetch	fit	foot	fun	feet	phone	food	fail	find
g	gone	gap	get	give	good	gun	geese	go	ghoul	gate	guy
h	hot	had	head	his	hood	hut	he	hold	who	hey	hi
j	jaw	Jack	Jeff	gin		jump	jeans	joke	jewel	jail	giant
k	call	cat	Ken	kid	could	come	key	cold	cool	cane	kite
l	law	laugh	left	lick	look	luck	lead	load	lose	lay	lie
m	Mom	mad	men	mix		much	me	most	moon	make	mine
n	not	Nan	net	knit	nook	none	need	note	new	name	knife
p	pot	pat	pet	pick	put	putt	peak	pole	pool	pay	pie
r	raw	ran	red	rib	rook	rub	reed	row	room	raise	rise
s	saw	sat	said	sin	soot	such	see	so	suit	say	sigh
sh	shawl	shack	shed	shill	should	shut	she	show	shoe	shape	shine
t	tall	tack	ten	tin	took	tub	tea	toe	tube	take	try
th	thought	that	then	this		the	these	though	through	they	thigh
v	Von	vat	vex	vim		vug	veal	voice	voodoo	veil	vie
w	walk	wax	when	with	would	was	we	won't	woo	whales	why
y	yawn	yap	yes	yip	you'll	young	yield	yo-yo	you	Yale	yikes
z	czar	zap	zen	zig		zug	zeal	Zoey	zoo	zany	zygote

The Most Common Sound in English: Uh

As you may know, the schwa ə is the most commonly used sound in English. **The** is the most commonly used word: **thə**. Just by mastering these two sounds—**th** and **ə**—you'll make a 30% improvement in your pronunciation.

Let's start with the schwa ə sound. Fortunately, it's an easy one. Don't move your lips or tongue, just let a completely neutral sound come out—**uh**. It's pretty much a little grunt. It's the sound Americans use when they're thinking—**um, uh, uh-huh, uh-uh, hum**. As you've seen on page 5, it's also used for agreeing, disagreeing, expressing interest, or conveying confusion. It appears as any vowel (act**u**al, happ**e**n, p**o**ssible, c**o**mmunity, **u**nusual) or even where there is no vowel (chasm, spasm, rhythm) just before the **m**. (See also Chapters 12 and 18.)

The Second Most Common Sound: Tee Aitch

To pronounce **Th** correctly, think about your tongue position. You don't want to take a big relaxed tongue, throw it out of your mouth for a long distance, and leave it out there for a long time. Make only a very quick, sharp little movement. Keep your tongue's tip very tense. It darts out between your teeth and snaps back very quickly—**thing, that, this**. The tongue tip is pressed against the back of your top teeth, and the sound

pops out. It's not a breathy sound at all. Just as with most of the other consonants, there are two types—*voiced* and *unvoiced*. The voiced **Th** is like a **D**, but instead of being on the roof of the mouth, it's ¼ inch forward, *against* the teeth. The unvoiced **Th** is like a **T** between the teeth. If you mistakenly replace the unvoiced **Th** with **S** or **T** and the voiced one with **Z** or **D**, instead of *thing,* you'll say *sing* or *ting,* and instead of *that,* you'll say *zat* or *dat.* (See also Chapter 13.)

Exercise 3-11: Theodore Thurston's Theory

I'm going to read the following paragraph once straight through, so you can hear that no matter how fast I read it, all the Ths are still there. It is a distinctive sound, but when you repeat it, don't put too much effort into it. Listen to my reading.

The theory **th**at **Th**eodore **Th**urston **th**ought **th**at **th**ree-**th**irds was wor**th th**ree **th**ousand dollars meant **th**at one-**th**ird was wor**th** a **th**ousand dollars.

I'd like you to consider words as rocks for a moment. When a rock first rolls into the ocean, it is sharp and well-defined. After tumbling about for a few millennia, it becomes round and smooth. A word goes through a similar process. When it first rolls into English, it may have a lot of sharp, well-defined vowels or consonants in it, but after rolling off a few million tongues, it becomes round and smooth. This smoothing process occurs when a tense vowel becomes reduced and when an unvoiced consonant becomes voiced. The most common words are the smoothest, the most reduced, the most often voiced. There are several very common words that are all voiced: *this, that, the, those, them, they, their, there, then, than, though*. The strong words such as *thank, think,* or *thing,* as well as long or unusual words such as *thermometer* or *theologian,* stay unvoiced.

Four More Important Sounds

CD 1 Track 58

Earlier, you learned the ə sound (*uh*), and now we're going to take a look at two related sounds. First say **uh**, then drop your jaw and say **ah**. This **ah** sound is used for the letter **O** in one-syllable words (**hot**, **lost**, **cop**) and with the **O** in stressed syllables (**possible**, **hospital**, **college**). (See also Chapter 12.)

Now say **ah** again, but pull your lips back a bit. This gives you the **æ** sound, used for the letter **a** in one-syllable words (**chance**, **laugh**, **dance**) and in stressed syllables (**plastic**, **fantastic**, **imaginable**). (See also Chapter 12.)

Another high value sound is the **R**. This growly sound is so very American. It always sounds the same, whether it's at the beginning, middle, or end of the word, and it's always pronounced, especially at the end of a word, such as **carrr**, **doorrr**, and **hearrr**. In most languages the **R** is a consonant because the tip of the tongue touches the roof of the mouth. This is **not** the case in American English. The tongue does not touch **anywhere** in the mouth, and the sound is formed back in the throat. (See also Chapter 15.)

The letter **T**, as you will learn, has six different pronunciations, but right now we're only going to look at the case of **T** in the middle of a word, where it sounds like a **D**. This is why **metal, medal, mettle**, and **meddle** all sound identical, despite the wide variation in spelling. (See also Chapter 14.)

Anticipating the Next Word

CD 1 Track 59

The anticipation of each following sound brings me to the subject that most students raise at some point—one that explains their resistance to wholly embracing liaisons and general fluency. People feel that because English is not their native tongue, they can't anticipate the next sound because they never know what the next word is going to be. Accurate or not, for the sake of argument, let's say that you do construct sentences entirely word by word. This is where those pauses we'll study in Chapter 7 come in handy. During your pause, line up in your head all the words you want to use in order to communicate your thought, and then push them out in groups. If you find yourself slowing down and talking ... word ... by ... word, back up and take a running leap at a whole string of words.

Run Them All Together (runnemälld'gether)

As I was reading, I hope you heard that in a lot of places, the words ran together, such as *runnemälld'gether*. You don't have to go way out of your way to make a huge new sound, but rather create a smooth flowing from one word to the next by leaving your tongue in an anticipatory position. (See also Chapter 11.)

> Change pitch
> on important information.

The American Speech Music

What to Do with Your Mouth to Sound American

One of the main differences between the way an American talks and the way the rest of the world talks is that we don't really move our lips. (So, when an American says, "Read my lips!" what does he really mean?) We create most of our sounds in the throat, using our tongue very actively. If you hold your fingers over your lips or clench your jaws when you practice speaking American English, you will find yourself much closer to native-sounding speech than if you try to pronounce every ... single ... sound ... very ... carefully.

If you can relate American English to music, remember that the indigenous music is jazz. Listen to their speech music, and you will hear that Americans have a melodic, jazzy way of producing sounds. Imagine the sound of a cello when you say *Beddy bada bida bedder budder* (Betty bought a bit of better butter), and you'll be close to the native way of saying it.

Because most Americans came from somewhere else, American English reflects the accent contributions of many lands. The speech music has become much more exaggerated than British English, developing a strong and distinctive intonation. If you use this intonation, not only will you be easier to understand, but you will sound much more confident, dynamic, and persuasive.

Intonation, or speech music, is the sound that you hear when a conversation is too far away to be clearly audible but close enough for you to tell the nationality of the speakers. The American intonation dictates liaisons and pronunciation, and it indicates mood and meaning. Without intonation, your speech would be flat, mechanical, and very confusing for your listener. What is the American intonation pattern? How is it different from other languages? *Foa egzampuru, eefu you hea ah Jahpahneezu pahsohn speakingu Ingurishu*, the sound would be very choppy, mechanical, and unemotional to an American. *Za sem vey vis Cheuman pipples*, it sounds too stiff. *A mahn frohm Paree ohn zee ahzer ahnd, eez intonashon goes up at zee end ov evree sentence* and has such a strong intonation that he sounds romantic and highly emotional, but this may not be appropriate for a lecture or business meeting in English.

American Intonation Do's and Don'ts

Do Not Speak Word by Word

Bob... is... on... the... phone

Connect Words to Form Sound Groups

bä bizän the foun

Use Staircase Intonation to Stress Important Information

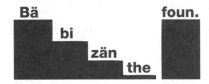

Start a new staircase
when you want to emphasize
that information, generally a *noun.*

▶ **Do not speak word by word.**

If you speak word by word, as many people who learned "printed" English do, you'll end up sounding mechanical and foreign. You may have noticed the same thing happens in your own language: when someone reads a speech, even a native speaker, it sounds stiff and stilted, quite different from a normal conversational tone.

▶ **Connect words to form sound groups.**

This is where you're going to start doing something *completely different* than what you have done in your previous English studies. This part is the most difficult for many people because it goes against everything they've been taught. Instead of thinking of each word as a unit, think of *sound units.* These sound units may or may not correspond to a word written on a page. Native speakers don't say *Bob is on the phone,* but say *bäbizän the foun.* Sound units make a sentence flow smoothly, like peanut butter—never really ending and never really starting, just flowing along. Even chunky peanut butter is acceptable. So long as you don't try to put plain peanuts directly onto your bread, you'll be OK. (See also Chapters 8 and 11.)

▶ **Use staircase Intonation.**

Let those sound groups floating on the wavy river in the figure flow downhill and you'll get the staircase. Staircase intonation not only gives you that American sound, it also makes you sound much more confident. Not every American uses the downward staircase. A certain segment of the population uses rising staircases—generally, teenagers on their way to a shopping mall: *"Hi, my name is Tiffany. I live in La Cañada. I'm on the pep squad."*

What Exactly Is Staircase Intonation?

In saying your words, imagine that they come out as if they were bounding lightly down a flight of stairs. Every so often, one jumps up to another level and then starts down again. Americans tend to stretch out their sounds longer than you may think is natural. So to lengthen your vowel sounds, put them on two stairsteps instead of just one.

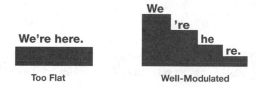

The sound of an American speaking a foreign language is very distinctive, because we double sounds that should be single. For example, in Japanese or Spanish, the word *no* is, to our ear, clipped or abbreviated.

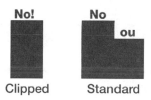

When you have a word ending in an *unvoiced consonant*—one that you "whisper" (t, k, s, x, f, sh)—you will notice that the preceding vowel is said quite quickly, and on a single stair step. When a word ends in a vowel or a *voiced consonant*—one that you "say" (b, d, g, z, v, zh, j), the preceding vowel is said more slowly, and on a double stair step.

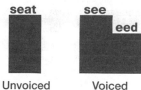

There are two main consequences of not doubling the second category of words: either your listener will hear the wrong word, or even worse, you will always sound upset. Consider that the words *curt, short, terse, abrupt,* and *clipped* all literally mean *short*. When applied to a person or to language, they take on the meaning of *upset* or *rude*. For example, the expressions *"His curt reply ...," "Her terse response ...,"* or *"He was very short with me"* all indicate a less than sunny situation.

Three Ways to Make Intonation

About this time, you're coming to the point where you may be wondering, what exactly are the mechanics of intonation? What changes when you go to the top of the staircase or when you put stress on a word? There are three ways to stress a word:

▸ The first way is to just get *louder* or raise the volume. This is not a very sophisticated way of doing it, but it will definitely command attention.

▸ The second way is to *streeeeetch* the word out or lengthen the word that you want to draw attention to (which sounds very insinuating).

▸ The third way, which is the most refined, is to change *pitch.* Although pausing just before changing the pitch is effective, you don't want to do it every time, because then it becomes an obvious technique. However, it will make your audience stop and listen because they think you're going to say something interesting.

Exercise 4-1: Rubber Band Practice with Nonsense Syllables   CD 2 Track 2

Take a rubber band and hold it with your two thumbs. Every time you want to stress a word by changing pitch, pull on the rubber band. Stretch it out gently, don't jerk it sharply. Make a looping ∞ figure with it and do the same with your voice. Use the rubber band and stretch it out every time you change pitch. Read first across, then down.

	A		B		C		D
1.	**duh** duh **duh**	1.	**la** la **la**	1.	**mee** mee **mee**	1.	**ho** ho **ho**
2.	duh duh **duh**	2.	la la **la**	2.	mee mee **mee**	2.	ho ho **ho**
3.	duh **duh** duh	3.	la **la** la	3.	mee **mee** mee	3.	ho **ho** ho
4.	**duh** duh duh	4.	**la** la la	4.	**mee** mee mee	4.	**ho** ho ho

Read each column down, keeping the same intonation pattern.

	A		B		C		D
1.	**duh** duh **duh**	1.	duh duh **duh**	1.	duh **duh** duh	1.	**duh** duh duh
2.	**ABC**	2.	impre**cise**	2.	con**di**tion	2.	**al**phabet
3.	**123**	3.	a hot **dog**	3.	a **hot** dog	3.	**hot** dog stand
4.	**Dogs** eat **bones**.	4.	They eat **bones**.	4.	They **eat** them.	4.	**Give** me one.

The American Speech Music
CD 2 Track 3

All cultures gesture. A developmental physiologist at University of Wisconsin, Dr. Alibali, put forth that gestures accompany speech because our mouths and hands are closely linked in the brain. You may have noticed babies saying **ga-ga-ga** and moving their hands to the beat. It's not necessary for you to gesticulate wildly, but it **is** important to integrate the rhythm of your speech music with physical gestures. To this end, you'll be tapping the table, snapping your fingers, and maybe even stretching a rubber band.

Not in My Language

A Pakistani database analyst said, "I didn't think about my own language in this way before. There is intonation when we speak, but not as much as in American English. Now that I've analyzed it, I found my language to be rhythmic too. In many places, we do the same up and down intonation. I must not have realized it because I speak without thinking about the language itself! It's really interesting to compare both language styles and then to extract certain resemblances from them. I never thought of it in that way."

Staircase Intonation
CD 2 Track 4

So what is intonation in American English? What do Americans do? We go up and down staircases. We start high and end low.

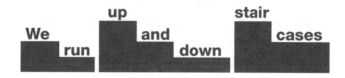

Every time we want to stress a word or an idea, we just start a new staircase. That sounds simple enough, but when and where do you start a new staircase?

Statement Intonation with Nouns

Intonation or pitch change is primarily used to introduce *new information.* This means that when you are making a statement for the first time, you will stress the *nouns.*

Exercise 4-2: Noun Intonation CD 2 Track 5

Practice the noun stress pattern after me, using pitch change. Add your own examples.

1.	**Dogs** eat **bones.**	11.	**Jerry** makes **music.**
2.	**Mike** likes **bikes.**	12.	**Jean** sells some **apples.**
3.	**Elsa** wants **a book.**	13.	**Carol** paints the **car.**
4.	**Adam** plays **pool.**	14.	**Bill** and I fix the **bikes.**
5.	**Bobby** needs some **money.**	15.	**Ann** and **Ed** call the **kids.**
6.	**Susie** combs **her hair.**	16.	The **kids** like the **candy.**
7.	**John** lives in **France.**	17.	The **girls** have a **choice.**
8.	**Nelly** teaches **French.**	18.	The **boys** need some **help.**
9.	**Ben** writes **articles.**	19.	_____
10.	**Keys** open **locks.**	20.	_____

✖ Pause the CD.

▶ Practice the patterns five more times on your own, using your rubber band.

Statement Intonation with Pronouns CD 2 Track 6

When you replace the nouns with pronouns (i.e., *old information*), stress the verb.

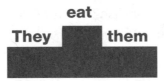

As we have seen, *nouns* are *new* information; *pronouns* are *old* information. In a nutshell, these are the two basic intonation patterns.

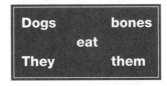

Exercise 4-3: Noun and Pronoun Intonation CD 2 Track 7

In the first column, stress the nouns. In the second column, stress the verb. Fill in your own examples at the bottom.

1.	**Bob** sees **Betty.**	1.	He **sees** her.
2.	**Betty** knows **Bob.**	2.	She **knows** him.
3.	**Ann** and **Ed** call the **kids.**	3.	They **call** them.
4.	**Jan** sells some **apples.**	4.	She **sells** some.
5.	**Jean** sells **cars.**	5.	She **sells** them.
6.	**Bill** and I fix the **bikes.**	6.	We **fix** them.

7.	**Carl** hears **Bob** and me.	7.	He **hears** us.
8.	**Dogs** eat **bones**.	8.	They **eat** them.
9.	The **girls** have a **choice**.	9.	They **have** one.
10.	The **kids** like the **candy**.	10.	They **like** it.
11.	The **boys** need some **help**.	11.	They **need** something.
12.	**Ellen** should call her **sister**.	12.	She should **call** someone.
13.	The **murderer** killed the **plumber**.	13.	He **killed** a man.
14.	The **tourists** went **shopping**.	14.	They **bought** stuff.
15.	_____	15.	_____
16.	_____	16.	_____
17.	_____	17.	_____
18.	_____	18.	_____
19.	_____	19.	_____
20.	_____	20.	_____

Statement Versus Question Intonation

CD 2 Track 8

You may have learned at some point that questions have a rising intonation. They do, but usually a question will step upward until the very end, where it takes one quick little downward step. A question rises a little higher than a statement with the same intonation pattern.

Emotional or Rhetorical Question Intonation

If you know that your car is parked outside, however, and someone doesn't see it and asks you where it is, you might think that it has been stolen, and your emotion will show in your intonation as you repeat the question. As your feelings rise in an emotional situation, your intonation rises up along with them.

Exercise 4-4: Sentence Intonation Test   CD 2 Track 9

Pause the CD and underline or highlight the words that you think should be stressed. Check Answer Key, beginning on page 210.

1. Sam sees Bill.	11. He sees him.
2. She wants one.	12. Mary wants a car.
3. Betty likes English.	13. She likes it.
4. They play with them.	14. They eat some.
5. Children play with toys.	15. Len and Joe eat some pizza.
6. Bob and I call you and Bill.	16. We call you.
7. You and Bill read the news.	17. You read it.
8. It tells one.	18. The news tells a story.
9. Bernard works in a restaurant.	19. Mark lived in France.
10. He works in one.	20. He lived there.

Exercise 4-5: Four Main Reasons for Intonation   CD 2 Track 10

Depending on the situation, a word may be stressed for any of the following reasons:

New Information   **Opinion**   **Contrast**   **"Can't"**

1. New Information

*It sounds like **rain**.*

   Rain is the new information. It's the most important word in that sentence and you could replace everything else with *duh-duh-duh*. *Duh-duh-duh **rain*** will still let you get your point across.

▸ Repeat: *Duh-duh-duh **rain**. I It sounds like **rain**.*

▸ Make *rain* very musical and put it on two notes: *ray-ayn*.
   *Duh-duh-duh **ray-ayn** / It sounds like **ray-ayn**.*

2. Opinion

*It **sounds** like rain, but I don't think it is.*

   In this case, intonation makes the meaning the opposite of what the words say: *It **looks** like a diamond, but I think it's a **zircon**. It **smells** like Chanel, but at that price, it's a **knock**-off. It **feels** like... It **tastes** like...* These examples all give the impression that you mean the *opposite* of what your senses tell you.

▸ Practice the intonation difference between *new information* and *opinion*:

   *It sounds like **rain**.* (It's rain.)
   *It **sounds** like rain,* (but it's not.)

3. Contrast

*He **likes** rain, but he **hates** snow.*

>*Like* and *hate* are contrasted and are the stronger words in the sentence.

4. Can't

*It **can't rain** when there're no **clouds**.*

>Contractions *(shouldn't, wouldn't)* and negatives *(no, not, never)* are important words since they totally negate the meaning of a sentence, but they are not usually stressed.

>*Can't* is the exception.

Exercise 4-6: Pitch and Meaning Change   CD 2 Track 11

Practice saying the four sentences after me. Pay close attention to the changes in pitch that you must make to convey the different meanings intended. The words to be stressed are indicated in boldface.

1. It sounds like **rain**.

2. It **sounds** like rain.

3. He **likes** rain, but he **hates** snow.

4. It **can't rain** on my **parade**! He **can't do** it. *(See also Exercise 4-17 for negatives.)*

Exercise 4-7: Individual Practice   CD 2 Track 12

*Practice saying the sentences after the suggestion and the beep tone. You will be given only a **short** time in which to reply so that you won't have the leisure to overthink. Start speaking as soon as you hear the tone because I'll be saying the sentence only a few seconds later.*

1. Convey the information that it really does sound as if rain is falling. ◀

2. Convey the opinion that although it has the sound of rain, it may be something else. ◀

3. Convey the different feelings that someone has about rain and snow. ◀

4. Convey the fact that rain is an impossibility right now. ◀

- ✗ Pause the CD.
- ▶ Practice the four sentences on your own ten times.
- ✗ Once you're familiar with moving the stress around and feeling how the meaning changes, turn the CD on to continue with the next exercise.

Exercise 4-8: Meaning of "Pretty"   CD 2 Track 13

*Native speakers make a clear distinction between pretty **easily** (easily) and **pretty** easily (a little difficult). Repeat the answers after me, paying close attention to your stress.*

Question:	How did you like the movie?
Answer:	1. *It was pretty **good**.* (She liked it.)
	2. *It was **pretty** good.* (She didn't like it much.)

Exercise 4-9: Inflection   CD 2 Track 14

Notice how the meaning changes, while the actual words stay the same.

1. **I** didn't say he stole the money. Someone **else** said it.
2. I **didn't** say he stole the money. **That's** not true at **all**.
3. I didn't **say** he stole the money. I only **suggested** the **possibility**.
4. I didn't say **he** stole the money. I think someone **else** took it.
5. I didn't say he **stole** the money. Maybe he just **borrowed** it.
6. I didn't say he stole **the** money, but rather some **other** money.
7. I didn't say he stole the **money**. He may have taken some **jewelry**.

I	**I** didn't say he stole the money. Someone **else** said it. It's true that somebody said it, but I wasn't that person.
Didn't	I **didn't** say he stole the money. **That's** not true at **all**. Someone has accused me, and I'm protesting my innocence.
Say	I didn't **say** he stole the money. I only **suggested** the **possibility**. Maybe I hinted it. Maybe I wrote it. In some way, I indicated that he stole the money, *but* I didn't say it.
He	I didn't say **he** stole the money. I think someone **else** took it. I think someone stole the money, only not the person you suspect did it.
Stole	I didn't say he **stole** the money. Maybe he just **borrowed** it. I agree that he took it, but I think his motive was different.
The	I didn't say he stole **the** money, but rather some **other** money. We agree that he stole some money, but I don't think it's this money.
Money	I didn't say he stole the **money**. He may have taken some **jewelry**. We agree that he's a thief, but we think he stole different things.

Notice that in the first half of these sentences nothing changes but the intonation.

▶ Repeat after me.

Exercise 4-10: Individual Practice CD 2 Track 15

Now, let's see what you can do with the same sentence, just by changing the stress around to different words. I'll tell you which meaning to express. When you hear the tone ◀, say the sentence as quickly as you can, then I'll say the sentence for you. To test your ear, I'm going to repeat the sentences in random order. Try to determine which word I'm stressing. The answers are given in parentheses, but don't look unless you really have to. Here we go.

1. Indicate that he borrowed the money and didn't steal it. (5) ◀
2. Indicate that you are denying having said that he stole it. (2) ◀
3. Indicate that you think he stole something besides money. (7) ◀
4. Indicate that you were not the person to say it. (1) ◀
5. Indicate that you don't think that he was the person who stole it. (4) ◀
6. Indicate that you didn't say it outright but did suggest it in some way. (3) ◀
7. Indicate that he many have stolen a different amount of money. (6) ◀

Exercise 4-11: Sticky Note Exercise CD 2 Track 16

Imagine that you are being held hostage by a mad bomber, and the only way to communicate with the outside is with notes stuck to the bank window.

If you give each word of your plea equal value, the message will be lost in the barrage of information.

To clearly convey your message, you'll need to emphasize the most important words. This way, any random passerby can, at a glance, immediately catch your meaning.

This is the same with intonation. Repeat the sentence, clearly stressing the marked words.

Please **help** me! I'm being held **captive** by a mad **bomber**!

Overdo It

Practice these sentences on your own, really exaggerating the word that you think should be stressed. In the beginning, you're going to feel that this is ridiculous. *(Nobody stresses this hard! Nobody talks like this! People are going to laugh at me!)* Yet as much as you may stress, you're probably only going to be stressing about half as much as you should.

✘ Pause the CD and practice the sentences in random order ten times.

Another reason you must overexaggerate is because when you get tired, emotional, or relaxed, you will stop paying attention. When this happens, like a rubber band, you're going to snap back to the way you originally were sounding (10%). So, if you just stretch yourself to the exact position where you ideally want to be, you'll go back almost completely to the old way when you relax. For practice, then, stretch yourself far *beyond* the normal range of intonation (150%), so when you relax, you relax back to a standard American sound (100%). (See also Chapter 1.)

We All Do It

Possibly about this time you're thinking, *Well, maybe you do this in English, but in* **my** *language, I just really don't think that we do this.* I'd like you to try a little exercise.

Exercise 4-12: Translation

Take the sentence **I didn't say he stole the money** *and translate it into your native language. Write it down below, using whatever letters or characters you use in your language.*

Now that you have written your sentence down, try shifting the stress around in your own language by going through the stress patterns 1–7 in Exercise 4-9. Don't try to put on a particularly American or other accent; just concentrate on stressing a different word in the sentence each time you say it.

For example, if your language is German, *Ich habe nicht gesagt daß er das Geld gestohlen hat,* you would change the stress to: **Ich** *habe nicht gesagt daß er das Geld gestohlen hat,* or *Ich habe* **nicht** *gesagt daß er das Geld gestohlen hat.*

If you translated it into French, you would say, *Je* **n'ai pas** *dit qu'il a volé l'argent,* or *Je n'ai pas dit qu'il a* **volé** *l'argent.*

In Japanese, many people think that there are no intonation changes, but if you hear someone say, *wak**ka**nai,* you'll realize that it has similarities to every other language. *Watashi wa* **kare** *ga okane o nusunda to wa iimasen deshita.* Or perhaps, *Watashi wa kare ga okane o nusunda to wa* **iimasen** *deshita.*

No matter how strange it may sound to you, stress each different word several times in your language. You may notice that with some words it sounds perfectly normal, but with other words it sounds very strange. Or you may find that in your language, rather than stressing a word, you prefer to change the word order or substitute another word. Whatever you do is fine, as long as you realize where your language patterns are similar to and different from the American English intonation patterns. Then, when you do it again, in English, it will be much easier.

Note *An excellent exercise is to practice speaking your native language with an American accent. If you can sound like an American speaking your native language, imagine how easy it would be to speak English with an American accent.*

✘ Pause the CD and practice shifting the stressed words in your native language.

Intonation Contrast

CD 2 Track 20

Below are two sentences—the first is stressed on the most common, everyday word, *book*. Nine times out of ten, people will stress the sentence in this way. The second sentence has a less common, but perfectly acceptable intonation, since we are making a distinction between two possible locations.

Normal intonation	Where's the **book**? It's on the **table**.
Changed intonation	Is the book **on** the table or **under** it? It's **on** the table.

✘ Pause the CD and repeat the sentences.

Exercise 4-13: Create Your Own Intonation Contrast　　　　CD 2 Track 21

Write a short sentence and indicate where you think the most normal intonation would be placed. Then, change the meaning of the sentence slightly and change the intonation accordingly.

Normal intonation　　　_____

Changed intonation　　　_____

Question Types

CD 2 Track 22

There are three types of questions: *Yes/No, Either/Or,* and *The Five W Questions*. They each have a different inflection pattern, so even if you don't catch all of the words, you can still tell what type of question it was. The Five W Questions are *Who?, What?, Where?, When?,* and *Why?* (and *How?*).

As you heard in the question and response above, "Where's the book? It's on the table.", the inflection goes up on the question and down on the statement. A query like "Would you like tea or coffee?" could be an Either/Or question (Tea? Coffee?) or a Yes/No question (Hot beverage?).

A classic, probably apocryphal story spells out the consequences of misinterpreting the question type. An immigrant was passing through Ellis Island and was asked the then-standard question, "Are you planning to overthrow the United States by force or violence?"

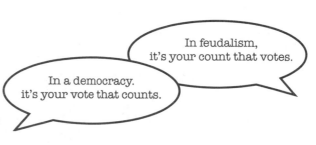

In feudalism, it's your count that votes.

In a democracy. it's your vote that counts.

The man pondered deeply for a moment and tentatively replied, "By force?" Of course, he was not let in, as the only acceptable answer was, "No."

Exercise 4-14: Variable Stress   CD 2 Track 23

Notice how the meaning of the following sentence changes each time we change the stress pattern. You should be starting to feel in control of your sentences now.

1. **What would you like?**

This is the most common version of the sentence, and it is just a simple request for information.

2. **What would you like?**

This is to single out an individual from a group.

3. **What would you like?**

You've been discussing the kinds of things he might like, and you want to determine his specific desires: "*Now that you mention it, what **would** you like?*"
or
He has rejected several things, and a little exasperated, you ask, "*If you don't want any of these, what **would** you like?*"

4. **What would you like?**

You didn't hear, and you would like the speaker to repeat herself.
or
You can't believe what you heard: "*I'd like strawberry jam on my asparagus.*" — "***What** would you like?*"

◀ Turn off the CD and repeat the four sentences.

Exercise 4-15: Make a Variable Stress Sentence   CD 2 Track 24

*Now **you** decide which words should be emphasized. Write a normal, everyday sentence with at least seven words and put it through as many changes as possible. Try to make a pitch change for each word in the sentence and think about how it changes the meaning of the entire sentence.*

1. _____
2. _____
3. _____
4. _____
5. _____
6. _____
7. _____

Exercise 4-16: Yes, You *Can* or No, You *Can't*?

Next you use a combination of intonation and pronunciation to make the difference between **can** *and* **can't**. *Reduce the positive* **can** *to* **k'n** *and stress the verb. Make the negative* **can't** *(kæn*[(t)]*) sound very short, and stress both* **can't** *and the verb. This will contrast with the positive, emphasized* **can**, *which is doubled—and the verb is not stressed. If you have trouble with* **can't** *before a word that starts with a vowel, such as* **open**, *put in a very small* [(d)]*— The keys* **kæn**[(d)] **open** *the locks. Repeat.*

I can **do** it.	I k'n **do** it	positive
I **can't do** it.	I **kæn**[(t)]**do** it	negative
I **can** do it.	I **kææn** do it	extra positive
I **can't** do it.	I **kæn**[(t)]**do** it	extra negative

Exercise 4-17: Can or Can't Quiz

Listen to how each sentence is said, and select positive, negative, extra positive, or extra negative. Check Answer Key beginning on page 210.

1. I can see it. ◀
   - ❑ A. positive
   - ❑ B. negative
   - ❑ C. extra positive
   - ❑ D. extra negative

2. I can't see it. ◀
   - ❑ A. positive
   - ❑ B. negative
   - ❑ C. extra positive
   - ❑ D. extra negative

3. I can see it. ◀
   - ❑ A. positive
   - ❑ B. negative
   - ❑ C. extra positive
   - ❑ D. extra negative

4. I can't see it. ◀
   - ❑ A. positive
   - ❑ B. negative
   - ❑ C. extra positive
   - ❑ D. extra negative

5. He can try it. ◀
   - ❑ A. positive
   - ❑ B. negative
   - ❑ C. extra positive
   - ❑ D. extra negative

6. I can't understand him. ◀
   - ❑ A. positive
   - ❑ B. negative
   - ❑ C. extra positive
   - ❑ D. extra negative

7. We can call you. ◀
   - ❑ A. positive
   - ❑ B. negative
   - ❑ C. extra positive
   - ❑ D. extra negative

8. She can't buy one. ◀
   - ❑ A. positive
   - ❑ B. negative
   - ❑ C. extra positive
   - ❑ D. extra negative

9. She can do it. ◀
   - ❑ A. positive
   - ❑ B. negative
   - ❑ C. extra positive
   - ❑ D. extra negative

Rule of Grammar

Double negatives are a no-no.

Application of Intonation

CD 2 Track 27

There is always at least one stressed word in a sentence, and frequently you can have quite a few if you are introducing a lot of new information or if you want to contrast several things. Look at the paragraph in Exercise 4-18. Take a pencil and mark every word that you think should be stressed or sound stronger than the words around it. I'd like you to make just an accent mark (') to indicate a word you think should sound stronger than others around it.

Reminder: The three ways to change your voice for intonation are:

(1) **Volume** (speak louder)
(2) **Length** (stretch out a word)
(3) **Pitch** (change your tone)

✘ Pause the CD and work on the paragraph below.

Exercise 4-18: Application of Stress

CD 2 Track 28

Mark every word or syllable with ´ where you think that the sound is stressed. Use the first sentence as your example. Check Answer Key beginning on page 210. Pause the CD.

Héllo, **my'** name is_____. I'm taking American Accent Training. There's a lot to learn, but I hope to make it as enjoyable as possible. I should pick up on the American intonation pattern pretty easily, although the only way to get it is to practice all of the time. I use the up and down, or peaks and valleys, intonation more than I used to. I've been paying attention to pitch, too. It's like walking down a staircase. I've been talking to a lot of Americans lately, and they tell me that I'm easier to understand. Anyway, I could go on and on, but the important thing is to listen well and sound good. Well, what do you think? Do I?

▸ Listen and make any corrections. After you've put in the accent marks where you think they belong, take a highlighter, and as I read very slowly, mark the words that I stress. I am going to exaggerate the words far more than you'd normally hear in a normal reading of the paragraph. You can mark either the whole word or just the strong syllable, whichever you prefer, so that you have a bright spot of color for where the stress should fall.

Note *If you do the exercise only in pencil, your eye and mind will tend to skip over the accent marks. The spots of color, however, will register as "different" and thereby encourage your pitch change. This may strike you as unusual, but trust me, it works.*

✘ Pause the CD and practice reading the paragraph out loud three times on your own.

How You Talk Indicates to People How You Are

Beware of "Revealing" a Personality that You Don't Have!

There is no absolute right or wrong in regard to intonation because a case can be made for stressing just about any word or syllable, but you actually reveal a lot about yourself by the elements you choose to emphasize. For example, if you say, *Hello,* this intonation would indicate doubt. This is why you say, *Hello?* when answering the telephone because you don't know who is on the other end. Or when you go into a house and you don't know who's there because you don't see anyone. But if you're giving a speech or making a presentation and you stand up in front of a crowd and say *Hello,* the people would probably laugh because it sounds so uncertain. This is where you'd confidently want to say *Hello,* **my** *name is* **So-and-so**.

A second example is, **my** *name is*—as opposed to *my* **name** *is.* If you stress *name,* it sounds as if you are going to continue with more personal information: *My* **name** *is So-and-so, my* **address** *is such-and-such, my* **blood** *type is O.* Since it may not be your intention to give all that information, stay with the standard—*Hello,* **my** *name is* **So-and-so**.

If you stress *I* every time, it will seem that you have a very high opinion of yourself. Try it: **I'm** *taking American Accent Training.* **I've** *been paying attention to pitch, too.* **I** *think I'm quite wonderful.*

An earnest, hard-working person might emphasize words this way: *I'm* **taking** *American Accent Training* (Can I learn this stuff?). *I hope to* **make** *it as enjoyable as possible* (I'll force myself to enjoy it if I have to). *Although the only way to get it is to practice* **all** *of the time* (24 hours a day).

A Doubting Thomas would show up with: *I* **should** *pick up on* (but I might not) *the American intonation pattern* **pretty** *easily* (but it looks pretty hard, too). *I've been talking to a lot of Americans lately, and they* **tell** *me that I'm easier to understand* (but I think they're just being polite). (See also Chapter 1.)

Exercise 4-19: Paragraph Intonation Practice

▸ *From your color-marked copy, read each sentence of the paragraph in Exercise 4-18 after me. Use your rubber band, give a clear pitch change to the highlighted words, and think about the meaning that the pitch is conveying.*

✖ *Back up the CD and practice this paragraph three times.*

✖ *Pause the CD and practice three times on your own.*

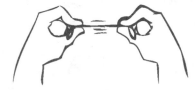

Exercise 4-20: Reading with Staircase Intonation CD 2 Track 31

Read the following with clear intonation where marked.

Hello, **my** name is_____. I'm taking American **Accent** Training. There's a **lot** to **learn**, but I **hope** to make it as **enjoyable** as possible. I should pick **up** on the American **intonation** pattern pretty **easily,** although the **only** way to **get** it is to **practice** all of the time. I use the **up** and down, or **peaks** and valleys, **intonation** more than I **used** to. I've been paying attention to **pitch, too.** It's like **walking** down a **stair**case. I've been **talking** to a lot of **Americans** lately, and they tell me that I'm **easier** to under**stand. Any**way, I could go **on** and on, but the **important** thing is to **listen** well and sound **good. Well,** what do you **think**? **Do** I?

Exercise 4-21: Spelling and Numbers CD 2 Track 32

Just as there is stress in words or phrases, there is intonation in spelling and numbers. Americans seem to spell things out much more than other people. In any bureaucratic situation, you'll be asked to spell names and give all kinds of numbers—your phone number, your birth date, and so on. There is a distinct stress and rhythm pattern to both spelling and numbers—usually in groups of three or four letters or numbers, with the stress falling on the last member of the group. Acronyms (phrases that are represented by the first letter of each word) and initials are usually stressed on the last letter. Just listen to the words as I say them, then repeat the spelling after me.

Acronym	Pronunciation	Spelling	Pronunciation
IBM	Eye Bee **Em**	Box	Bee Oh **Ex**
MIT	Em Eye **Tee**	Cook	See Oh Oh **Kay**
Ph.D.	Pee Aitch **Dee**	Wilson	Dubya You Eye **El**, Ess Oh **En**
MBA	Em Bee **εi**		
LA	Eh **Lay**		
IQ	Eye **Kyu**	**Numbers**	**Pronunciation**
RSVP	Are Ess Vee **Pee**	Area Code	**213**
TV	Tee **Vee**	Zip Code	**91604**
USA	You Ess **εi**	Date	**9/6/62**
ASAP	εi Ess εi **Pee**	Phone Number	**1**(800)-**475-4255**
CIA	See Eye **εi**		
FBI	Eff Bee **Eye**		
USMC	You Ess Em **See**	**Time**	**Pronunciation**
COD	See Oh **Dee**	Nine-fifteen	9:**15**
SOS	Ess Oh **Ess**	Two-thirty	2:**30**
X, Y, Z	Ex, Why, **Zee**	Names	**mid**night, after**noon**

Exercise 4-22: Sound/Meaning Shifts   CD 2 Track 33

Intonation is powerful. It can change meaning and pronunciation. Here you will get the chance to play with the sounds. Remember, in the beginning, the meaning isn't that important—just work on getting control of your pitch changes. Use your rubber band for each stressed word.

my **tie**	**mai**-tai	**Might** I?
my **keys**	**Mi**key's	My **keys**?
inn **key**	in **key**	**ink**y
my **tea**	**might**y	My **D**
I have **two**.	I have, **too**.	I **have** to.

How many **kids** do you have?	I have **two**.
I've been to **Europe**.	I have, **too**.
Why do you **work** so hard?	I **have** to.

Exercise 4-23: Squeezed-Out Syllables   CD 2 Track 34

Intonation can also completely get rid of certain entire syllables. Some longer words that are stressed on the first syllable squeeze weak syllables right out. Cover up the regular spelling and read the phonetics.

accidentally	æk•sə•**dent**•lee	favorite	**fāv**•rit
actually	**æk**•chully	finally	**fyn**•lee
aspirin	**æs**prin	general	**jɛn**r'l
average	**æv**r'j	groceries	**gross**reez
bakery	**bā**•kree	history	**hiss**tree
basically	**ba**•sə•klee	interest	**intr**'st
beverage	**bev**•r'j	jewelry	**jool**ree
boundary	**bound**•ree	liberal	**libr**'l
broccoli	**brä**klee	mathematics	**mæth**mædix
business	**biz**ness	memory	**mɛm**ree
cabinet	**cæb**•net	natural	**næch**•rul
camera	**kæm**ruh	Niagara	**nyæ**•grə
catholic	**cæth**•l'k	nursery	**nr**•sree
chocolate	**chäk**l't	onion	**ən**y'n
comfortable	**k'mf**•t'bl	opera	**äp**rə
conference	**cän**frns	orange	**ornj**
corporal	**cor**pr'l	preference	**pref**•rənce
coverage	**c'v**r'j	probably	**präb**lee
desperate	**dɛs**pr't	realize	**ri**•lize
diamond	**däi**m'nd	restaurant	**rɛs**tränt
diaper	**däi**per	separate	**sɛp**r't
different	**diff**r'nt	several	**sɛv**r'l
emerald	**ɛm**r'ld	theory	**thi**ree
emory	**ɛm**ree	threatening	**thrɛt**ning
every	**ɛv**ree	vegetable	**vej**•t'bl
family	**fæm**lee	victory	**vic**•tree

Note *The **-cally** ending is always pronounced **-klee**; **-tory** turns into **-tree**.*

Exercise 4-24: Regular Transitions of Nouns and Verbs CD 2 Track 35

*In the list below, change the stress from the first syllable for **nouns** to the second syllable for **verbs**. This is a regular, consistent change. Intonation is so powerful that you'll notice that when the stress changes, the pronunciation of the vowels do, too.*

Nouns		Verbs	
an accent	**æk**s'nt	to accent	æk**sɛnt**
a concert	**kän**sert	to concert	k'n**sert**
a conflict	**kän**flikt	to conflict	k'n**flikt**
a contest	**kän**test	to contest	k'n**test**
a contract	**kän**træct	to contract	k'n**trækt**
a contrast	**kän**træst	to contrast	k'n**træst**
a convert	**kän**vert	to convert	k'n**vert**
a convict	**kän**vikt	to convict	k'n**vict**
a default	**dee**fält	to default	d'**fält**
a desert*	**dɛz**'rt	to desert	d'**z'rt**
a discharge	**dis**chärj	to discharge	d'**schärj**
an envelope	**än**v'lop	to envelop	en**vel**'p
an incline	**in**kline	to incline	in**kline**
an influence	**in**flu(w)'ns	to influence	in**flu**(w)ns†
an insert	**in**sert	to insert	in**sert**
an insult	**in**s'lt	to insult	in**səlt**
an object	**äb**ject	to object	ə**bject**
perfect	**prf**'ct	to perfect	pr**fekt**
a permit	**pr**mit	to permit	pr**mit**
a present	**prɛz**'nt	to present	pr'**zɛnt**
produce	**pro**duce	to produce	pr'**duce**
progress	**prä**gr's	to progress	pr'**grɛss**
a project	**prä**ject	to project	pr'**jɛct**
a pronoun	**pro**noun	to pronounce	pr'**nounce**
a protest	**pro**test	to protest	pr'**test**
a rebel	**rɛ**bəl	to rebel	r'**bɛl**
a recall	**ree**käll	to recall	r'**käll**
a record	**rɛk**'rd	to record	r'**cord**
a reject	**re**ject	to reject	r'**jɛct**
research	**re**s'rch	to research	r'**srch**
a subject	**s'b**jekt	to subject	s'**bjekt**
a survey	**s'r**vei	to survey	s'**rvei**
a suspect	**s's**pekt	to suspect	s's**pekt**

* The **désert** is hot and dry. A **dessért** is ice cream. To **desért** is to abandon.

† *Pronunciation symbols (w) and (y) represent a glide sound. This is explained on page 87.*

Exercise 4-25: Regular Transitions of Adjectives and Verbs   CD 2 Track 36

*A different change occurs when you go from an adjective or a noun to a verb. The stress stays in the same place, but the -**mate** in an adjective is completely reduced to -**m't**, whereas in a verb, it is a full **ā** sound: -**mɛit**.*

Nouns/Adjectives		Verbs	
advocate	**æd**v'k't	to advocate	**æd**v'kɛit
animate	**æn**'m't	to animate	**æn**'mɛit
alternate	**äl**tern't	to alternate	**äl**ternɛit
appropriate	ə**pro**pre⁽ʸ⁾'t	to appropriate	ə**pro**pre⁽ʸ⁾ɛit
approximate	ə**präk**s'm't	to approximate	ə**präk**s'mɛit
articulate	är**tic**yul't	to articulate	är**tic**yəlɛit
associate	ə**sso**sey't	to associate	ə**sso**seyɛit
deliberate	d'**libr**'t	to deliberate	d'**libe**rɛit
discriminate	d'**skrim**'n't	to discriminate	d'**skrim**'nɛit
duplicate	**dup**l'k't	to duplicate	**dup**l'kɛit
elaborate	e**læb**r't	to elaborate	ə**læb**erɛit
an estimate	**ɛst**'m't	to estimate	**ɛst**'mɛit
graduate	**græ**jyu⁽ʷ⁾'t	to graduate	**græ**jyu⁽ʷ⁾ɛit
intimate	**int**'m't	to intimate	**int**'mɛit
moderate	**mä**der't	to moderate	**mä**derɛit
predicate	**prɛ**d'k't	to predicate	**prɛ**d'kɛit
separate	**sɛp**r't	to separate	**sɛp**erɛit

Exercise 4-26: Regular Transitions of Adjectives and Verbs   CD 2 Track 37

Mark the intonation or indicate the long vowel on the boldfaced word, depending which part of speech it is. Pause the CD and mark the proper syllables. Check Answer Key, beginning on page 210.

1. You need to **insert** a paragraph here on this newspaper **insert**.
2. How can you **object** to this **object**?
3. I'd like to **present** you with this **present**.
4. Would you care to **elaborate** on his **elaborate** explanation?
5. The manufacturer couldn't **recall** if there'd been a **recall**.
6. The religious **convert** wanted to **convert** the world.
7. The political **rebels** wanted to **rebel** against the world.
8. The mogul wanted to **record** a new **record** for his latest artist.
9. If you **perfect** your intonation, your accent will be **perfect**.
10. Due to the drought, the fields didn't **produce** much **produce** this year.
11. Unfortunately, City Hall wouldn't **permit** them to get a **permit**.
12. Have you heard that your **associate** is known to **associate** with gangsters?
13. How much do you **estimate** that the **estimate** will be?
14. The facilitator wanted to **separate** the general topic into **separate** categories.

> Whenever there is more than one syllable, one will be stronger.

Syllable Count Intonation Patterns

CD 2 Track 38

In spoken English, if you put the em**pha**sis on the wrong sy**lla**ble, you totally lose the meaning, when you need to put the em**pha**sis on the right **sy**llable.

At this point, we won't be concerned with *why* we are stressing a particular syllable—that understanding will come at the end of this chapter.

Exercise 5-1: Syllable Patterns
CD 2 Track 39

In order to practice accurate pitch change, repeat the following columns. Each syllable will count as one musical note. Remember that words that end in a vowel or a voiced consonant will be longer than ones ending in an unvoiced consonant (p, f, s, t, k, x, sh, th, ch).

1 Syllable	A	B	C
Pattern 1a	la!	get	stop
	cat	quick	which
	jump	choice	bit
	box	loss	beat
Pattern 1b	la-a	law	bid
	dog	goes	bead
	see	choose	car
	plan	lose	know

2 Syllables	A	B	C
Pattern 2a	la-**la**	Bob **Smith**	for **you**
	a **dog**	my **car**	Who **knows**?
	a **cat**	some **more**	cas**sette**
	des**troy**	red **tape**	bal**let**
	a **pen**	en**close**	va**let**
	pre**tend**	con**sume**	to **do**
	your **job**	my **choice**	to**day**
	pea **soup**	How's **work**?	to**night**
Pattern 2b	la-la	**wrist**watch	**phone** book
	hot dog	**text**book	**door**knob
	icy	**book**shelf	**note**book
	suitcase	**sun**shine	**house** key
	project	**place** mat	**ballot**
	sunset	**stapler**	**valid**
	Get one!	**mo**dern	**dog** show
	Do it!	**mo**dem	**want** ad

a hot *dog* is an overheated canine 🐕 ; a *hot*dog is a frankfurter 🍴

45

Exercise 5-1: Syllable Patterns *continued*

3 Syllables	A	B	C
Pattern 3a	la-la-**la**	**Worms** eat **dirt.**	**Joe** has **three.**
♪♪♩	**Bob's** hot **dog** 🐕	**Inch**worms **inch.**	**Bob** has **eight.**
	Bob won't **know.**	**Pets** need **care.**	**Al** jumped **up.**
	Sam's the **boss.**	**Ed's** too **late.**	**Glen** sat **down.**
	Susie's nice.	**Paul** threw **up.**	**Tom** made **lunch.**
	Bill went **home.**	**Wool** can **itch.**	**Kids** should **play.**
	Cats don't **care.**	**Birds** sing **songs.**	**Mom** said, **"No!"**
	Stocks can **fall.**	**Spot** has **fleas.**	**Mars** is **red.**
	School is **fun.**	**Nick's** a **punk.**	**Ned** sells **cars.**
Pattern 3b	la-la-**la**	Make a **cake.**	IB**M**
♪♪♩	a hot **dog** 🐕	He for**got.**	a good **time**
	I don't **know.**	Take a **bath.**	Use your **head!**
	He's the **boss.**	We're too **late.**	How are **you?**
	We cleaned **up.**	I love **you.**	We came **home.**
	in the **bag**	over **here**	on the **bus**
	for a **while**	What a **jerk!**	engi**neer**
	I went **home.**	How's your **job?**	She fell **down.**
	We don't **care.**	How'd it **go?**	They called **back.**
	It's in **March.**	Who'd you **meet?**	You goofed **up.**
Pattern 3c	la-**la**-la	per**cen**tage (%)	O**hi**o
♩♪♪	a **hot**dog 🍴	ad**van**tage	his **foot**ball
	I **don't** know!	It's **start**ing.	They're **leav**ing.
	Jim **killed** it.	Let's **try** it.	How **are** you?
	to**mor**row	fi**nan**cial	em**phat**ic
	a **fruit**cake	I **thought** so.	Dale **planned** it.
	the **en**gine	on **Wednes**day	You **took** it.
	a **wine**glass	in **A**pril	ex**ter**nal
	po**ta**to	I **love** you.	a **bar**gain
	what**ev**er	Let's **tell** him.	Don't **touch** it.
Pattern 3d	**la**-la-la	**al**phabet	**phone** number
♩♪♪	**hot**dog stand	**pos**sible	**think** about
	I don't know.	**Show** me one.	**com**fortable
	analyze	**ar**ea	**wait**ing for
	article	**punc**tuate	**pit**iful
	dinnertime	**em**phasis	**ev**erything
	digital	**syl**lable	**or**chestra
	analog	**Post**-It note	**ig**norant
	cell structure	**Ro**lodex	**Ru**bbermaid

Exercise 5-1: Syllable Patterns *continued*   **CD 2 Track 39**

4 Syllables	A	B	C
Pattern 4a	la-la-la-**la**	**Nate** needs a **break**.	**Max** wants to **know**.
	Spot's a hot **dog**.	**Ed** took my **car**.	**Al's** kitchen **floor**
	Jim killed a **snake**.	**Jill** ate a **steak**.	**Bill's** halfway **there**.
	Joe doesn't **know**.	**Spain's** really **far**.	**Roses** are **red**,
	Nate bought a **book**.	**Jake's** in the **lake**.	**Violets** are **blue**,
	Al brought some **ice**.	**Sam's** in a **bar**.	**Candy** is **sweet**,
			and *so* are *you*.
Pattern 4b	la-la-la-**la**	She asked for **help**.	I want to **know**.
	It's a hot **dog**.	We took my **car**.	the kitchen **floor**
	He killed a **snake**.	We need a **break**.	We watched **TV**.
	He doesn't **know**.	It's really **far**.	She's halfway **there**.
	We came back **in**.	I love you, **too**.	We played all **day**.
	He bought a **book**.	They got a**way**.	Please show me **how**.
Pattern 4c	**la**-la-**la**-la	**Boys** ring **door**bells.	**Phil** knows **mail**men.
	Bob likes **hot**dogs.	**Bill** ate **break**fast.	**Joe** grew **egg**plants.
	Ann eats **pan**cakes.	**Guns** are **le**thal.	**Hump**ty **Dump**ty
	Cats eat **fish** bones.	**Inch**worms **bug** me.	**Hawks** are **vi**cious.
	Bears are **fuzz**y.	**Rag**tops **cost** more.	**Home**work **bores** them.
	Planets **ro**tate.	**Sales**men **sell** things.	**Mike** can **hear** you.
Pattern 4d	la-la-**la**-la	an a**larm** clock	He said, "**Light**bulb."
	It's my **hot**dog.	I don't **need** one.	What does **"box"** mean?
	imi**ta**tion	Ring the **door**bell.	Put your **hands** up.
	ana**ly**tic	What's the **mat**ter?	Where's the **mail**man?
	We like **sci**ence.	intro**duc**tion	an as**sem**bly
	my to-**do** list	my re**port** card	defi**ni**tion
Pattern 4e	la-**la**-la-la	po**ta**to chip	What **time** is it?
	a **hot** dog stand	Whose **turn** is it?	my **phone** number
	Jim **killed** a man.	We **worked** on it.	Let's **eat** something.
	a**nal**ysis	How **tall** are you?	How **old** are you?
	in**vis**ible	in**san**ity	un**touch**able
	a **plat**ypus	a**bil**ity	a **man**iac
Pattern 4f	**la**-la-la-la	**su**pervisor	**light**house keeper
	permanently	**win**dow cleaner	**cough** medicine
	demonstrated	**race** car driver	**bus**iness meeting
	category	**Jan**uary (jæn-yə-wery)	**Feb**ruary (feb•yə•wery)
	office supplies	**prog**ress report	**ba**by-sitter
	educator	**thing**amajig	**dic**tionary

Syllable Rules

The good news is that most of the words used in English are only one syllable.

Rule of Thumb: Stress **nouns** on the **first** syllable and **verbs** on the **second** syllable.

The 95% Rule: When in doubt, stress the **next to last**.

2 Syllables	3 Syllables	1 Syllable Suffix	2 Syllable Suffix	Multiple Syllable Suffix
paper	po**ta**to	eco**nom**ic ic	**pos**sible ible	**crit**ically i+cal+ly
napkin	com**pu**ter	ad**mon**ish ish	**syl**lable able	**ver**ifying i+fy+ing
hotdog	per**sua**sive	**vi**sion ion	com**mu**nity ity	astro**nom**ical nom+i+cal
contest	con**di**tion	**cru**cial ial	bi**ol**ogy logy	edu**ca**tionally tion+al+ly
angry	di**ver**sion	**pho**tograph graph	pho**tog**raphy graphy	photo**graph**ically ic+al+ly

The 5% Rule: Stress the **last syllable**.

Most **two-syllable verbs** stress the **last** syllable, as well as words starting with the prefixes **a-** and **be-**, and words that end in **French suffixes**.

2-Syllable Verbs	Prefixes a- and be-	French Suffixes
be**gin**	a**bove**	refer**ee**
con**test**	be**low**	engin**eer**
de**ny**	a**bout**	client**ele**
con**tain**	be**neath**	bal**let**
re**fuse**	a**cross**	gar**age**

Exercise 5-2: Intonation Shifts

Practice the following intonation shifts.

1st to 3rd	1st to 4th	1st to 2nd to 3rd	2nd to 3rd
accident	**quan**tity	**an**alyze	con**demn**
acci**den**tal	**quan**tify	a**nal**ysis	con**demn**atory
acci**den**tally	quantifi**ca**tion	ana**lyt**ic	condem**na**tion
president	**max**imum	**cat**alyze	re**volve**
presi**den**tial	**max**imize	ca**tal**ysis	re**volv**er
presi**den**tially	maximi**za**tion	cata**lyt**ic	revo**lu**tionary
de**velop***	**or**igin	**real**	cre**ate**
de**vel**opment	o**rig**inal	**real**ize	cre**a**tive
develop**men**tal	o**rig**inate	re**al**ity	cre**a**tion
develop**men**tally	origi**na**tion	reali**za**tion	crea**tiv**ity

*This is a key word stress issue for Indians, who tend to stress the first syllable, **de**velop, instead of the second, de**vel**op. This is the same situation in com**po**nent and be**gin**ning.

Chapter 6

Complex Intonation

CD 2 Track 42

This is the beginning of an extremely important part of spoken American English—the rhythms and intonation patterns of the long streams of nouns and adjectives that are so commonly used. These exercises will tie in the intonation patterns of **adjectives** *(nice, old, best,* etc.), **nouns** *(dog, house, surgeon,* etc.), and **adverbs** *(very, really, amazingly,* etc.).

One way of approaching sentence intonation is not to build each sentence from scratch. Instead, use patterns, with each pattern similar to a mathematical formula. Instead of plugging in numbers, however, plug in words.

In Exercise 4-2, we looked at simple noun•verb•noun patterns, and in Exercises 5-1 and 5-2, the syllable-count intonation patterns were covered. Here, we'll examine intonation patterns in two-word phrases.

It's important to note that there's a major difference between *syllable stress* and *compound noun stress* patterns. In the syllable count exercises, each *syllable* was represented by a single musical note. In the noun phrases, each individual *word* will be represented by a single musical note—no matter how many total syllables there may be.

At times, what appears to be a single-syllable word will have a "longer" sound to it—*seed* takes longer to say than *seat,* for example. This was introduced on page 25, where you learned that a final voiced consonant causes the previous vowel to double.

Exercise 6-1: Single-Word Phrases   CD 2 Track 43

Repeat the following noun and adjective sentences.

	Noun	Adjective
1.	It's a **nail**.	It's **short**.
2.	It's a **cake**.	It's **chocolate**. (chäkl't)
3.	It's a **tub**.	It's **hot**. (hät)
4.	It's a **drive**.	It's **härd**.
5.	It's a **door**.	It's in **back**. (bæk)
6.	It's a **cärd**.	There are **four**.
7.	It's a **spot**. (spät)	It's **smäll**.
8.	It's a **book**. (bük)	It's **good**. (güd)

Write your own noun and adjective sentences below. You will be using these examples throughout this series of exercises.

9. It's a _____ It's _____

10. It's a _____ It's _____

11. It's a _____ It's _____

Two-Word Phrases

Descriptive Phrases

CD 2 Track 44

Nouns are "heavier" than adjectives; they carry the weight of the new information. An adjective and a noun combination is called a *descriptive phrase,* and in the absence of contrast or other secondary changes, the stress will always fall naturally on the noun. In the absence of a noun, you will stress the adjective, but as soon as a noun appears on the scene, it takes immediate precedence—and should be stressed.

| Exercise 6-2: Sentence Stress with Descriptive Phrases | CD 2 Track 45 |

Repeat the following phrases.

	Adjective	Noun and Adjective
1.	It's **short**.	It's a short **nail**.
2.	It's **chocolate**.	It's a chocolate **cake**.
3.	It's **good**.	It's a good **plan**.
4.	It's **guarded**.	It's a guarded **gate**.
5.	It's **wide**.	It's a wide **river**.
6.	There're **four**.	There're four **cards**.
7.	It was **small**.	It was a small **spot**.
8.	It's the **best**.	It's the best **book**.

Pause the CD and write your own adjective and noun/adjective sentences. Use the same words from Example 6-1.

9. It's_____   It's a _____
10. It's_____   It's a _____
11. It's_____   It's a _____

| Exercise 6-3: Two Types of Descriptive Phrases | CD 2 Track 46 |

Repeat.

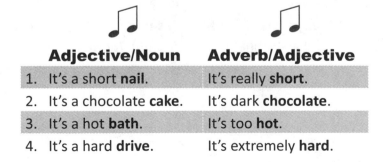

	Adjective/Noun	Adverb/Adjective
1.	It's a short **nail**.	It's really **short**.
2.	It's a chocolate **cake**.	It's dark **chocolate**.
3.	It's a hot **bath**.	It's too **hot**.
4.	It's a hard **drive**.	It's extremely **hard**.

Exercise 6-3: Two Types of Descriptive Phrases *continued* CD 2 Track 46

5.	It's the back **door**.	It's far **back**.
6.	There are four **cards**.	There are only **four**.
7.	It's a small **spot**.	It's laughably **small**.
8.	It's a good **book**.	It's amazingly **good**.

Pause the CD and write your own adjective/noun and adverb/adjective sentences, carrying over Example 6-2.

9. It's a _____ It's _____

10. It's a _____ It's_____

11. It's a _____ It's_____

Exercise 6-4: Descriptive Phrase Story – The Ugly Duckling CD 2 Track 47

The following well-known story has been rewritten to contain only descriptions. Stress the second word of each phrase. Repeat after me.

There is a *mother duck.* She lays *three eggs.* Soon, there are three *baby birds.* Two of the birds are *very beautiful.* One of them is *quite ugly.* The *beautiful ducklings* make fun of their *ugly brother.* The *poor thing* is *very unhappy.* As the *three birds* grow older, the *ugly duckling* begins to change. His *gray feathers* turn *snowy white.* His *gangly neck* becomes *beautifully smooth.*

In *early spring,* the *ugly duckling* is swimming in a *small pond* in the *backyard* of the *old farm.* He sees his *shimmering reflection* in the *clear water.* What a *great surprise*! He is no longer an *ugly duckling.* He has grown into a *lovely swan.*

Set Phrases
CD 2 Track 48

A Cultural Indoctrination to American Norms

When I learned the alphabet as a child, I *heard* it before I *saw* it. I heard that the last four letters were *dubba-you, ex, why, zee.* I thought that *dubbayou* was a long, strange name for a letter, but I didn't question it anymore than I did *aitch.* It was just a name. Many years later, it struck me that it was a *double U.* Of course, a **W** is really **UU**. I had such a funny feeling, though, when I realized that something I had taken for granted for so many years had a background meaning that I had completely overlooked. This "funny feeling" is exactly what most native speakers get when a two-word phrase is stressed on the wrong word. When two individual words go through the cultural process of becoming a set phrase, the original sense of each word is more or less forgotten and the new meaning completely takes over. When we hear the word *pain**killer,*** we think *anesthetic.* If, however, someone says *pain**killer,*** it brings up the strength and almost unrelated meaning of *kill.*

When you have a two-word phrase, you have to either stress on the first word, or on the second word. If you stress both or neither, it's not clear what you are trying to say. Stress on the first word is more noticeable and one of the most important concepts of intonation that you are going to study. At first glance, it doesn't seem significant, but the more you look at this concept, the more you are going to realize that it reflects how we Americans think, what concepts we have adopted as our own, and what things we consider important.

Set phrases are our "cultural icons," or word images; they are indicators of a *determined use* that we have internalized. These set phrases, with stress on the first word, have been taken into everyday English from descriptive phrases, with stress on the second word. As soon as a descriptive phrase becomes a set phrase, the emphasis shifts from the *second* word to the *first*. The original sense of each word is more or less forgotten, and the new meaning takes over.

Set phrases indicate that we have internalized this phrase as an *image,* that we all agree on a concrete idea that this phrase represents. A hundred years or so ago, when Levi Strauss first came out with his denim pants, they were described as *blue **jeans***. Now that we all agree on the image, however, they are ***blue** jeans*.

A more recent example would be the descriptive phrase, *He's a real party animal.* This slang expression refers to someone who has a great time at a party. When it first became popular, the people using it needed to explain (with their intonation) that he was an *animal* at a *party.* As time passed, the expression became cliché and we changed the intonation to *He's a real **party** animal* because "everyone knew" what it meant.

Clichés are hard to recognize in a new language because what may be an old and tired expression to a native speaker may be fresh and exciting to a newcomer. One way to look at English from the inside out, rather than always looking from the outside in, is to get a feel for what Americans have already accepted and internalized. This starts out as a purely language phenomenon, but you will notice that as you progress and undergo the relentless cultural indoctrination of standard intonation patterns, you will find yourself expressing yourself with the language cues and signals that will mark you as an insider—not an outsider.

When the interpreter was translating for the former Russian president Mikhail Gorbachev about his trip to San Francisco in 1990, his pronunciation was good, but he placed himself on the outside by repeatedly saying, *cable **car***. The phrase ***cable** car* is an image, an established entity, and it was very noticeable to hear it stressed on the second word as a mere description.

An important point that I would like to make is that the "rules" you are given here are not meant to be memorized. This discussion is only an introduction to give you a starting point in understanding this phenomenon and in recognizing what to listen for. Read it over; think about it; then listen, try it out, listen some more, and try it out again.

As you become familiar with intonation, you will become more comfortable with American norms, thus the cultural orientation, or even cultural indoctrination, aspect of the following examples.

Note *When you get the impression that a two-word description could be hyphenated or even made into one word, it is a signal that it could be a set phrase—for example, **flash** light, **flash**-light, **flash**light. Also, stress the first word with Street (**Main** Street) and nationalities of food and people (**Mexican** food, **Chinese** girls).*

Exercise 6-5: Sentence Stress with Set Phrases

Repeat the following sentences.

	Noun	Noun/Adj.	Set Phrase
1.	It's a **finger**.	It's a **nail**.	It's a **finger**nail.
2.	It's a **pan**.	It's a **cake**.	It's a **pan**cake.
3.	It's a **tub**.	It's **hot**.	It's a **hot** tub. (Jacuzzi)
4.	It's a **drive**.	It's **hard**.	It's a **hard** drive.
5.	It's a **bone**.	It's in **back**.	It's the **back**bone. (spine)
6.	It's a **card**.	It's a **trick**.	It's a **card** trick.
7.	It's a **spot**.	It's a **light**.	It's a **spot**light.
8.	It's a **book**.	It's a **phone**.	It's a **phone** book.

Pause the CD and write your own noun and set phrase sentences, carrying over the same nouns you used in Exercise 6-2. Remember, when you use a noun, include the article (a, an, the); when you use an adjective, you don't need an article.

9. It's a_____ It's a_____ It's a_____

10. It's a_____ It's a_____ It's a_____

11. It's a_____ It's a_____ It's a_____

Exercise 6-6: Making Set Phrases

Pause the CD and add a noun to each word as indicated by the picture. Check Answer Key, beginning on page 210.

1. a chair   a **chair**man
2. a phone   _____
3. a house   _____
4. a base   _____
5. a door   _____
6. the White   _____
7. a movie   _____
8. the Bullet   _____
9. a race   _____
10. a coffee   _____

11. a wrist   _____
12. a beer   _____
13. a high   _____
14. a hunting   _____
15. a dump   _____
16. a jelly   _____
17. a love   _____
18. a thumb   _____
19. a lightning   _____
20. a pad   _____

Exercise 6-7: Set Phrase Story – The Little Match Girl   CD 2 Track 51

The following story contains only set phrases, as opposed to the descriptive story in Exercise 6-4. Stress the first word of each phrase.

The little *match girl* was out in a *snow*storm. Her feet were like *ice cubes* and *her fingertips* had *frostbite.* She hadn't sold any matches since *daybreak,* and she had a *stomachache* from the *hunger pangs,* but her *stepmother* would beat her with a *broomstick* if she came home with an empty *coin purse.* Looking into the bright *living rooms,* she saw *Christmas trees* and warm *fireplaces.* Out on the *snowbank,* she lit a match and saw the image of a grand *dinner table* of food before her. As the *matchstick* burned, the illusion slowly faded. She lit *another one* and saw a room full of happy *family members.* On the last match, her *grandmother* came down and carried her home. In the morning, the *passersby* saw the little *match girl.* She had frozen during the *nighttime,* but she had a smile on her face.

Contrasting a Description and a Set Phrase

We now have two main intonation patterns—*first word stress* and *second word stress.* In the following exercise, we will contrast the two.

Exercise 6-8: Contrasting Descriptive and Set Phrases   CD 2 Track 52

Repeat after me.

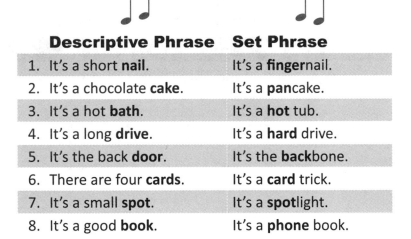

Descriptive Phrase	Set Phrase
1. It's a short **nail**.	It's a **finger**nail.
2. It's a chocolate **cake**.	It's a **pan**cake.
3. It's a hot **bath**.	It's a **hot** tub.
4. It's a long **drive**.	It's a **hard** drive.
5. It's the back **door**.	It's the **back**bone.
6. There are four **cards**.	It's a **card** trick.
7. It's a small **spot**.	It's a **spot**light.
8. It's a good **book**.	It's a **phone** book.

Pause the CD and rewrite your descriptive phrases (Example 6-2) and set phrases (Example 6-5).

9. It's a _____	It's a _____
10. It's a _____	It's a _____
11. It's a _____	It's a _____

Repeat the following pairs.

Descriptive Phrase	**Set Phrase**
a light **bulb**	a **light**bulb
blue **pants**	**blue** jeans
a cold **fish**	a **gold**fish
a gray **hound**	a **grey**hound
an old **key**	an **inn** key
a white **house**	the **White** House
a nice **watch**	a **wrist**watch
a sticky **web**	a **spider** web
a clean **cup**	a **coffee** cup
a sharp **knife**	a **steak** knife
a baby **alligator**	a **baby** bottle
a shiny **tack**	**thumb**tacks
a wire **brush**	a **hair**brush
a new **ball**	a **foot**ball
a toy **gun**	a **machine** gun
a silk **bow**	a **Band**-Aid
a bright **star**	a **fire**cracker
Mary **Jones**	a **mail**box
Bob **Smith**	a **spray** can
foreign **affairs**	a **wine**glass
down **payment**	a **foot**print
New **York**	a **straw**berry
Social **Security**	a **fig** leaf
City **Hall**	an **ice** cream

Summary of Stress in Two-Word Phrases   CD 2 Track 54

First Word	set phrases	*light*bulb
	streets	*Main* Street
	Co. or Corp.	*Xerox* Corporation
	nationalities of food	*Chinese* food
	nationalities of people	*French* guy
Second Word	descriptive phrases	new *information*
	road designations	Fifth *Avenue*
	modified adjectives	really *big*
	place names and parks	New *York*, Central *Park*
	institutions, or Inc.	Oakland *Museum*; Xerox, *Inc.*
	personal-names and titles	Bob *Smith*, Assistant *Manager*
	personal pronouns and possessives	his *car*, Bob's *brother*
	articles	the *bus*, a *week*, an *hour*
	initials and acronyms	U.S., I*Q*
	chemical compounds	zinc *oxide*
	colors and numbers	red *orange*, 2*6*
	most compound verbs	go *away*, sit *down*, fall *off*
	percent and dollar	10 *percent*, 50 *dollars*
	hyphenated nationalities	African-*American*
	descriptive nationalities	Mexican *restaurant*

Nationalities   CD 2 Track 55

When you are in a foreign country, the subject of nationalities naturally comes up a lot. It would be nice if there were a simple rule that said that all the words using nationalities are stressed on the first word. There isn't, of course. Take this preliminary quiz to see if you need to do this exercise. For simplicity's sake, we will stick with one nationality—American.

Exercise 6-10: Nationality Intonation Quiz   CD 2 Track 56

Pause the CD and stress one word in each of the following examples. Repeat after me. (See also Chapter 5.)

1. an American guy
2. an American restaurant
3. American food
4. an American teacher
5. an English teacher

When you first look at it, the stress shifts may seem arbitrary, but let's examine the logic behind these five examples and use it to go on to other, similar cases.

1. an Américan guy

The operative word is *American; guy* could even be left out without changing the meaning of the phrase. Compare *I saw two **American** guys yesterday,* with *I saw two **Americans** yesterday.* Words like *guy, man, kid, lady, people* are de facto pronouns in an anthropocentric language. A strong noun, on the other hand, would be stressed—*They flew an American **flag**.* This is why you have the pattern change in Exercise 5-1: 4e, *Jim **killed** a man;* but 4b, *He killed a **snake**.*

2. an American réstaurant

Don't be sidetracked by an ordinary descriptive phrase that happens to have a nationality in it. You are describing the restaurant: *We went to a good **restaurant** yesterday* or *We went to an American **restaurant** yesterday.* You would use the same pattern where the nationality is more or less incidental in *I had French **toast** for breakfast.* **French** *fry,* on the other hand, has become a set phrase.

3. Américan food

Food is a weak word. *I never ate **American** food when I lived in Japan. Let's have **Chinese** food for dinner.*

4. an American téacher

This is a description, so the stress is on *teacher.*

5. an Énglish teacher

This is a set phrase. The stress is on the subject being taught, not the nationality of the teacher: *a **French** teacher, a **Spanish** teacher, a **history** teacher.*

Exercise 6-11: Contrasting Descriptive and Set Phrases   CD 2 Track 57

Repeat the following pairs.

Set Phrase	Descriptive Phrase
An **English** teacher...	An English **teacher**...
...teaches English.	...is from England.
An **English** book...	An English **book**...is on any subject,
...teaches the English language.	but it came from England.
An **English** test...	An English **test**... is on any subject,
...tests a student on the English language.	but it deals with or came from England.
English food...	An English **restaurant**...
...is kippers for breakfast.	...serves kippers for breakfast.

Intonation can indicate completely different meanings for otherwise similar words or phrases. For example, an **English** teacher teaches English, but an *English* **teacher** is from England; **French** class is where you study French, but *French* **class** is Gallic style and sophistication; an **orange** tree grows oranges, but an *orange* **tree** is any kind of tree that has been painted orange. To have your intonation tested, call (800) 457-4255.

Exercise 6-12: Contrast of Compound Nouns   CD 2 Track 58

In the following list of words, underline the element that should be stressed. Pause the CD. Check Answer Key, beginning on page 210. Repeat after me.

1.	the **White** House	21.	convenience store	41.	a doorknob
2.	a white **house**	22.	convenient store	42.	a glass door
3.	a darkroom	23.	to pick up	43.	a locked door
4.	a dark room	24.	a pickup truck	44.	ice cream
5.	Fifth Avenue	25.	six years old	45.	I scream.
6.	Main Street	26.	a six-year-old	46.	elementary
7.	a main street	27.	six and a half	47.	a lemon tree
8.	a hot dog 🐕	28.	a sugar bowl	48.	Watergate
9.	a hotdog 🍴	29.	a wooden bowl	49.	the back gate
10.	a baby blanket	30.	a large bowl	50.	the final year
11.	a baby's blanket	31.	a mixing bowl	51.	a yearbook
12.	a baby bird	32.	a top hat	52.	United States
13.	a blackbird	33.	a nice hat	53.	New York
14.	a black bird	34.	a straw hat	54.	Long Beach
15.	a greenhouse	35.	a chairperson	55.	Central Park
16.	a green house	36.	Ph.D.	56.	a raw deal
17.	a green thumb	37.	IBM	57.	a deal breaker
18.	a parking ticket	38.	MIT	58.	the bottom line
19.	a one-way ticket	39.	USA	59.	a bottom feeder
20.	an unpaid ticket	40.	ASAP	60.	a new low

Exercise 6-13: Description and Set Phrase Test   CD 3 Track 1

Let's check and see if the concepts are clear. Pause the CD and underline or highlight the stressed word. Check Answer Key, beginning on page 210. Repeat after me.

1. He's **a nice guy**.
2. He's an **American guy** from **San Francisco**.
3. The **cheerleader** needs a **rubber band** to hold her **ponytail**.
4. The **executive assistant** needs a **paper clip** for the **final report**.
5. The **law student** took an **English test** in a **foreign country**.
6. The **policeman** saw a **red car** on the **freeway** in **Los Angeles**.
7. My **old dog** has **long ears** and a **flea problem**.
8. The **new teacher** broke his **coffee cup** on the **first day**.
9. His **best friend** has a **broken cup** in his **other office**.
10. Let's play **football** on the **weekend** in **New York**.
11. **"Jingle Bells"** is a **nice song**.
12. Where are my **new shoes**?
13. Where are my **tennis shoes**?
14. I have a **headache** from the **heat wave** in **South Carolina**.
15. The **newlyweds** took a **long walk** in **Long Beach**.
16. The **little dog** was sitting on the **sidewalk**.
17. The **famous athlete** changed clothes in the **locker room**.
18. The **art exhibit** was held in an **empty room**.
19. There was a **class reunion** at the **high school**.
20. The **headlines** indicated a **new policy**.
21. We got **online** and went to AmericanAccent **dot com**.
22. The **stock options** were listed in the **company directory**.
23. All the **second graders** were out on the **playground**.

Exercise 6-14: Descriptions and Set Phrases – Goldilocks   CD 3 Track 2

*Read the story and stress the indicated words. Notice if they are a **description**, a **set phrase**, or con-trast. Repeat after me. (For the next level of this topic, go to page 141.)*

There is a *little girl.* Her name is *Goldilocks.* She is in a *sunny forest.* She sees a *small house.* She *knocks on* the door, but *no one* answers. She *goes inside.* In the *large room,* there are *three chairs. Goldilocks* sits on the *biggest chair,* but it is *too high.* She sits on the *middle-sized* one, but it is *too low.* She sits on the *small chair* and it *is just right.* On the table, there are *three bowls.* There is *hot porridge* in the bowls. She tries *the first one,* but it is *too hot;* the *second one* is *too cold;* and the *third one* is *just right,* so she eats it all. *After that,* she *goes upstairs.* She *looks around.* There are *three beds,* so she *sits down.* The *biggest bed* is *too hard.* The *middle-sized* bed is *too soft.* The *little one is just right,* so she *lies down.* Soon, she *falls asleep.* In the *meantime,* the family of *three bears* comes home — the *Papa bear,* the *Mama bear,* and the *Baby bear.* They *look around.*

They say, "Who's been sitting in our chairs and eating our porridge?" Then they *run upstairs.* They say, "Who's been sleeping in our beds?" *Goldilocks wakes up.* She is *very scared.* She *runs away. Goldilocks* never *comes back.*

Phrasal Verbs   CD 3 Track 3

When you have a *verb* and a *preposition*, it's called a *phrasal verb*. These are idiomatic expressions that can't be translated literally. They tend to be stressed on the second word, such as sit **down**, fall **off**, get **up**, put **away**, come **back**, etc. If you have a phrasal verb, such as pick **up**, and you put the stress on the first word, it turns into a noun meaning **truck**, as in, "He was driving a **pick**up truck."

Don't come **back**!	He's planning his big **come**back.
Let's back **up** and start again.	Do you have a **back**up plan?
The children have run **off**.	The sewer **run**off polluted the stream.
Could you print this **out**?	Could you make a **print**out?
They broke **up** last week.	It was a terrible **break**up.
Could you call me **back**?	I'm still waiting for a **call**back.
We're going to have to cut **back**.	The **cut**backs are ruining the program.
Sure, go **ahead**.	We got the **go**-ahead.
We need to work **around** the problem.	He came up with a good **work**-around.
The heirlooms were handed **down**.	I won't wear **hand**-me-downs!
How much was left **over**?	What? **Left**overs again!
It didn't work **out**.	It was a great **work**out.
The dogs ran **away**.	It was a **run**away best seller.
He knocked me **down** and dragged me **out**.	It was a **knock**-down, **drag**-out fight.

Chapter 7

Phrasing

Word Groups and Phrasing

CD 3 Track 4

Pauses for Related Thoughts, Ideas, or for Breathing

By now you've begun developing a strong intonation, with clear peaks and reduced valleys, so you're ready for the next step. You may find yourself reading the paragraph in Exercise 4-18 like this:

*Hello**my**nameisSo-and-SoI'mtakingAmerican**Accent**Training.
There's**a****lot**tolearnbutI**hope**tomakeitasen**joy**ableaspossible.*

If so, your audience won't completely comprehend or enjoy your presentation.

In addition to intonation, there is another aspect of speech that indicates meaning. This can be called *phrasing* or *tone*. Have you ever caught just a snippet of a conversation in your own language and somehow known how to piece together what came before or after the part you heard? This has to do with phrasing.

In a sentence, phrasing tells the listener where the speaker is at the moment, where the speaker is going, and if the speaker is finished or not. Note that the intonation stays on the nouns. (See also Chapter 4.)

Exercise 7-1: Phrasing

CD 3 Track 5

Repeat after me.

Statement	**Dogs** eat **bones**.
Clauses	**Dogs** eat **bones**, but **cats** eat **fish**, *or* As we all **know**, **dogs** eat **bones**.
Listing	**Dogs** eat **bones**, **kibbles**, and **meat**.
Question	Do **dogs** eat **bones**?
Repeated Question	Do **dogs** eat **bones**?!!
Tag Question	**Dogs** eat bones, **don't** they?
Tag Statement	**Dogs** eat **bones**, **DON'T** they!
Indirect Speech	He asked if **dogs** ate **bones**.
Direct Speech	"Do **dogs** eat **bones**?" he **asked**.

For clarity, break your sentences with pauses between natural word groups of related thought or ideas. Of course, you will have to break at every comma and every period, but besides those breaks, add other little pauses to let your listeners catch up with you or think over the last burst of information and to allow you time to take a breath. Let's work on this technique. In doing the following exercise, you should think of using *breath groups* and *idea groups*.

Exercise 7-2: Creating Word Groups
CD 3 Track 6

Break the paragraph into natural word groups. Mark every place where you think a pause is needed with a slash.

Hello, **my** name is_____. I'm taking American **Accent** Training. There's a **lot** to **learn**, but I **hope** to make it as **enjoyable** as possible. I should pick **up** on the American **intonation** pattern pretty **easily**, although the **only** way to **get** it is to **practice** all of the time. I use the **up** and down, or **peaks** and valleys **intonation** more than I **used** to. I've been paying attention to **pitch, too**. It's like **walking** down a **stair**case. I've been **talking** to a lot of **Americans** lately, and they tell me that I'm **easier** to under**stand**. **Any**way, I could go on and on, but the **important** thing is to **listen** well and sound **good**. **Well**, what do you **think**? **Do** I?

Note *In the beginning, your word groups should be very short. It'll be a sign of your growing sophistication when they get longer.*

✖ Pause the CD to do your marking.

Exercise 7-3: Practicing Word Groups
CD 3 Track 7

When I read the paragraph this time, I will exaggerate the pauses. Although we're working on word groups here, remember, I don't want you to lose your intonation. Repeat each sentence group after me.

Hello, my name is _____ . I'm taking American Accent Training. There's a lot to learn, but I hope to make it as enjoyable as possible. I should pick up on the American intonation pattern pretty easily, although the only way to get it is to practice all of the time. I use the up and down, or peaks and valleys intonation more than I used to. I've been paying attention to pitch, too. It's like walking down a staircase. I've been talking to a lot of Americans lately, and they tell me that I'm easier to understand. Anyway, I could go on and on, but the important thing is to listen well and sound good. Well. What do you think? Do I?

✖ Next, back up the CD and practice the word groups three times using strong intonation.

✖ Then, pause the CD and practice three more times on your own. When reading, your pauses should be neither long nor dramatic — just enough to give your listener time to digest what you're saying. Be sure to take a breath for each phrase, not for each word or indeed the entire paragraph.

Exercise 7-4: Punctuation & Phrasing	CD 3 Track 8

Take this quick quiz to make sure you can hear the punctuation-based phrasing. Check Answer Key, beginning on page 210.

1. I did it
   A. ☐ . B. ☐ , C. ☐ ? D. ☐ !
2. I did it
   A. ☐ . B. ☐ , C. ☐ ? D. ☐ !
3. I did it
   A. ☐ . B. ☐ , C. ☐ ? D. ☐ !
4. I did it
   A. ☐ . B. ☐ , C. ☐ ? D. ☐ !

Exercise 7-5: Tag Endings	CD 3 Track 9

Pause the CD and complete each sentence with a tag ending. Use the same verb, but with the opposite polarity—positive becomes negative, and negative becomes positive. Check Answer Key, beginning on page 210. (See also Chapter 11.)

Intonation

With a *query*, the intonation rises.
With *confirmation*, the intonation drops.

Pronunciation

Did he?	**Di**dee?
Does he?	**Du**zzy?
Was he?	**Wu**zzy?
Has he?	**Ha**zzy?
Is he?	**Iz**zy?
Will he?	**Wi**lly?
Would he?	**Woo**dy?
Can he?	**Ca**nny?
Wouldn't you?	**Woo**den chew?
Shouldn't I?	**Shüd**n näi?
Won't he?	**Woe** knee?
Didn't he?	**Did**n knee?
Hasn't he?	**Has** a knee?
Wouldn't he?	**Woo**den knee?
Isn't he?	**Is** a knee?
Isn't it?	**Is** a nit?
Doesn't it?	**Duz**za nit?
Aren't I?	**Are** näi?
Won't you?	**Wone** chew?
Don't you?	**Done** chew?
Can't you?	**Can** chew?
Could you?	**Cü**joo?
Would you?	**Wü**joo?

1. The new **clerk** is very **slow**, <u>isn't he</u>!
2. But he can **improve**, _____ ?
3. She doesn't **type** very well, _____ !
4. They lost their **way**, _____ ?
5. You don't **think** so, _____ !
6. I don't think it's **easy**, _____ ?
7. I'm your **friend**, _____ ?
8. You won't be **coming**, _____ !
9. He keeps the **books**, _____ !
10. We have to close the **office**, _____ ?
11. We have closed the **office**, _____ ?
12. We had to close the **office**, _____ !
13. We had the **office** closed, _____ ?
14. We had already closed the **office**, _____ ?
15. We'd better close the **office**, _____ !
16. We'd rather close the **office**, _____ ?
17. The office has **closed**, _____ ?
18. You couldn't **tell**, _____ !
19. You'll be working **late** tonight, _____ ?
20. He should have **been** here by now, _____ !
21. He should be **promoted**, _____ !
22. I didn't send the **fax**, _____ ?
23. I won't get a **raise** this year, _____ ?
24. You use the **computer**, _____ ?
25. You're used to the **computer**, _____ !
26. You used to use the **computer**, _____ ?
27. You never used to work **Saturdays**, _____ ?
28. That's **better**, _____ !

The basic techniques introduced so far, are *pitch, stress,* the *staircase* and *musical notes, reduced sounds,* and *word groups and phrasing.* In Chapters 12 through 25, we refine and expand this knowledge to cover every sound of the American accent.

Chapter 8

> Listen for the actual sounds,
> not what you *think* they are.

The Miracle Technique

CD 3 Track 10

As you saw in Chapter 1 with **Bobby bought a bike (bäbee bädə bäik)**, and in Chapter 2 with **Got it (gäddit)**, there is a difference between pure sound and spelling.

Regaining Long-Lost Listening Skills

The trouble with starting accent training after you know a great deal of English is that you know a great deal *about* English. You have a lot of preconceptions and, unfortunately, misconceptions about the sound of English.

A Child Can Learn Any Language

Every sound of every language is within every child. So, what happens with adults? People learn their native language and stop listening for the sounds that they never hear; then they lose the ability to hear those sounds. Later, when you study a foreign language, you learn a lot of spelling rules that take you still further away from the real sound of that language—in this case, English.

What we are going to do here is teach you to *hear* again. So many times, you've heard what a native speaker said, translated it into your own accent, and repeated it with your accent. Why? Because you "knew" how to say it.

Exercise 8-1: Tell Me Wədai Say CD 3 Track 11

*The first thing you're going to do is write down exactly what I say. It will be nonsense to you for two reasons: First, because I will be saying **sound units**, not **word units**. Second, because I will be starting at the **end** of the sentence instead of the **beginning**. Listen carefully and write down exactly what you hear, regardless of meaning. The first sound is given to you—**kit**.*

_____ _____´ kit

▶ *Once you have written it down, check with the version below.*

*äi **lie** kit*

▶ *Read it out loud to yourself and try to hear what the regular English is. Don't look ahead until you've figured out the sense of it.*

*I **like** it.*

Exercise 8-2: Listening for Pure Sounds
CD 3 Track 12

Again, listen carefully and write the sounds you hear. Start at the end and fill in the blanks right to left, then read them back left to right. Write whichever symbols are easiest for you to read back. The answers are below.

1. _____ _____ dəp´.

2. _____ _____ dæout´.

3. _____ _____ _____´.

4. _____ _____ _____ _____´.

Exercise 8-3: Extended Listening Practice
CD 3 Track 13

Let's do a few more pure sound exercises to fine-tune your ear. Remember, start at the end and fill in the blanks right to left, then read them back left to right. You will only need five non-alphabet symbols: **æ, ä, ə, ü,** *and* **ɛ**. *There are clues sprinkled around for you and all the answers are in the Answer Key, beginning on page 210.*

1. _____´ _____ !

2. thæng´ _____ .

3. _____ _____´ _____´ _____ _____ _____´ _____ !

4. wə _____ _____ _____´ ?

5. kwee _____ _____ _____ _____ ?

6. _____ _____ _____ _____ _____´ _____ _____ _____ _____ ?

7. _____ _____ _____ _____´ _____ _____ _____ bæou _____ .

8. _____ _____ _____´ _____ _____ !

9. _____ _____ _____ _____ _____´ _____ wən.

10. wyn _____ _____ _____ _____´ ?

11. _____ _____ _____´ _____ _____ frə _____ ?

| 1. Yoo zih **dəp**. | 2. Wɛ rih **dæout**. | 3. May kit **doo**. | 4. Orr doo with **æout**. |
| Use it up. | Wear it out. | Make it do. | Or do without. |

Chapter 9

Even in complex sentences,
stress the noun
(unless there is contrast).

Grammar in a Nutshell

Everything You Ever Wanted to Know About Grammar... But Were Afraid to Use
CD 3 Track 14

English is a chronological language. We just love to know when something happened, and this is indicated by the range and depth of our verb tenses.

*I **had** already **seen** it by the time she **brought** it in.*

As you probably learned in your grammar studies, "the past perfect is an action in the past that occurred before a separate action in the past." Whew! Not all languages do this. For example, Japanese is fairly casual about when things happened, but being a hierarchical language, it is very important to know what *relationship* the two people involved had. A high-level person with a low-level one, two peers, a man and a woman, all these things show up in Japanese grammar. Grammatically speaking, English is democratic.

The confusing part is that in English the verb tenses are very important, but instead of putting them up on the *peaks* of a sentence, we throw them all deep down in the *valleys*! Therefore, two sentences with strong intonation—such as, "***Dogs eat bones***" and "*The **dogs**'ll've eaten the **bones***" sound amazingly similar. Why? Because it takes the same amount of time to say both sentences since they have the same number of stresses. The three original words and the rhythm stay the same in these sentences, but the meaning changes as you add more stressed words. Articles and verb tense changes are usually not stressed.

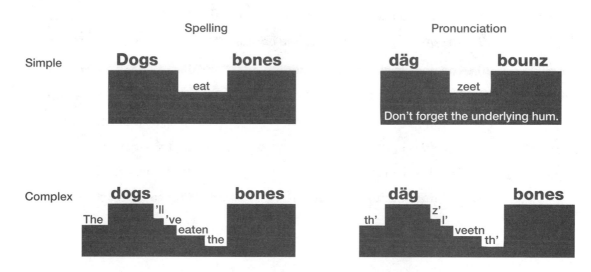

Now let's see how this works in the exercises that follow.

Exercise 9-1: Consistent Noun Stress in Changing Verb Tenses   CD 3 Track 15

This is a condensed exercise for you to practice simple intonation with a wide range of verb tenses. When you do the exercise the first time, go through stressing only the nouns: **Dogs** *eat* **bones.** *Practice this until you are quite comfortable with the intonation. The pronunciation and word connections are on the right, and the full verb tenses are on the far left.*

eat	1.	The **dogs** eat the **bones.**	the **däg** zeet the **bounz**
ate	2.	The **dogs** ate the **bones.**	the **däg** zɛit the **bounz**
are eating	3.	The **dogs**'re eating the **bones.**	the **däg** zr reeding the **bounz**
will eat	4.	The **dogs**'ll eat the **bones** (if)	the **däg** zə leet the **bounz** (if)
would eat	5.	The **dogs**'d eat the **bones** (if)	the **däg** zə deet the **bounz** (if)
would have eaten	6.	The **dogs**'d've eaten the **bones** (if)	the **däg** zədə veetn the **bounz** (if)
that have eaten	7.	The **dogs** that've eaten the **bones** (are)	the **däg** zədə veetn the **bounz** (are)
have eaten	8.	The **dogs**'ve eaten the **bones.**	the **däg** zə veetn the **bounz**
had eaten	9.	The **dogs**'d eaten the **bones.**	the **däg** zə deetn the **bounz**
will have eaten	10.	The **dogs**'ll've eaten the **bones.**	the **däg** zələ veetn the **bounz**
ought to eat	11.	The **dogs** ought to eat the **bones.**	the **däg** zädə eat the **bounz**
should eat	12.	The **dogs** should eat the **bones.**	the **dägz** sh'deet the **bounz**
should not eat	13.	The **dogs** shouldn't eat the **bones.**	the **dägz** sh'dn•neet the **bounz**
should have eaten	14.	The **dogs** should've eaten the **bones.**	the **dägz** sh'də veetn the **bounz**
should not have eaten	15.	The **dogs** shouldn't've eaten the **bones.**	the **dägz** sh'dn•nə veetn the **bounz**
could eat	16.	The **dogs** could eat the **bones.**	the **dägz** c'deet the **bounz**
could not eat	17.	The **dogs** couldn't eat the **bones.**	the **dägz** c'dn•neet the **bounz**
could have eaten	18.	The **dogs** could've eaten the **bones.**	the **dägz** c'də veetn the **bounz**
could not have eaten	19.	The **dogs** couldn't've eaten the **bones.**	the **dägz** c'dn•nə veetn the **bounz**
might eat	20.	The **dogs** might eat the **bones.**	the **dägz** mydeet the **bounz**
might have eaten	21.	The **dogs** might've eaten the **bones.**	the **dägz** mydəveetn the **bounz**
must eat	22.	The **dogs** must eat the **bones.**	the **dägz** məss deet the **bounz**
must have eaten	23.	The **dogs** must've eaten the **bones.**	the **dägz** məsdəveetn the **bounz**
can eat	24.	The **dogs** can eat the **bones.**	the **dägz** c'neet the **bounz**
can't eat	25.	The **dogs can't eat** the **bones.**	the **dägz cæn**(d)**eet** the **bounz**

Exercise 9-2: Consistent Pronoun Stress in Changing Verb Tenses　　CD 3 Track 16

*This is the same as the previous exercise, except you now stress the verbs: They **eat** them. Practice this until you are quite comfortable with the intonation. Notice that in fluent speech, the **th** of **them** is frequently dropped (as is the **h** in the other object pronouns, **him**, **her**). The pronunciation and word connections are on the right, and the tense name is on the far left.*

present	1.	They **eat** them.	they**eed**'m
past	2.	They **ate** them.	they**ɛid**'m
continuous	3.	They're **eating** them.	the**ree**ding'm
future	4.	They'll **eat** them (if...)	the**lee**d'm (if...)
present conditional	5.	They'd **eat** them (if...)	they **deed**'m (if...)
past conditional	6.	They'd've **eaten** them (if...)	they də**vee**tn'm (if...)
relative pronoun	7.	The ones that've **eaten** them (are...)	the wənzədə**vee**tn'm (are...)
present perfect	8.	They've **eaten** them (many times).	they **vee**tn'm (many times)
past perfect	9.	They'd **eaten** them (before...)	they **dee**tn'm (before...)
future perfect	10.	They'll have **eaten** them (by...)	they lə**vee**tn'm (by...)
obligation	11.	They ought to **eat** them.	they ädə**eed**'m
obligation	12.	They should **eat** them.	they sh'**dee**d'm
obligation	13.	They shouldn't **eat** them.	they sh'dn•**nee**d'm
obligation	14.	They should have **eaten** them.	they sh'də**vee**tn'm
obligation	15.	They shouldn't've **eaten** them.	they sh'dn•nə**vee**tn'm
possibility/ability	16.	They could **eat** them.	they c'**dee**d'm
possibility/ability	17.	They couldn't **eat** them.	they c'dn•**nee**d'm
possibility/ability	18.	They could have **eaten** them.	they c'də **vee**tn'm
possibility/ability	19.	They couldn't have **eaten** them.	they c'dn•nə **vee**tn'm
possibility	20.	They might **eat** them.	they my**dee**d'm
possibility	21.	They might have **eaten** them.	they my də **vee**tn'm
probability	22.	They must **eat** them.	they məss **dee**d'm
probability	23.	They must have **eaten** them.	they məsdə**vee**tn'm
ability	24.	They can **eat** them.	they c'**nee**d'm
ability	25.	They **can't eat** them.	they cæn(d)**eed**'m

Exercise 9-3: Writing Your Own Phonetics   CD 3 Track 17

In the blanks below, fill in the phonetic pronunciation, using the guidelines from Example 9-1. Remember, don't rely on spelling, and use the contracted forms whenever possible. Turn off the CD. Check the Answer Key, beginning on page 210.

1.	Bob	writes	a letter.
	bä	· bry	· tsə ledder
2.	Bob	wrote	a letter.
	bä	· bro	· də ledder
3.	Bob	is writing	a letter.
	bä	· _____	· _____ ledder
4.	Bob	will write	a letter.
	bä	· _____	· _____ ledder
5.	Bob	would write	a letter, if...
	bä	· bədry	· də ledderif...
6.	Bob	would have written	a letter.
	bä	· _____	· _____ ledder
7.	The guy	that has written	a letter...
	thə gäi	· _____	· _____ ledder...
8.	Bob	has written	a letter.
	bä	· _____	· _____ ledder
9.	Bob	had written	a letter.
	bä	· _____	· _____ ledder
10.	Bob	will have written	a letter.
	bä	· _____	· _____ ledder
11.	Bob	ought to write	a letter.
	bä	· bädə ry	· də ledder
12.	Bob	should write	a letter.
	bäb	· _____	· _____ ledder

13.	Bob	shouldn't write	a letter.
	bäb ·	_____ ·	_____ ledder

14.	Bob	should've written	a letter.
	bäb ·	_____ ·	_____ ledder

15.	Bob	shouldn't've written	a letter.
	bäb ·	shüdnə vri(t)n ·	nə ledder

16.	Bob	could write	a letter.
	bäb ·	_____ ·	_____ ledder

17.	Bob	couldn't write	a letter.
	bäb ·	_____ ·	_____ ledder

18.	Bob	could've written	a letter.
	bäb ·	_____ ·	_____ ledder

19.	Bob	couldn't've written	a letter.
	bäb ·	_____ ·	_____ ledder

20.	Bob	might write	a letter.
	bäb ·	_____ ·	_____ ledder

21.	Bob	might've written	a letter.
	bäb ·	_____ ·	_____ ledder

22.	Bob	must write	a letter.
	bäb ·	_____ ·	_____ ledder

23.	Bob	must've written	a letter.
	bäb	_____	_____ ledder

24.	Bob	can write	a letter.
	bäb	_____	_____ ledder

25.	Bob	can't write	a letter.
	bäb	_____	_____ ledder

Exercise 9-4: Supporting Words

For this next part of the intonation of grammatical elements, each sentence has a few extra words to help you get the meaning. Keep the same strong intonation that you used before and add the new stress where you see the boldface. Use your rubber band.

1.	The **dogs** eat the **bones** every **day**.	th' **däg** zeet th' **bounz**evree **day**
2.	The **dogs** ate the **bones** last **week**.	th' **däg** zɛit th' **bounz**læss **dweek**
3.	The **dogs**'re eating the **bones** right **now**.	th' **däg** zr reeding th' **bounz** räit **næo**
4.	The **dogs**'ll eat the **bones** if they're **here**.	th' **däg** zə leet th' **bounz**if thɛr **hir**
5.	The **dogs**'d eat the **bones** if they were **here**.	th' **däg** zə deet th' **bounz**if they wr **hir**
6.	The **dogs**'d've eaten the **bones** if they'd **been** here.	th' **däg** zədə veetn th' **bounz**if theyd **bin** hir
7.	The **dogs** that've eaten the **bones** are **sick**.	th' **däg** zədə veetn th' **bounz**r **sick**
8.	The **dogs**'ve eaten the **bones** every **day**.	th' **däg** zə veetn th' **bounz**ɛvry **day**
9.	The **dogs**'d eaten the **bones** by the time we **got** there.	th' **däg** zə deetn th' **bounz** by th' time we **gät** thɛr
10.	The **dogs**'ll have eaten the **bones** by the time we **get** there.	th' **däg** zələ veetn th' **bounz** by th' time we **get** thɛr

English has a fixed word order that does not change with additional words.

	auxiliary	negative	perfect auxiliary	adverb	passive	continuous	main verb
Draw!							
							Draw!
He draws.							
He							draws.
He does draw.							
He	does						draw.
He is drawing.							
He	is						drawing.
He is not drawing.							
He	is	not					drawing.
He is not always drawing.							
He	is	not		always			drawing.
He is not always being drawn.							
He	is	not		always		being	drawn.
He has not always been drawn.							
He	has	not		always	been		drawn.
He has not always been being drawn.							
He	has	not		always	been	being	drawn.
He will not have always been being drawn.							
He	will	not	have	always	been	being	drawn.

Exercise 9-5: Contrast Practice — CD 3 Track 20

Now, let's work with contrast. For example, **The dogs'd eat the bones,** *and* **The dogs'd eaten the bones,** *are so close in sound, yet so far apart in meaning, that you need to make a special point of recognizing the difference by listening for content. Repeat each group of sentences using sound and intonation for contrast. (See also Chapter 4.)*

would eat	The **dogs**'d eat the **bones**.	the **däg** zə deet the **bounz**
had eaten	The **dogs**'d eaten the **bones**.	the **däg** zə deetn the **bounz**
would have eaten	The **dogs**'d've eaten the **bones**.	the **däg** zədə veetn the **bounz**
that have eaten	The **dogs** that've eaten the **bones**.	the **däg** zədə veetn the **bounz**
will eat	The **dogs**'ll eat the **bones**.	the **däg** zə leet the **bounz**
would eat	The **dogs**'d eat the **bones**.	the **däg** zə deet the **bounz**
would have eaten	The **dogs**'d've eaten the **bones**.	the **däg** zədə veetn the **bounz**
have eaten	The **dogs**'ve eaten the **bones**.	the **däg** zə veetn the **bounz**
had eaten	The **dogs**'d eaten the **bones**.	the **däg** zə deetn the **bounz**
will have eaten	The **dogs**'ll have eaten the **bones**.	the **däg** zələ veetn the **bounz**
would eat	The **dogs**'d eat the **bones**.	the **däg** zə deet the **bounz**
ought to eat	The **dogs** ought to eat the **bones**.	the **däg** zädə eat the **bounz**
can eat	The **dogs** can eat the **bones**.	the **dägz** c'neet the **bounz**
can't eat	The dogs **can't eat** the **bones**.	the dägz **cæn**(d)**eet** the **bounz**

Exercise 9-6: Building an Intonation Sentence — CD 3 Track 21

Repeat after me.

1. I bought a **sand**wich.
2. I **said** I bought a **sand**wich.
3. I **said** I think I bought a **sand**wich.
4. I said I **really** think I bought a **sand**wich.
5. I said I **really** think I bought a chicken **sand**wich.
6. I said I **really** think I bought a **chicken** salad **sand**wich.
7. I said I **really** think I bought a **half** a chicken salad **sand**wich.
8. I said I **really** think I bought a **half** a chicken salad **sand**wich this after**noon**.
9. I **actually** said I **really** think I bought a **half** a chicken salad **sand**wich this after**noon**.
10. I **actually** said I **really** think I bought another **half** a chicken salad **sand**wich this after**noon**.
11. Can you **believe** I **actually** said I **really** think I bought another **half** a chicken salad **sand**wich this after**noon**?

1. I **did** it.
2. I did it **again**.
3. I already **did** it again.
4. I think I already **did** it again.

5. I **said** I think I already **did** it again.

6. I **said** I think I already did it again **yes**terday.

7. I **said** I think I already **did** it again the day before **yes**terday.

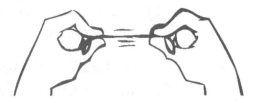

1. I want a **ball**.
2. I want a large **ball**.
3. I want a **large, red ball**.
4. I want a **large,** red, bouncy **ball**.
5. I want a **large,** red bouncy rubber **ball**.
6. I want a **large,** red bouncy rubber **basket**ball.

1. I want a **raise**.
2. I want a **big raise**.
3. I want a **big**, impressive raise.
4. I want a **big**, impressive, annual **raise**.
5. I want a **big**, impressive, annual cost of **living** raise.

Exercise 9-7: Building Your Own Intonation Sentences   CD 3 Track 22

Build your own sentence, using everyday words and phrases, such as **think**, **hope**, **nice**, **really**, **actually**, **even**, **this afternoon**, **big**, **small**, **pretty**, *and so on.*

1.
2.
3.
4.
5.
6.
7.
8.
9.
10.

Breathing Exercises   CD 3 Track 23

Different languages have different breathing patterns. Because Americans are a little louder than you may expect, in order to emulate this projection of the voice, you're going to have to take deeper breaths than you're accustomed to. Stand up straight, chest out, inhale deeply, and in a deep voice say, "Hi! How's it going?"

As you saw with *Phrasing* on page 61, your breathing should be in sync with the phrasing and punctuation. If you're saying something short, you can get away with a more shallow inhale, but short panting breaths are interpreted as nervous or impatient, whereas long, deep exhalations of sound are considered calm and confident. Take deeper breaths than usual, and push the sound out from deep in your chest.

Pay particular attention that you do not push the air out through your nose, which would create a very unattractive nasal quality to your speech.

Practice with the long sentences on pages 68–74, 141, and 169.

Chapter 10

Reduced Sounds

CD 3 Track 24

The Down Side of Intonation

Reduced sounds are all those extra sounds created by an absence of lip, tongue, jaw, and throat movement. They are a principal function of intonation and are truly indicative of the American sound. (See also Chapter 4.)

Reduced Sounds Are "Valleys"

American intonation is made up of peaks and valleys—tops of staircases and bottoms of staircases. To have strong *peaks,* you will have to develop deep *valleys.* These deep valleys should be filled with all kinds of reduced vowels, one in particular—the completely neutral *schwa.* Ignore spelling. Since you probably first became acquainted with English through the printed word, this is going to be quite a challenge. The position of a syllable is more important than spelling as an indication of correct pronunciation. For example, the words *photograph* and *photography* each have two **O**'s and an **A**. The first word is stressed on the first syllable so *photograph* sounds like *fod'græf.* The second word is stressed on the second syllable, *photography,* so the word comes out *f'tahgr'fee.* You can see here that their spelling doesn't tell you how they sound. Word stress or intonation will determine the pronunciation. Work on listening to words. Concentrate on hearing the pure sounds, not in trying to make the word fit a familiar spelling. Otherwise, you will be taking the long way around and giving yourself both a lot of extra work and an accent!

Syllables that are perched atop a peak or a staircase are strong sounds; that is, they maintain their original pronunciation. On the other hand, syllables that fall in the valleys or on a lower stair step are weak sounds; thus they are reduced. Some vowels are reduced completely to schwas, a very relaxed sound, while others are only toned down. In the following exercises, we will be dealing with these "toned down" sounds.

In the Introduction ("Read This First," page iv) I talked about *overpronouncing.* This section will handle that overpronunciation. You're going to skim over words; you're going to dash through certain sounds. Your peaks are going to be quite strong, but your valleys, blurry—a very intuitive aspect of intonation that this practice will help you develop.

Articles (such as *the, a*) are usually very reduced sounds. Before a consonant, *the* and *a* are both schwa sounds, which are reduced. Before a vowel, however, you'll notice a change—for example, the schwa of *the* turns into a long *e* plus a connecting ⁽ʸ⁾—*Th' book* changes to *thee⁽ʸ⁾only book. A hat* becomes *a nugly hat:* The article *a* becomes *an.* Think of ə•nornj rather than *an orange;* ə•nop'ning, ə•neye; ə•nimaginary animal.

Exercise 10-1: Reducing Articles				CD 3 Track 25
Consonants			**Vowels**	
the man	a girl	thee⁽ʸ⁾apple	an orange	ə•nornj
the best	a banana	thee⁽ʸ⁾egg	an opening	ə•nop'ning
the last one	a computer	thee⁽ʸ⁾easy way	an interview	ə•ninerview

When you used the rubber band with *Däg zeet bounz* and when you built your own sentence, you saw that intonation reduces the unstressed words. Intonation is the peak and reduced sounds are the valleys. In the beginning, you should make extra-high peaks and long, deep valleys. When you are not sure, reduce. In the following exercise, work with this idea. Small words such as articles, prepositions, pronouns, conjunctions, relative pronouns, and auxiliary verbs are lightly skimmed over and almost not pronounced.

You have seen how intonation changes the meaning in words and sentences. Inside a one-syllable word, it distinguishes between a final voiced or unvoiced consonant *be-ed* and *bet.* Inside a longer word, *éunuch* vs. *uníque,* the pronunciation and meaning change in terms of vocabulary. In a sentence (He seems **nice**; He **seems** nice.), the meaning changes in terms of intent.

In a sentence, intonation can also make a clear vowel sound disappear. When a vowel is *stressed,* it has a certain sound; when it is *not stressed,* it usually sounds like *uh,* pronounced ə. Small words like *to, at,* or *as* are not usually stressed, so the vowel disappears.

Exercise 10-2: Reduced Sounds

Read aloud from the right-hand column. The intonation is marked for you.

To	**Looks Like ...**	**Sounds Like ...**
The preposition **to** usually reduces so much that it's like dropping the vowel.	today	t'**day**
	tonight	t'**night**
	tomorrow	t'**märou**
	to work	t' **wrk**
	to school	t' **school**
	to the store	t' th' **store**
Use a **t'** or **tə** sound to replace **to**.	We have to go now.	we hæftə **go** næo
	He went to work.	he wentə **work**
	They hope to find it.	they houptə **fine** dit
	I can't wait to find out.	äi **cæn**⁽ᵗ⁾wai⁽ᵗ⁾tə fine **dæot**
	We don't know what to do.	we dont know w'⁽ᵗ⁾t' **do**
	Don't jump to conclusions.	dont j'm t' c'n**cloo**zh'nz
	To be or not to be...	t' **bee**⁽ʸ⁾r **nät** t' bee
	He didn't get to go.	he din ge⁽ᵗ⁾tə **gou**
If that same **to** follows a vowel sound, it will become **d'** or **də**.	He told me to help.	he told meedə **help**
	She told you to get it.	she tol joodə **ged**dit
	I go to work.	ai goudə **wrk**
	at a quarter to two	ædə kworder də **two**
	The only way to get it is...	thee⁽ʸ⁾**ounly** waydə **ged**didiz
	You've got to pay to get it.	yoov gäddə paydə **ged**dit
	We plan to do it.	we plæn də **do** it
	Let's go to lunch.	lets goudə **lunch**
	The score was 4–6.	th' score w'z for də **six**

Exercise 10-2: Reduced Sounds *continued*   **CD 3 Track 27**

To	Looks Like ...	Sounds Like ...
	It's the only way to do it.	its thee^(y)**ounly** weidə **do**^(w)'t
	So to speak...	soda **speak**
	I don't know how to say it.	äi don^(t)know hæwdə **say**^(y)it
	Go to page 8.	goudə pay **jate**
	Show me how to get it.	shou me hæodə **gedd**it
	You need to know when to do it.	you nee^(d)də nou wendə **do**^(w)it
	Who's to blame?	hooz də **blame**

At

At is just the opposite of **to**. It's a small grunt followed by a reduced **t**.

	Looks Like ...	Sounds Like ...
	We're at home.	wir^ət **home**
	I'll see you at lunch.	äiyəl see you^(w)ət **lunch**
	Dinner's at five.	d'nnerz^{ə(t)} **five**
	Leave them at the door.	leev^əm^{ə(t)}th^ə **door**
	The meeting's at one.	th' meeding z't **w'n**
	He's at the post office.	heez^{ə(t)}th' **pouss**däff^əs
	They're at the bank.	thɛr^{ə(t)}th' **bænk**
	I'm at school.	äim^{ə(t)}**school**

If **at** is followed by a vowel sound, it will become **'d** or **əd**.

	Looks Like ...	Sounds Like ...
	I'll see you at eleven.	äiyəl see you^(w)ədə **lɛv'n**
	He's at a meeting.	heez'ə də **meeding**
	She laughed at his idea.	she **læf** dədi zy **dee**yə
	One at a time.	wənədə **time**
	We got it at an auction.	we gädidədə **näksh'n**
	The show started at eight.	th' **show** stardədə **date**
	The dog jumped out at us.	th' däg jump **dæo** dədəs
	I was at a friend's house.	äi w'z'd' **frenz** hæos

It

It and **at** sound the same in context — **'t**.

	Looks Like ...	Sounds Like ...
	Can you do it?	k'niu **do**^(w)'t
	Give it to me.	g'v'^(t)t' me
	Buy it tomorrow.	bäi^{(y)ə(t)}t' **märrow**
	It can wait.	't c'n **wait**
	Read it twice.	ree d'^(t)**twice**
	Forget about it!	frgedd' **bæo**dit

...and they both turn to **'d** or **əd** between vowels or voiced consonants.

	Looks Like ...	Sounds Like ...
	Give it a try.	givdə **try**
	Let it alone.	ledidə **lone**
	Take it away.	tay kida **way**
	I got it in London.	äi gädidin **l'**nd'n
	What is it about?	w'd'z'd'**bæot**
	Let's try it again.	lets try'd' **gen**
	Look! There it is!	**lük** there'd'**z**

Exercise 10-2 Reduced Sounds *continued*   CD 3 Track 27

	Looks Like ...	Sounds Like ...
For	This is for you.	th's'z fr **you**
	It's for my friend.	ts fr my **friend**
	A table for four, please.	ə table fr **four**, pleeze
	We planned it for later.	we **plan** dit fr **layd'r**
	For example, for instance	fregg **zæmple frin** st'nss
	What is this for?	w'd'z **this** for *(for is not reduced at*
	What did you do it for?	w'j' **do**^(w)it for *the end of a sentence)*
	Who did you get it for?	hoojya **gedd**it for
From	It's from the IRS.	ts frm thee^(y)äi^(y)ä **ress**
	I'm from Arkansas.	äim fr'm **ärk'** nsä
	There's a letter from Bob.	therzə **ledder** fr'm **Bäb**
	This letter's from Alaska!	this **ledderz** frəmə **læskə**
	Who's it from?	hoozit **frəm**
	Where are you from?	wher'r you **frəm**
In	It's in the bag.	tsin thə **bæg**
	What's in it?	w'**ts**'n't
	I'll be back in a minute.	äiyəl be **bæk**'nə **m'n't**
	This movie? Who's in it?	this **movie** ... hooz**'n't**
	Come in.	c '**min**
	He's in America.	heez'ən **mɛrəkə**
An	He's an American.	heez'ən **mɛrəkən**
	I got an A in English.	äi gäddə **nay** ih **nin**glish
	He got an F in Algebra.	hee gäddə **neff**inæl jəbrə
	He had an accident.	he hædə **næk**səd'nt
	We want an orange.	we want'n **nornj**
	He didn't have an excuse.	he didnt hævə neks **kyooss**
	I'll be there in an instant.	äiyəl be there inə **nin**stnt
	It's an easy mistake to make.	itsə **nee**zee m' stake t' **make**
And	ham and eggs	hæmə **neggz**
	bread and butter	bredn **buddr**
	Coffee? With cream and sugar?	**käffee** ... with creem'n **sh'g'r**
	No, lemon and sugar.	**nou** ... **lem**'n'n sh'g'r
	... And some more cookies?	'n s'more **cükeez**
	They kept going back and forth.	they kep going bækn **forth**
	We watched it again and again.	we **wäch** didə **gen**'n' **gen**
	He did it over and over.	he di di **dov**erə **nov**er
	We learned by trial and error.	we lrnd by tryələ**ner**ər

Exercise 10-2: Reduced Sounds *continued*   CD 3 Track 27

Or	Looks Like ...	Sounds Like ...
	Soup or salad?	super **salad**
	now or later	næ(w)r **lay**dr
	more or less	**mor**'r less
	left or right	**lef**ter **right**
	For here or to go?	f'r **hir**'r d'**go**
	Are you going up or down?	are you going **úp**per **dówn**

*This is an **either** / **or** question: **Up? Down?***
*Notice how the intonation is different from "Cream and **sugar**?", which is a **yes** / **no** question.*

Are		
	What are you doing?	w'dr you **do**ing
	Where are you going?	wer'r you **go**ing
	What're you planning on doing?	w'dr yü planning än **do**ing
	How are you?	hæwr **you**
	Those are no good.	thozer no **good**
	How are you doing?	hæwer you **do**ing
	The kids are still asleep.	the **kid**zer stillə **sleep**

Your		
	How's your family?	hæozhier **fæm**lee
	Where're your keys?	wher'r y'r **keez**
	You're American, aren't you?	yrə **mer**'k'n, arn choo
	Tell me when you're ready.	tell me wen yr **red**dy
	Is this your car?	izzis y'r **cär**
	You're late again, Bob.	yer lay də **gen**, Bäb

One		
	Which one is yours?	which w'n'z **y'rz**
	Which one is better?	which w'n'z **bed**der
	One of them is broken.	w'n'v'm'z **brok**'n
	I'll use the other one.	æl yuz thee(y)**ə**ther w'n
	I like the red one, Edwin.	äi like the **red**w'n, edw'n
	That's the last one.	thæts th' lass **dw'n**
	The next one'll be better.	the **necks** dw'n'll be **bedd'r**
	Here's one for you.	**hir** zw'n f'r **you**
	Let them go one by one.	led'm gou **w'n** by **w'n**

The		
	It's the best.	ts th' **best**
	What's the matter?	w'ts th' **mad**der
	What's the problem?	w'tsə **präb**l'm
	I have to go to the bathroom.	äi hæf t' go d' th' **bæth**room
	Who's the boss around here?	hoozə **bäss** səræond hir
	Give it to the dog.	g'v'(t)tə th' **däg**
	Put it in the drawer.	püdidin th' **dror**

Exercise 10-2: Reduced Sounds *continued*		CD 3 Track 27

	Looks Like ...	**Sounds Like ...**
A	It's a present.	tsə **pre**znt
	You need a break.	you needə **bray-eek**
	Give him a chance.	g'v'mə **chæns**
	Let's get a new pair of shoes.	lets geddə new perə **shooz**
	Can I have a Coke, please?	c'nai hævə **kouk**, pleez
	Is that a computer?	izzædə k'm**pyoo**dr
	Where's a public telephone?	wherzə pəblic **tel**əfoun
Of	It's the top of the line.	tsə täp'v th' **line**
	It's a state of the art printer.	tsə **stay** də thee⁽ʸ⁾ärt **prin**ner
	As a matter of fact, ...	z'mædderə **fækt** ...
	Get out of here.	ged**dæow** də hir
	Practice all of the time.	**præk**t'säll'v th' time
	Today's the first of May.	t'**dayz** th' frss d'v **May**
	What's the name of that movie?	w'ts th' **nay** m'v thæt **movie**
	That's the best of all!	**thæts** th' bess d'**väll**
	some of them	**sə**məvəm
	all of them	**äll**əvəm
	most of them	**mos**dəvəm
	none of them	**nə**nəvəm
	any of them	**enn**yəvəm
	the rest of them	th' **res**dəvəm
Can	Can you speak English?	k'new spee **king**lish
	I can only do it on Wednesday.	äi k'**noun**ly du⁽ʷ⁾idän **wen**zday
	A can opener can open cans.	ə **kæn**op'ner k'nopen **kænz**
	Can I help you?	k'näi **hel** piu
	Can you do it?	k'niu **do**⁽ʷ⁾'t
	We can try it later.	we k'n **try** it **layder**
	I hope you can sell it.	äi **hou** piu k'n **sell**'t
	No one can fix it.	nou w'n k'n **fick** sit
	Let me know if you can find it.	lemme no⁽ʷ⁾'few k'n **fine** dit
Had	Jack had had enough.	jæk'd hæd' **n'f**
	Bill had forgotten again.	bil'd frga⁽ᵗ⁾n nə **gen**
	What had he done to deserve it?	w'd'dee d'nd'd' **zr** vit
	We'd already seen it.	weedäl reddy **see** nit
	He'd never been there.	heed never **bin** there
	Had you ever had one?	h'jou⁽ʷ⁾ever **hæd**w'n
	Where had he hidden it?	wer dee **hid**n●nit
	Bob said he'd looked into it.	bäb sedeed lük**din** tu⁽ʷ⁾it

	Looks Like ...	Sounds Like ...
Would	He would have helped, if ...	he wüda **help** dif ...
	Would he like one?	woody **lye** kw'n
	Do you think he'd do it?	dyiu thing keed **du**(w)'t
	Why would I tell her?	why wüdäi **tell**er
	We'd see it again, if...	weed see(y)idəgen, if...
	He'd never be there on time.	heed never **be** therän tyme
	Would you ever have one?	w'jou(w)ever **hæv**w'n
Was	He was only trying to help.	he w'zounly trying də **help**
	Mark was American.	**mär** kw'z'**mer**'k'n
	Where was it?	wer **w'z**'t
	How was it?	hæo**w'z**'t
	That was great!	thæt w'z **great**
	Who was with you?	hoow'z **with** you
	She was very clear.	she w'z very **clear**
	When was the war of 1812?	wen w'z th' **wor**'v ei(t)teen **twelv**
What	What time is it?	w't **tye** m'z't
	What's up?	w'ts'**p**
	What's on your agenda?	w'tsänyrə **jen**də
	What do you mean?	w'd'y' **mean**
	What did you mean?	w'j'**mean**
	What did you do about it?	w'j' **du**(w)əbæodit
	What took so long?	w't **tük** so läng
	What do you think of this?	w'ddyə thing k'v **this**
	What did you do then?	w'jiu do **then**
	I don't know what he wants.	I dont know wədee **wänts**
Some	Some are better than others.	**s'm**r beddr thənəth**erz**
	There are some leftovers.	ther'r s'm **lef** doverz
	Let's buy some ice cream.	let spy s' **mice** creem
	Could we get some other ones?	kwee get s' **mother** w'nz
	Take some of mine.	**take** səməv **mine**
	Would you like some more?	w' joo like s'**more**
	(or very casually)	jlike s'**more**
	Do you have some ice?	dyü hæv sə**mice**
	Do you have some mice?	dyü hæv sə**mice**

"You can fool some of the people some of the time,
but you can't fool all of the people all of the time."

yük'n **fool səmə** thə peepᵊl **səmə** thə time, b'choo **kænt fool** ällthə peepᵊl **äll**thə time

Exercise 10-3: Intonation and Pronunciation of "That"   CD 3 Track 28

That is a special case because it serves three different grammatical functions. The **relative pronoun** and the **conjunction** are reducible. The **demonstrative pronoun** cannot be reduced to a schwa sound. It must stay *æ*.

Relative Pronoun	The car that she ordered is red.	th' **car** th't she order diz **red**
Conjunction	He said that he liked it.	he sed the dee **läik**dit.
Demonstrative	Why did you do that?	why dijoo **do** thæt?
Combination	I know that he'll read that book that I told you about.	äi **know** the dill read thæt **bük** the dai **tol**joo⁽ʷ⁾' bæot

Exercise 10-4: Crossing Out Reduced Sounds   CD 3 Track 29

Pause the CD and cross out any sound that is not clearly pronounced, including **to**, **for**, **and**, **that**, **than**, **the**, **a**, *the* **soft i**, *and unstressed syllables that do not have strong vowel sounds.*

He̶llo, **my** name i̶s̶_____. I'm tak̶i̶ng A̶me̶ri̶ca̶n **Accent** Trai̶ni̶ng. There's a **lot** to **learn**, but I **hope** to make it as en**joy**able as possible. I should pick **up** on the American into**na**tion pattern pretty **easily**, although the **only** way to **get** it is to **practice** all of the time. I use the **up** and down, or **peaks** and valleys, intonation more than I **used** to. I've been paying atten-tion to **pitch**, **too**. It's like **walk**ing down a **stair**case. I've been **talk**ing to a lot of **Americans** lately, and they tell me that I'm **ea**sier to under**stand**. **Any**way, I could go **on** and on, but the im**port**ant thing is to **listen** well and sound **good**. **Well**, what do you **think**? **Do** I?

Exercise 10-5: Reading Reduced Sounds   CD 3 Track 30

Repeat the paragraph after me. Although you're getting rid of the vowel sounds, you want to maintain a strong intonation and let the sounds flow together. For the first reading of this paragraph, it is helpful to keep your teeth clenched together to reduce excess jaw and lip movement. Let's begin.

Hello, **my** name'z_____. I'm taking 'mer'k'n **Acc**'nt Train'ng. Therez' **lot** t̯ **learn**, b't I **hope** t̯ make 'tz 'n**joy**'bl'z poss'bl. I sh'd p'ck **'p** on the 'mer'k'n 'nt̯**na**sh'n pattern pretty **ea**s'ly, although the **on**ly way t̯ **get** 't 'z t̯ **prac**t̯s all 'v th' time. I use the **'p**'n down, or **peaks** 'n valleys, 'nt̯nash'n more th'n I **used** to. Ive b'n pay'ng 'ttensh'n t̯ **p'ch, too**. 'Ts like **walk**'ng down' **stair**case. Ive b'n **talk**'ng to' lot 'v**mer**'k'ns lately, 'n they tell me th't Im **ea**sier to 'nder**stand**. **Any**way, I k'd go **on** 'n on, b't the 'm**port**'nt th'ng 'z t̯ **l's**'n wel'n sound **g'd. W'll**, wh' d'y' **th'nk**? **Do** I?

Chapter 11

Word Connections

CD 3 Track 31

As mentioned in the previous chapter, in American English, words are not pronounced one by one. Usually, the end of one word attaches to the beginning of the next word. This is also true for initials, numbers, and spelling. Part of the glue that connects sentences is an underlying hum or drone that only breaks when you come to a period, and sometimes not even then. You have this underlying hum in your own language, and it helps a great deal toward making you sound like a native speaker.

Once you have a strong intonation, you need to connect all those stair steps together so that each sentence sounds like one long word. This chapter is going to introduce you to the idea of liaisons, the connections between words, which allow us to speak in sound groups rather than in individual words. Just as we went over where to put intonation, here you're going to learn how to connect words. Once you understand and learn to use this technique, you can make the important leap from this practice book to other materials and your own conversation.

To make it easier for you to read, liaisons are written like this: **They tell me the dai measier.** (You've already encountered some liaisons in Exercises 8-1, 9-1, 10-2.) It could also be written **theytellmethedaimeasier**, but it would be too hard to read. (See also Chapters 1 and 7.)

Exercise 11-1: Spelling and Pronunciation   CD 3 Track 32

*Read the following sentences. The last two sentences should be pronounced exactly the same, no matter how they are written. It is the **sound** that is important, not the spelling.*

The dime.
The dime easier.
They tell me the dime easier.
They tell me **the dime** easier to understand.
They tell me **that I'm** easier to understand.

Words are connected in four main situations:

1. Consonant / Vowel
2. Consonant / Consonant
3. Vowel / Vowel
4. T, D, S, or Z + Y

Liaison Rule 1: Consonant / Vowel   CD 3 Track 33

Words are connected when a word ends in a consonant sound and the next word starts with a vowel sound, including the semivowels **W**, **Y**, and **R**.

Exercise 11-2: Word Connections   CD 3 Track 34

My name is...	my nay●miz
because I've	b'k'zäiv
pick up on the American intonation	pi●kə pän the⁽ʸ⁾əmer'kə ninətənashən

In the preceding example, the word *name* ends in a consonant sound **m** (the *e* is silent and doesn't count), and *is* starts with a vowel sound *i*, so *naymiz* just naturally flows together. In *because I've,* the **z** sound at the end of *because* and the **äi** sound of *I* blend together smoothly. When you say the last line *pi●kəpän the⁽ʸ⁾əmer'kəninətənashən*, you can feel each sound pushing into the next.

Exercise 11-3: Spelling and Number Connections   CD 3 Track 35

You also use liaisons in spelling and numbers. (See also Chapter 4.)

| LA (Los Angeles) | eh●lay |
| 902-5050 | nai●no●too fai●vo●fai●vo |

What's the Difference Between a Vowel and a Consonant?

In pronunciation, a consonant touches at some point in the mouth. Try saying **p** with your mouth open—you can't do it because your lips must come together to make the **p** sound. A vowel, on the other hand, doesn't touch anywhere. You can easily say **e** without any part of the mouth, tongue, or lips coming into contact with any other part. This is why we are calling **W**, **Y**, and **R** semivowels, or glides.

Exercise 11-4: Consonant / Vowel Liaison Practice   CD 3 Track 36

Pause the CD and reconnect the following words. On personal pronouns, it is common to drop the H. Check Answer Key, beginning on page 210. Repeat.

hold on	hol don
turn over	tur nover
tell her I miss her	tellerl misser

1. read only
2. fall off
3. follow up on
4. come in
5. call him
6. sell it
7. take out
8. fade away
9. 6–0
10. MA

Llaison Rule 2: Consonant / Consonant   CD 3 Track 37

Words are connected when a word ends in a consonant sound and the next one starts with a consonant that is in a similar position. What is a similar position? Let's find out.

Exercise 11-5: Consonant / Consonant Liaisons   CD 3 Track 38

Say the sound of each group of letters out loud (the sound of the letter, not the name: **b** *is* **buh** *not* **bee**). *There are three general locations—the lips, behind the teeth, or in the throat. If a word ends with a sound created in the throat and the next word starts with a sound from that same general location, these words are going to be linked together. The same with the other two locations. Repeat after me.*

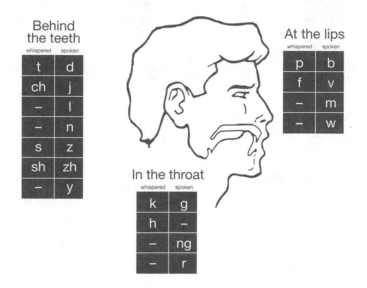

Exercise 11-6: Consonant / Consonant Liaisons   CD 3 Track 39

| I just didn't get the chance. | I•jusdidn't•ge⁽ᵗ⁾the•chance. |
| I've been late twice. | I'vbinla⁽ᵗ⁾twice. |

In the preceding examples you can see that because the ending **st** *of just* and the beginning **d** of *didn't* are so near each other in the mouth, it's not worth the effort to start the sound all over again, so they just flow into each other. You don't say *I justə didn'tə getə the chance* but do say *Ijusdidn' ge⁽ᵗ⁾the chance.* In the same way, it's too much work to say *I'və beenə lateə twice,* so you say it almost as if it were a single word, *I'vbinla⁽ᵗ⁾twice.*

The sound of **TH** is a special case. It is a floater between areas. The sound is sometimes created by the tongue popping out from between the teeth and other times on the back of the top teeth, combining with various letters to form a new composite sound. For instance, **s** moves forward and the **th** moves back to meet at the midpoint between the two.

Note *Each of the categories in the drawing contains two labels—voiced and unvoiced. What does that mean? Put your thumb and index fingers on your throat and say* **z***; you should feel a vibration from your throat in your fingers. If you whisper that same sound, you end up with* **s** *and you feel that your fingers don't vibrate. So,* **z** *is a voiced sound,* **s***, unvoiced. The consonants in the two left columns are paired like that. (See also Chapters 17, 19, 21, 24, and 25.)*

Consonants

Voiced	Unvoiced		Voiced	Unvoiced
b	p		—	h
d	t		l	—
v	f		r	—
g	k		m	—
j	ch		n	—
z	s		ng	—
<u>th</u>	th		y	—
zh	sh		w	—

Exercise 11-7: Liaisons with TH Combination   CD 3 Track 40

*When the **TH** combination connects with certain sounds, the two sounds blend together to form a composite sound. In the following examples, see how the **TH** moves back and the **L** moves forward, to meet in a new middle position. Repeat after me. (See also Chapter 13.)*

th	+	l	with lemon	th	+	ch	both charges
th	+	n	with nachos	th	+	j	with juice
th	+	t	both times				
th	+	d	with delivery	n	+	th	in the
th	+	s	both sizes	z	+	th	was that
th	+	z	with zeal	d	+	th	hid those

Exercise 11-8: Consonant / Consonant Liaison Practice   CD 3 Track 41

Pause the CD and reconnect the following words as shown in the models. Check Answer Key, beginning on page 210. Repeat.

hard times	hardtimes
with luck	withluck

1. business deal
2. credit check
3. the top file
4. sell nine new cars
5. sit down
6. some plans need luck
7. check cashing
8. let them make conditions
9. had the
10. both days

Liaison Rule 3: Vowel / Vowel

CD 3 Track 42

When a word ending in a *vowel* sound is next to one beginning with a *vowel* sound, they are connected with a glide between the two vowels. A glide is either a slight **y** sound or a slight **w** sound. How do you know which one to use? This will take care of itself—the position your lips are in will dictate either **y** or **w**.

Go away.	Go⁽ʷ⁾away.
I also need the other one.	I⁽ʸ⁾also need the⁽ʸ⁾other one.

For example, if a word ends in **o** your lips are going to be in the forward position, so a **w** quite naturally leads into the next vowel sound—*Go⁽ʷ⁾away*. You don't want to say: *Go...away* and break the undercurrent of your voice. Run it all together: *Go⁽ʷ⁾away*.

After a long **ē** sound, your lips will be pulled back far enough to create a **y** glide or liaison: *I⁽ʸ⁾also need the⁽ʸ⁾other one*. Don't force this sound too much, though. It's not a strong pushing sound. *I(y) also need the(y)other one* would sound really weird.

Exercise 11-9: Vowel / Vowel Liaison Practice

CD 3 Track 43

*Pause the CD and reconnect the following words as shown in the models. Add a (y) glide after an **e** sound, and a (w) glide after a **u** sound. Don't forget that the sound of the American **O** is really **ou**. Check Answer Key, beginning on page 210.*

she isn't	she⁽ʸ⁾isn't
who is	who⁽ʷ⁾iz

1. go anywhere
2. so honest
3. through our
4. you are
5. he is
6. do I?
7. I asked
8. to open
9. she always
10. too often

Liaison Rule 4: T, D, S, or Z + Y   CD 3 Track 44

When the letter or sound of **T**, **D**, **S**, or **Z** is followed by a word that starts with **Y**, or its sound, both sounds are connected. These letters and sounds connect not only with **y**, but they do so as well with the initial unwritten **y**. (See also Chapter 21, The Ridge.)

Exercise 11-10: T, D, S, or Z + Y Liaisons   CD 3 Track 45

Repeat the following.

T + Y = CH	What's your **name**?	wəcher **name**
	Can't you **do** it?	kænt chew **do**(w)it
	Actually	**æk**·chully
	Don't you **like** it?	dont chew **lye** kit
	Wouldn't you?	**wood**en chew
	Haven't you? No, not **yet**.	**hæv**en chew? nou, nä **chet**
	I'll let you **know**.	I'll letcha **know**
	Can I get you a **drink**?	k'näi getchewə **drink**
	We thought you weren't **coming**.	we thä chew wrnt **kəm**ing
	I'll bet you **ten** bucks he for**got**.	æl betcha **ten** buxee fr**gät**
	Is **that** your final **answer**?	is **thæ**chr fin'**læn** sr
	natural	**næ**chrəl
	per**pe**tual	per**pe**chə(w)əl
	virtual	**vr**chə(w)əl

D + Y = J	Did you **see** it?	didjə **see**(y)it
	How did you **like** it?	hæo•jə **lye** kit
	Could you **tell**?	küjə **tell**
	Where did you send your **check**?	wɛrjə senjer **check**
	What did your **fam**ily think?	wəjer **fæm**lee think
	Did you find your **keys**?	didjə fine jer **keez**
	We followed your **instructions**.	we fallow jerin **strɑc**shunz
	Congratu**la**tions!	k'ngræj'**la**shunz
	edu**ca**tion	edjə·**ca**shun
	indi**vid**ual	ində**vij**ə(w)əl
	gradu**a**tion	græjə(w)**a**shun
	gradual	**græ**jə(w)əl

S + Y = SH	**Yes**, you are.	**yesh**u are
	In**sur**ance	in**shur**ance
	Bless you!	**bless**hue
	Press your **hands** together.	pressure **hanz** d'gethr
	Can you **dress** yourself?	c'new **dresh**ier self
	You can pass your **exams** this year.	yuk'n pæsher eg**zæmz** thisheer
	I'll try to guess your **age**.	æl trydə geshier**age**
	Let him gas your **car** for you.	leddim gæshier **cär** fr you

Exercise 11-10: T, D, S, or Z + Y Liaisons *continued* CD 3 Track 45

Z + Y = ZH	How's your **family**?	hæozhier **fæm**lee
	How was your **trip**?	hæo•wəzhier **trip**
	Who's your **friend**?	hoozhier **frend**
	Where's your **mom**?	wɛrzh'r **mäm**
	When's your **birthday**?	wɛnzh'r **brth**day
	She says you're O**K**.	she sɛzhierou **kay**
	Who does your **hair**?	hoo dəzhier **hɛr**
	casual	**kæ**•zhyə^(w)əl
	visual	**vi**•zhyə^(w)əl
	usual	**yu**•zhyə^(w)əl
	version	**vr**zh'n
	vision	**vi**zh'n

Exercise 11-11: T, D, S, or Z + Y Liaison Practice CD 3 Track 46

*Reconnect or rewrite the following words. Remember that there may be a **y** sound that is not written. Check Answer Key, beginning on page 210. Repeat.*

| put your | pücher |
| gradual | gradjyə^(w)l |

1. did you
2. who's your
3. just your
4. gesture
5. miss you
6. tissue
7. got your
8. where's your
9. congratulations
10. had your

This word exchange really happened.

Now that you have the idea of how to link words, let's do some liaison work.

Exercise 11-12: Finding Liaisons and Glides — CD 3 Track 47

In the following paragraph connect as many of the words as possible. Mark your liaisons as we have done in the first two sentences. Add the (y) and (w) glides between the words.

He**llo**, **my** name is_____. I'm taking American **Accent** Training. There's a **lot** to **learn**, but I **hope** to make it as **enjoyable** as possible. I should pick **up** on the American **intonation** pattern pretty **easily**, although the^(y)**only** way to **get** it is to **practice** all of the time. I use the **up** and down, or **peaks** and valleys, **intonation** more than I **used** to. I've been paying attention to **pitch, too**. It's like **walking** down a **stair**case. I've been **talking** to^(w)a lot of **Americans** lately, and they tell me that I'm **easier** to under**stand**. **Any**way, I could go **on** and on, but the **important** thing is to **listen** well and sound **good**. **Well**, what do you **think**? **Do** I?

▸ Prac**tice** reading the paragraph three times, focusing on running your words together.

◂ Turn the CD back on and repeat after me as I read. I'm going to exaggerate the linking of the words, drawing it out much longer than would be natural.

Exercise 11-13: Practicing Liaisons — CD 3 Track 48

Back up the CD to the last paragraph just read and repeat again. This time, however, read from the paragraph below. The intonation is marked for you in boldface. Use your rubber band on every stressed word.

He**llo**, **my nay** miz _____. **I'm** taking**ə** merica **næccent**(t)raining. There z**ə lätt**ə learn, b**ə** däi **hope** t' ma ki desen **joy**ablez pässible. I shüd pi **kə**pän the^(y)əmerica nint**ə**nash'n pæddern pridy^(y)**ezily**, although thee^(y)**ounly** wayd**ə ged**didiz t' **præk**ti sälläv th' time. I^(y)use thee^(y)**up**'n down, or **peak** s'n valley zint**ə**nashen more th**ə** näi **used** to. Ivbn paying**ə** tenshen t' **pitch, too**. Itsläi **kwäl**king dow n**ə stair**case. Ivbn **täl**king to^(w)ə läddəv**ə meri**can zla^(t)ely, 'n they tell me the däi**mee**zier to^(w)under**stænd**. **Any**way, I could go^(w)**ä** n**ə** nän, bu^(t)thee^(y)im**port**ant thingiz t' **lis**ənwellən soun^(d) **good**. Well, whəddyü **think**? **Do**^(w)I?

> When a clock is hungry ...

> It goes back four seconds.

Exercise 11-14: Additional Liaison Practice CD 3 Track 49

▶ Use these techniques on texts of your own and in conversation.
(1) Take some written material and mark the *intonation,* then the *word groups,* and finally the *liaisons.*
(2) Practice saying it out loud.
(3) Record yourself and listen back.

▶ In conversation, think which word you want to make stand out, and change your pitch on that word. Then, run the in-between words together in the valleys. Listen carefully to how Americans do it and copy the sound.

Exercise 11-15: Colloquial Reductions and Liaisons CD 3 Track 50

In order for you to recognize these sounds when used by native speakers, they are presented here, but I don't recommend that you go out of your way to use them yourself. If, at some point, they come quite naturally of their own accord in casual conversation, you don't need to resist, but please don't force yourself to talk this way. Repeat. (See also Chapter 1.)

I have got to **go.**	I've gotta **go.**
I have got a **book.**	I've gotta **book.**
Do you want to **dance**?	Wanna **dance**?
Do you want a **banana**?	Wanna **banana**?
Let me **in.**	Lemme **in.**
Let me **go.**	Lemme **go.**
I'll let you **know.**	I'll letcha **know.**
Did you **do** it?	Dija **do** it?
Not **yet.**	Nä **chet.**
I'll meet you **later.**	I'll meechu **lay**der.
What do you **think**?	Whaddyu **think**?
What did you **do** with it?	Whajoo **do** with it?
How did you **like** it?	Howja **like** it?
When did you **get** it?	When ju **ge**ddit?
Why did you **take** it?	Whyju **tay** kit?
Why don't you **try** it?	Why don chu **try** it?
What are you **waiting** for?	Whaddya **wait**in' for?
What are you **doing**?	Whatcha **do**in'?
How is it **going**?	Howzit **going**?
Where's the **what**-you-may-call-it?	Where's the **what**chamacallit?
Where's **what**-is-his-name?	Where's **what**siizname?
How **about** it?	How **'bout** it?
He has got to **hurry** because he is **late.**	He's gotta **hurry** 'cuz he's **late.**
I could've been a **contender.**	I coulda bina con**ten**der.

Exercise 11-15: Colloquial Reductions and Liaisons *continued*	CD 3 Track 50

Could you speed it **up**, please?	Couldjoo spee di **dup**, pleez?
Would you mind if I **tried** it?	Would joo mindifai **try** dit?
Aren't you Bob **Barker**?	Arnchoo Bäb **Bar**ker?
Can't you see it **my** way for a change?	Kænchoo see it **my** way for a change?
Don't you **get** it?	Doancha **ged**dit?
I should have **told** you.	I shoulda **tol**joo.
Tell her (that) I **miss** her.	Teller I **mis**ser.
Tell him (that) I **miss** him.	Tellim I **mis**sim.

Extreme reductions

Did you **eat**?	**Jeet**?
No, did **you**?	No, **joo**?
Why don't you **get a job**?	Whyncha **getta job**?
I don't know, **it's** too **hard**.	I dunno, stoo **härd**.
Could **we go**?	Kwee **gou**?
Let's **go**!	**Sko**!
I'm **going** to	**äi**mana

Spoon or Sboon?

CD 3 Track 51

An interesting thing about liaisons is that so much of it has to do with whether a consonant is voiced or not. The key thing to remember is that the vocal cords don't like switching around at the midpoint. If the first consonant is voiced, the next one will be as well. If the first one is unvoiced, the second one will sound unvoiced, no matter what you do. For example, say the word *spoon*. Now, say the word *sboon*. Hear how they sound the same? This is why I'd like you to always convert the preposition *to* to **də** when you're speaking English, no matter what comes before it. In the beginning, to get you used to the concept, we made a distinction between **tə** and **də**, but now that your schwa is in place, use a single **d'** sound everywhere, except at the very beginning of a sentence.

After a voiced sound:	He had to **do** it.	he hæ$^{(d)}$d' **du**$^{(w)}$'t
After an unvoiced sound:	He got to **do** it.	he gä$^{(t)}$d' **du**$^{(w)}$'t
At the beginning of a sentence:	To **be** or **not** to be.	t' **bee**$^{(y)}$r nä$^{(t)}$d'bee

To have your liaisons tested, call (800) 457-4255.

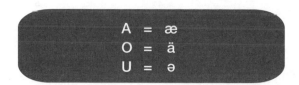

```
A  =  æ
O  =  ä
U  =  ə
```

Chapter 12

Cat? Caught? Cut?

CD 3 Track 52

After laying our foundation with intonation and liaisons, here we finally begin to refine your pronunciation! We are now going to work on the differences between **æ**, **ä**, and **ə**, as well as **ō**, **ā**, and **ɛ**. Let's start out with the **æ** sound. (See also page viii, Chapters 3, 18, 20, and the Nationality Guides.)

The æ Sound

Although not a common sound, **æ** is very distinctive to the ear and is typically American. In the practice paragraph in Exercise 12-2 this sound occurs five times. As its phonetic symbol indicates, **æ** is a combination of **ä** + **ɛ**. To pronounce it, drop your jaw down as if you were going to say **ä**; then from that position, try to say **ɛ**. The final sound is not two separate vowels but rather the end result of the combination. It is very close to the sound that a goat makes: *ma-a-a-a*!

▶ Try it a few times now: **ä** ▶ **æ**

If you find yourself getting too nasal with **æ**, pinch your nose as you say it. If **kæt** turns into **kɛæt**, you need to pull the sound out of your nose and down into your throat.

Note *As you look for the **œ** sound you might think that words like **down** or **sound** have an **æ** in them. For this diphthong, try **æ** + **oh**, or **æo**. This way, **down** would be written **dœon**. Because it is a combined sound, however, it's not included in the Cat? category. (See Pronunciation Point 4 on page ix.)*

The ä Sound

The **ä** sound occurs a little more frequently; you will find ten such sounds in the exercise. To pronounce **ä**, relax your tongue and drop your jaw as far down as it will go. As a matter of fact, put your hand under your chin and say **mä**, **pä**, **tä**, **sä**. Your hand should be pushed down by your jaw as it opens. Remember, it's the sound that you make when the doctor wants to see your throat, so open it up and ***dräp your jäw***.

The Schwa ə Sound

Last is the schwa ə, the *most common* sound in American English. When you work on Exercise 12-2, depending on how fast you speak, how smoothly you make liaisons, how strong your intonation is, and how much you relax your sounds, you will find from 50 to 75 schwas. Spelling doesn't help identify it, because it can appear as any one of the vowels, or a combination of them. It is a neutral vowel sound, *uh.* It is usually in an unstressed syllable, though it can be stressed as well. Whenever you find a vowel that can be crossed out and its absence wouldn't change the pronunciation of the word, you have probably found a schwa: *photography* **ph'togr'phy** (the two apostrophes show the location of the neutral vowel sounds).

Because it is so common, however, the wrong pronunciation of this one little sound can leave your speech strongly accented, even if you Americanized everything else.

Note *Some dictionaries use two different written symbols, ə and ʌ, but for simplicity we are only going to use the first one.*

Silent or Neutral?

A schwa is neutral, but it is not silent. By comparison, the silent **e** at the end of a word is a signal for pronunciation, but it is not pronounced itself: *code* is **kōd.** The **e** tells you to say an **o.** If you leave the **e** off, you have *cod,* **käd.** The schwa, on the other hand, is neutral, but it is an actual sound—*uh.* For example, you could also write *photography* as *phuh•tah•gruh•fee.*

Because it's a neutral sound, the schwa doesn't have any distinctive characteristics, yet it is *the most common sound in the English language.*

To make the **ə** sound, put your hand on your diaphragm and push until a grunt escapes. Don't move your jaw, tongue, or lips; just allow the sound to flow past your vocal cords. It should sound like *uh.*

Once you master this sound, you will have an even easier time with pronouncing *can* and *can't.* In a sentence, *can't* sounds like **kæn(t),** but *can* becomes **kən,** unless it is stressed, when it is **kæn** (as we saw in Example 4-17 on page 37). Repeat.

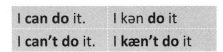

| I **can do** it. | I kən **do** it |
| I **can't do** it. | I **kæn't do** it |

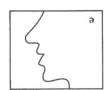

Vowel Chart

In the vowel chart that follows, the four corners represent the four most extreme positions of the mouth. The center box represents the least extreme position—the neutral schwa. For these four positions, only move your lips and jaw. Your tongue should stay in the same place—with the tip resting behind the bottom teeth.

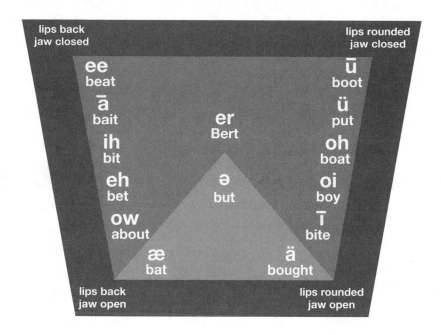

1. To pronounce *beat,* your lips should be drawn back, but your teeth should be close together. Your mouth should form the shape of a *banana.*

2. To pronounce *boot,* your lips should be fully rounded, and your teeth should be close together. Your mouth should form the shape of a *Cheerio.*

3. To pronounce *bought,* drop your jaw straight down from the *boot* position. Your mouth should form the shape of an *egg.*

4. To pronounce *bat,* keep your jaw down, pull your lips back, and try to simultaneously say **ä** and **ɛ**. Your mouth should form the shape of a *box.*

Note *Word-by-word pronunciation will be different than individual sounds within a sentence.* ***That, than, as, at, and, have, had, can****, and so on, are* **æ** *sounds when they stand alone, but they are weak words that reduce quickly in speech.*

Exercise 12-1: Word-by-Word and in a Sentence

CD 3 Track 53

Stressed		Unstressed		
that	thæt	th't	thət	He said th't it's OK.
than	thæn	th'n	thən	It's bigger th'n before.
as	æz	'z	əz	'z soon 'z he gets here
at	æt	't	ət	Look 't the time!
and	ænd	'n	ən	ham 'n eggs
have	hæv	h'v	həv	Where h'v you been?
had	hæd	h'd	həd	He h'd been at home.
can	cæn	c'n	cən	C'n you do it?

Exercise 12-2: Finding æ, ä, and ə Sounds

CD 3 Track 54

*There are five **æ**, ten **ä**, and 75 **ə** sounds in the following paragraph. Underscore them in pen or pencil. (The first one of each sound is marked for you.)*

Hello, **my** name is_____. I'm taking **ə**mer**ə**c**ə**n **æccent** Training. There's a l**ä**t to **learn**, but I **hope** to make it as **enjoyable** as possible. I should pick **up** on the American **intonation** pattern pretty **easily**, although the **only** way to **get** it is to **practice** all of the time. I use the **up** and down, or **peaks** and valleys, **intonation** more than I **used** to. I've been paying attention to **pitch**, **too**. It's like **walking** down a **stair**case. I've been **talking** to a lot of **Americans** lately, and they tell me that I'm **easier** to under**stand**. **Any**way, I could go **on** and on, but the **important** thing is to **listen** well and sound **good**. **Well**, what do you **think**? **Do** I?

▸ Next, check your answers with the Answer Key, beginning on page 210. Finally, take your markers and give a color to each sound. For example, mark **æ** green, **ä** blue, and **ə** yellow.

✗ Turn your CD off and read the paragraph three times on your own.

Note *It sounds regional to end a sentence with **ustə**. In the middle of a sentence, however, it is more standard: I **ustə** live there.*

Exercise 12-3: Vowel-Sound Differentiation

*Here we will read down from 1 to 24, then we will read each row across. Give the ā sound a clear double sound ɛ + ee. Also, the o is a longer sound than you might be expecting. Add the full **ooh** sound after each "o."*

	æ	ä	ə	ou	ā	ɛ
1.	Ann	on	un-	own	ain't	end
2.	ban	bond	bun	bone	bane	Ben
3.	can	con	come	cone	cane	Ken
4.	cat	caught/cot	cut	coat	Kate	ketch
5.	Dan	Don/dawn	done	don't	Dane	den
6.	fan	fawn	fun	phone	feign	fend
7.	gap	gone	gun	goat	gain	again
8.	hat	hot	hut	hotel	hate	het up
9.	Jan	John	jump	Joan	Jane	Jenny
10.	lamp	lawn	lump	loan	lane	Len
11.	man	monster	Monday	moan	main	men
12.	matter	motto	mutter	motor	made her	met her
13.	Nan	non-	none/nun	known	name	nemesis
14.	gnat	not/knot	nut	note	Nate	net
15.	pan	pawn	pun	pony	pain/pane	pen
16.	ran	Ron	run	roan	rain/reign	wren
17.	sand	sawn	sun	sewn/sown	sane	send
18.	shall	Sean	shut	show	Shane	Shen
19.	chance	chalk	chuck	choke	change	check
20.	tack	talk	tuck	token	take	tech
21.	van	Von	vug	vogue	vague	vent
22.	wax	want	won/one	won't	wane	when
23.	yam	yawn	young	yo!	yea!	yen
24.	zap	czar	result	zone	zany	zen

	single	double
ä	dock	dog
ə	duck	dug

To have your pronunciation tested, call (800) 457-4255.

Exercise 12-4: Reading the æ Sound CD 3 Track 56

The Tæn Mæn

A fashionably tan man sat casually at the bat stand, lashing a handful of practice bats. The manager, a crabby old bag of bones, passed by and laughed, "You're about average, Jack. Can't you lash faster than that?" Jack had had enough, so he clambered to his feet and lashed bats faster than any man had ever lashed bats. As a matter of fact, he lashed bats so fast that he seemed to dance. The manager was aghast. "Jack, you're a master bat lasher!" he gasped. Satisfied at last, Jack sat back and never lashed another bat.

✗ Pause the CD and read *The Tæn Mæn* aloud. Turn it back on to continue.

Exercise 12-5: Reading the ä Sound CD 3 Track 57

A Lät of Läng, Hät Wälks in the Gärden

John was not sorry when the boss called off the walks in the garden. Obviously, to him, it was awfully hot, and the walks were far too long. He had not thought that walking would have caught on the way it did, and he fought the policy from the onset. At first, he thought he could talk it over at the law office and have it quashed, but a small obstacle* halted that thought. The top lawyers always bought coffee at the shop across the lawn and they didn't want to stop on John's account. John's problem was not office politics, but office policy. He resolved the problem by bombing the garden.

lobster • a small lobster • lobstacle • a small obstacle

✗ Pause the CD and read *A Lät of Läng, Hät Wälks in the Gärden* aloud.

Exercise 12-6: Reading the ə Sound CD 3 Track 58

When you read the following schwa paragraph, try clenching your teeth the first time. It won't sound completely natural, but it will get rid of all of the excess lip and jaw movement and force your tongue to work harder than usual. Remember that in speaking American English we don't move our lips much, and we talk through our teeth from far back in our throats. I'm going to read with my teeth clenched together and you follow along, holding your teeth together.

What Must the Sun Above Wonder About?

Some pundits proposed that the sun wonders unnecessarily about sundry and assorted conundrums. One cannot but speculate what can come of their proposal. It wasn't enough to trouble us,* but it was done so underhandedly that hundreds of sun lovers rushed to the defense of their beloved sun. None of this was relevant on Monday, however, when the sun burned up the entire country. *ət wəzənənəf tə trəbələs

✗ Pause the CD and read *What Must the Sun Above Wonder About?* twice. Try it once with your teeth clenched the first time and normally the second time.

> **Th** is a popped sound.
> The tongue tip is pressed
> firmly against the top teeth.

Chapter 13

Tee Aitch

Exercise 13-1: Targeting the Th Sound

CD 3 Track 59

*In order to target the **Th** sound, first, hold a mirror in front of you and read our familiar paragraph silently, moving only your tongue. It should be visible in the mirror each time you come to a **Th**. Second, find all of the **Th**s, both voiced and unvoiced. Remember, a voiced sound makes your throat vibrate, and you can feel that vibration by placing your fingers on your throat. There are ten voiced and two unvoiced **Th**s here. You can mark them by underscoring the former and drawing a circle around the latter. Or, if you prefer, use two of your color markers. Pause the CD to mark the **Th** sounds. Don't forget to check your answers against the Answer Key, beginning on page 210. (See also Chapter 3 and Chapters 14 and 17 for related sounds.)*

Hello, **my** name is_____. I'm taking American **Accent** Training. There's a **lot** to **learn**, but I **hope** to make it as **enjoyable** as possible. I should pick **up** on the American **intonation** pattern pretty **easily**, although the **only** way to **get** it is to **practice** all of the time. I **use** the **up** and down, or **peaks** and valleys, **intonation** more than I **used** to. I've been paying attention to **pitch**, **too**. It's like **walking** down a staircase. I've been **talking** to a lot of **Americans** lately, and they tell me that I'm **easier** to under**stand**. Anyway, I could go **on** and on, but the **important** thing is to **listen** well and sound **good**. **Well**, what do you **think**? **Do** I?

Exercise 13-2: The Thuringian Thermometers

CD 3 Track 60

*I'm going to read the following paragraph once straight through, so you can hear that no matter how fast I read it, all the **Th**s are still there. It is a distinctive sound, but, when you repeat it, don't put too much effort into it. Listen to my reading.*

<u>Th</u>e throng of thermometers from <u>th</u>e Thuringian Thermometer Folks arrived on Thursday. <u>Th</u>ere were a **thousand thirty-three thick thermometers**, <u>though</u>, instead of a **thousand thirty-six thin thermometers**, which was **three thermometers** fewer <u>than</u> <u>the</u> **thousand thirty-six** we were expecting, not to mention <u>that</u> <u>they</u> were **thick** ones ra<u>ther</u> <u>than</u> **thin** ones. We **thoroughly thought** <u>that</u> we had ordered a **thousand thirty-six**, not a **thousand thirty-three**, thermometers, and asked <u>the</u> Thuringian Thermometer Folks to reship <u>th</u>e thermometers; **thin**, not **thick**. <u>Th</u>ey apologized for sending only a **thousand thirty-three thermometers** ra<u>ther</u> <u>than</u> a **thousand thirty-six** and promised to replace <u>the</u> **thick thermometers** with **thin thermometers**.

<u>th</u> = voiced (17)
th = unvoiced (44)

Exercise 13-3: Tongue Twisters · CD 3 Track 61

Feeling confident? Good! Try the following tongue twisters and have some fun.

1. The sixth sick Sheik's sixth thick sheep.

2. This is a zither. Is this a zither?

3. I thought a **thought**. But the thought I **thought** wasn't the thought I **thought** I thought. If the thought I **thought** I thought had been the thought I **thought**, I wouldn't have **thought** so much.

Exercise 13-4: Mr. Thingamajig

Sometimes, Americans have little mental pauses, where something's right on the tip of our tongue, but we can't think of the exact word—or when we want to euphemize unseemly speech. Fortunately, there's a way around this. We use substitution words that can mean anything and everything. Translation in Answer Key beginning on page 210.

I was rooting willy-nilly through a buncha stuff, looking every whichway for the dinky little whatchamacallit to fix the goldong thingamajig, but good ol' whatsizname had put it in the hooziwhatsit, as usual! Boy oh boy, what a load of hooey. Always the same old rigamarole with that cockamamie bozo. He's such a pipsqueak! If I found it, ka-ching, I'd be rich, which would be just jim dandy! I'd be totally discombobulated. You-know-who had done you-know-what with the goofy little gadget again, so whaddyaknow ... there was something-or-other wrong with it. What a snafu!

I had a heck of a time getting ahold of whatsername to come over and take care of it with her special little doohickey that she keeps there in the thingamabob. For the gazillionth time, the flightly little flibbertigibbit said alrighty, she wouldn't shilly shally, she'd schlep over with her widget fixer and whatnot to do a bodaciously whizbang job on the whole shebang. That's right, the whole kit 'n caboodle, no ifs, ands, or buts about it ... no malarkey. Okee dokey, but she was a skosh busy right then, yada, yada, yada. Yessirreebob, we usually have gadgets galore, but what with the this-and-that, and all the hooplah, it's all topsy turvy today, 'cuz that humungous nincompoop is still in the whatsit acting like everything's just hunky dory.

That's just a bunch, gobbledeegook. Pure gibberish. He's such an old rapscallion. Jeeminy Christmas, the shenanigans of that old fogey. Yackety schmackety, blah, blah, blah! Shucks, I wanted to find it on my own, and not be penalized for it—I'm just so darned tired of gimme's and gotcha's by a lotta has-been nosybones out hobnobbing with hoity toity wannabes.

The real nitty gritty is that, young and old, they're just a buncha happy-go-lucky whippersnappers and cantankerous old fuddyduddies who don't know diddly. I poked among the gewgaws, tchotchkes, gimcracks, and knickknacks, there in the doodad, but I found zilch, zero, zippo, nil, nada and null. So-and-so told me such-and-such about the deeleebob, but I just don't know where that little gizmo is. Sheesh! It's a big whoopdedoo when you can't even remember where the gosh diddly darned whaddyacallit is!

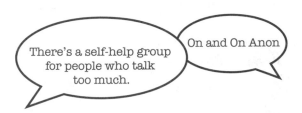

Chapter 14

The American T

CD 4 Track 1

The American **T** is influenced very strongly by intonation and its position in a word or phrase. At the *top* of a staircase, **T** is pronounced **T**, as in *Ted* or *Italian;* a **T** in the *middle* of a staircase is pronounced as **D**, *Beddy, Idaly;* whereas a **T** at the *bottom* of a staircase isn't pronounced at all, *ho(t)*. Look at *Italian* and *Italy* in the examples below. The **tæl** of *Italian* is at the top of the staircase and is strong: *Italian*. The **də** of *Italy* is in the middle and is weak: *Italy*. (See also Chapter 21.)

Exercise 14-1: Stressed and Unstressed T   CD 4 Track 2

Repeat after me.

Italian	Italy
attack	attic
atomic	atom
photography	photograph

Exercise 14-2: Betty Bought a Bit of Better Butter   CD 4 Track 3

*In the sentence **Betty bought a bit of better butter**, all of the Ts are in weak positions, so they all sound like soft **Ds**. Repeat the sentence slowly, word by word: **Beddy ... badə ... bidə ... bedder ... budder**. Feel the tip of your tongue flick across that area behind your top teeth. Think of the music of a cello again when you say, **Betty bought a bit of better butter**.*

Betty Bought a Bit of Better Butter

Betty bought a bit of better butter.	Beddy bädə bihda bedder budder.
But, said she,	Bu(t), said she,
This butter's bitter.	This budder'z bidder.
If I put it in my batter,	If I püdi din my bædder,
It'll make my batter bitter.	Id'll make my bædder bidder.

If you speak any language—such as Spanish, Japanese, Hindi, Italian, or Dutch, among others—where your **R** touches behind the teeth, you are in luck with the American **T**. Just fix the association in your mind so that when you see a middle position **T**, you automatically give it your native **R** sound. Say, *Beri bara bira...* with your native accent. (*Not* if you are French, German, or Chinese!) Along with liaisons, the American **T** contributes a great deal to the smooth, relaxed sound of English. When you say a word like *atom,* imagine that you've been to the dentist and you're a little numb, or that you've had a couple of drinks, or maybe that you're very sleepy. You won't be wanting to use a lot of energy saying **æ•tom**, so just relax everything and say **adəm**, like the masculine name, **Adam**. It's a very smooth, fluid sound. Rather than saying *BeTTy boughT a biT of beTTer buTTer,* which is physically more demanding, try *Beddy bada bidda bedder budder.* It's easy because you really don't need much muscle tension to say it this way.

The staircase concept will help clarify the various **T** sounds. The American **T** can be a little tricky if you base your pronunciation on spelling. Here are six rules to guide you.

1. **T is T** at the beginning of a word or in a stressed syllable.
2. **T is D** in the middle of a word.
3. **T is Held** at the end of a word.
4. **T is Held before N** in *-tain* and *-ten* endings.
5. **T is Silent after N** with lax vowels.
6. **T is Held** before glottal consonants **w, r, k, g** and **y**.

Exercise 14-3: Rule 1 – Top of the Staircase   CD 4 Track 4

*When a **T** or a **D** is at the top of a staircase, in a stressed position, it should be a clear popped sound.*

1. In the beginning of a word, **T** is **t**.
Ted took ten tomatoes.

2. With a stressed **T** and **ST, TS, TR, CT, LT**, sometimes **NT** combinations, **T** is **t**.
He was content with the contract

T replaces **D** in the past tense, after an unvoiced consonant sound—**f, k, p, s, ch, sh, th**—(except **T**).

T: laughed **læft**, *picked* **pikt**, *hoped* **houpt**, *raced* **rast**, *watched* **wächt**, *washed* **wäsht**, *unearthed* **uneartht**

D: halved **hœvd**, *rigged* **rigd**, *nabbed* **næbd**, *raised* **razd**, *judged* **j'jd**, *garaged* **garazhd**, *smoothed* **smoothd**

*Exceptions: wicked/***wikəd**, *naked/***nakəd**, *crooked/***krükəd**, *etc.*

Exercise 14-4: Rule 1 – Top of the Staircase Practice   CD 4 Track 5

Read the following sentences out loud. Make sure that the blue (stressed) Ts are sharp and clear.

1. It **took** Tim **ten** times **to try** the **telephone**.
2. **Stop touching Ted's toes**.
3. **Turn toward Stella** and **study** her **contract together**.
4. **Control** your **tears**.
5. It's **Tommy's turn to tell** the **teacher** the **truth**.

Exercise 14-5: Rule 2 – Middle of the Staircase   CD 4 Track 6

*An unstressed **T** in the middle of a staircase between two vowel sounds should be pronounced as a soft **D**.*

Betty bought a bit of better butter.	Beddy bädə bida bedder budder
Pat ought to sit on a lap.	pædädə sidänə læp

Read the following sentences out loud. Make sure that the blue (unstressed) Ts sound like a soft D.

1. What a good **idea**.	wədə gudai **dee**yə
2. Put it in a **bottle**.	püdidinə **bä**ddl
3. Write it in a **letter**.	räididinə **led**dr
4. Set it on the metal **gutter**.	sedidän thə medl **gə**ddr
5. Put all the **data** in the **computer**.	püdäl the **dei**də in the c'm**pyu**dr
6. Insert a **quarter** in the **meter**.	inserdə **kwor**der in the **mee**dr
7. Get a better **water** heater.	gedə beddr **wä**dr heedr
8. Let her put a **sweater** on.	ledr püdə **swe**der än
9. **Betty's** at a **meeting**.	**bed**dy's ædə **mee**ding
10. It's getting hotter and **hotter**.	its gedding häddr•rən **hä**ddr
11. **Patty** ought to write a better **letter**.	**pæd**dy(y)ädə ride a beddr **led**dr
12. **Frida** had a **little** metal **bottle**.	**free**də hædə **lid**dl medl **bä**ddl

---

Exercise 14-6: Rule 3 – Bottom of the Staircase CD 4 Track 7

T at the bottom of a staircase is in the held position. By held, I mean that the tongue is in the T position, but the air isn't released. To compare, when you say T as in Tom, there's a sharp burst of air over the tip of the tongue, and when you say Betty, there's a soft puff of air over the tip of the tongue. When you hold a T, as in hot, your tongue is in the position for T, but you keep the air in.

1. She hit the hot **hut** with her **hat**.
2. We went to that '**Net** site to get what we **needed.**
3. **Pat** was quite **right**, **wasn't** she?
4. **What**? Put my **hat** back!
5. hot, late, fat, goat, hit, put, not, hurt, what, set, paint,
   wait, sit, dirt, note, fit, lot, light, suit, point, incident, tight

---

Exercise 14-7: Rule 4 – "Held T" Before N CD 4 Track 8

The "held T" is, strictly speaking, not really a T at all. Remember t and n are very close in the mouth (see Liaisons, Example 11-5). If you have an N immediately after a T, you don't pop the T—the tongue is in the T position—but you release the air with the N, not the T. There is no t and no ə. Make a special point of not letting your tongue release from the top of your mouth before you drop into the n; otherwise, bu(tt)on would sound like two words: but-ton. An unstressed T or TT followed by N is held. Read the following words and sentences out loud. Make sure that the blue Ts are held. Remember, there is no uh sound before the n.

Note *Another point to remember is that you need a sharp upward sliding intonation up to the "held T," then a quick drop for the N. Just go to the T position and hum: writt•nnnn.*

	written	ri^(t)n		written	kitten
				sentence	patent
				forgotten	mutant
	sentence	sen^(t)ns		certain	latent
				curtain	mountain
				mitten	recently
	lately	la^(t)lee		Martin	lately
				bitten	partly
				button	frequently

t
n

1. He's **forgotten** the **carton** of satin **mittens**.
2. She's **certain** that he has **written** it.
3. The cotton **curtain** is not in the **fountain**.
4. The **hikers** went in the **mountains**.
5. **Martin** has gotten a **kitten**.
6. **Students** study **Latin** in **Britain**.
7. **Whitney** has **a patent** on those **sentences.**
8. He has not **forgotten** what was **written** about the **mutant** on the **mountain**.
9. It's not **certain** that it was gotten from the **fountain**.
10. You need to put an **orange** cotton **curtain** on that **window**.
11. We like that certain **satin** better than the **carton** of cotton **curtains**.
12. The intercontinental **hotel** is in **Seattle**.
13. The frightened **witness** had forgotten the **important** written **message**.
14. The child wasn't **beaten** because he had **bitten** the **button**.

Exercise 14-8: Rule 5 – The Silent T   CD 4 Track 9

*T and N are so close in the mouth that the **t** can simply disappear. Repeat.*

1.	**int**erview	**inn**erview
2.	**int**erface	**inn**erface
3.	**Int**ernet	**inn**ernet
4.	**int**erstate	**inn**erstate
5.	inter**rupt**	inner**rupt**
6.	inter**fere**	inner**fere**
7.	inter**acti**ve	inner**acti**ve
8.	inter**nati**onal	inner**nati**onal
9.	ad**van**tage	əd**væn**'j
10.	per**cen**tage	per**cen**'j
11.	**twen**ty	**twen**ny
12.	**print**out	**prin**nout or **prin**^dout
13.	**print**er	**prin**ner or **prin**^der
14.	**win**ter	**win**ner or **win**^der
15.	**ent**er	**en**ner or **en**^der
16.	**pen**tagon	**pen**nagon

Read the following sentences out loud. Make sure that the underlined Ts are silent.

1.	He had a great **int**erview.	he hædə gray ᵈ**in**nerview
2.	Try to enter the infor**ma**tion.	trydə enner the infrmation
3.	Turn the **print**er on.	trn thə **prin**nerän
4.	Finish the **print**ing.	f 'n'sh thə **prin**ning
5.	She's at the inter**na**tional center.	sheez' ⁽ᵗ⁾the⁽ʸ⁾inner**na**tional senner
6.	It's twenty de**grees** in Toronto.	'ts twenny d'**gree**zin **trän**no
7.	I don't under**stand** it.	I doe nənder **stæn** d't
8.	She in**vent**ed it in Santa **Mo**nica.	she⁽ʸ⁾in**ven**əd'din sænə **män**əkə
9.	He can't even **do** it.	he kæneevən **du**⁽ʷ⁾'t
10.	They don't even **want** it.	they doe neevən **wän**'t
11.	They won't ever **try**.	they woe never **try**
12.	What's the **point** of it?	w'ts the **poi** n'v't
13.	She's the intercont**inent**al repres**ent**ative.	shez thee⁽ʸ⁾innercän⁽ᵗ⁾n•**nen**l repr'**zen**'d'v
14.	**Has**n't he?	**hæz**ə nee
15.	**Is**n't he?	**iz**ə nee
16.	**Are**n't I?	**är** näi
17.	**Won**'t he?	**woe** nee
18.	**Does**n't he?	**də**zənee
19.	**Would**n't it?	**wüd**ənit
20.	**Did**n't I?	**did**n•näi

*Before a throat consonant, **T** is held by the back of the tongue. Repeat the following phrases.*

1.	bright white	11.	it can
2.	white car	12.	it runs
3.	rent control	13.	that we
4.	quit claim	14.	what we
5.	get one	15.	that one
6.	what was	16.	heat wave
7.	that when	17.	net worth
8.	it will	18.	but, yeah
9.	not really	19.	what could
10.	not good	20.	what would

Sometimes Americans will hear the expression **quit claim** as **quick claim**.

Exercise 14-11: Karina's T Connections

*Here are some extremely common middle **T** combinations. Repeat after me:*

	What	But	That
a	wədə	bədə	thədə
I	wədäi	bədäi	thədäi
I'm	wədäim	bədäim	thədäim
I've	wədäiv	bədäiv	thədäiv
if	wədif	bədif	thədif
it	wədit	bədit	thədit
it's	wədits	bədits	thədits
is	wədiz	bədiz	thədiz
isn't	wədizn[t]	bədizn[t]	thədizn[t]
are	wədr	bədr	thədr
aren't	wədärn[t]	bədärn[t]	thədärn[t]
he	wədee	bədee	thədee
he's	wədeez	bədeez	thədeez
her	wədr	bədr	thədr
you	wəchew	bəchew	thəchew
you'll	wəchül	bəchül	thəchül
you've	wəchoov	bəchoov	thəchoov
you're	wəchr	bəchr	thəchr

Exercise 14-12: Combinations in Context

Repeat the following sentences.

1.	I don't know what it **means**.	I don[t] know wədit **meenz**
2.	But it **look**s like what I **need**.	bədi[t] **lük** sly kwədäi **need**
3.	But you **said** that you **wouldn't**.	bəchew **sed** thəchew **wüdnt**
4.	I **know** what you **think**.	I **know** wəchew **think**
5.	But I don't **think** that he **will**.	bədäi don[t] **think** thədee **will**
6.	He said that if we can **do** it, he'll **help**.	he sed the diff we k'n **do**[w]it, hill **help**
7.	But isn't it **easier** this **way**?	bədizni **dee**zier thi **sway**?
8.	We **want** something that isn't **here**.	we **wänt** something thədizn[t] **here**
9.	You'll **like** it, but you'll **regret** it **later**.	yül **lye** kit, bəchül r'**gre** dit **laydr**
10.	But he's not **right** for what I **want**.	bədeez nät **right** fr wədäi **wänt**
11.	It's **amazing** what you've **accomplished**.	its amazing wəchoovəc**cäm**plisht
12.	What if he **forgets**?	wədifee fr**gets**
13.	**OK**, but aren't you **missing** something?	**OK**, bədärn[t] chew **miss**ing səmthing
14.	I think that he's **OK** now.	I think thədeez OK næo
15.	She **wanted** to, but her **car** broke down.	She **wän**əd to, bədr **cär** broke dæon
16.	We **think** that you're taking a **chance**.	We **think** thəchr taking a **chænce**
17.	They don't know what it's **about**.	They doe noe wədit sə**bæot**

Exercise 14-13: Voiced and Unvoiced Sounds with T CD 4 Track 14

This exercise is for the practice of the difference between words that end in either a vowel or a voiced consonant, which means that the vowel is lengthened or doubled. Therefore, these words are on a much larger, longer stairstep. Words that end in an unvoiced consonant are on a smaller, shorter stairstep. This occurs whether the vowel in question is tense or lax.

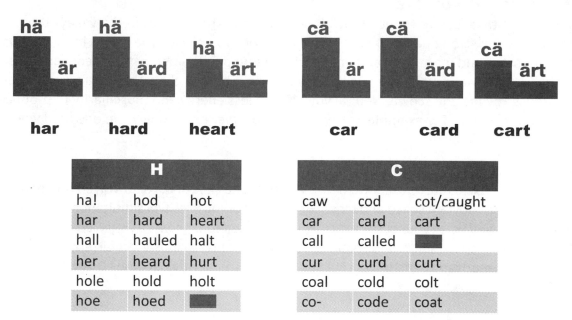

H		
ha!	hod	hot
har	hard	heart
hall	hauled	halt
her	heard	hurt
hole	hold	holt
hoe	hoed	

C		
caw	cod	cot/caught
car	card	cart
call	called	
cur	curd	curt
coal	cold	colt
co-	code	coat

Exercise 14-14: Finding American T Sounds CD 4 Track 15

Once again, go over the following familiar paragraph. First, find all the T's that are pronounced D (there are nine to thirteen here). Second, find all the held Ts (there are seven). The first one of each is marked for you. Pause the CD to do this and don't forget to check your answers with the Answer Key, beginning on page 210, when you finish.

He**llo, my** name is_____. I'm taking American **Accen(t)** Training. There's a **lo(t)** to **learn**, but[d] I **hope** to make it as **enjoyable** as possible. I should pick **up** on the American **intonation** pattern pretty **easily**, although the **only** way to **get** it is to **practice** all of the time. I use the **up** and down, or **peaks** and valleys, **intonation** more than I **used** to. I've been paying attention to **pitch, too**. It's like **walking** down a **stair**case. I've been **talking** to a lot of **Americans** lately, and they tell me that I'm **easier** to understand. **Any**way, I could go **on** and on, but the **important** thing is to **listen** well and sound **good. Well**, what do you **think**? **Do** I?

Voiced Consonants and Reduced Vowels

The strong intonation in American English creates certain tendencies in your spoken language. Here are four consistent conditions that are a result of intonation's tense peaks and relaxed valleys:

1. Reduced vowels

You were introduced to reduced vowels in Chapter 1. They appear in the valleys that are formed by the strong peaks of intonation. The more you reduce the words in the valleys, the smoother and more natural your speech will sound. A characteristic of reduced vowels is that your throat muscles should be very relaxed. This will allow the unstressed vowels to reduce toward the schwa. Neutral vowels take less energy and muscularity to produce than tense vowels. For example, the word *unbelievable* should only have one hard vowel: **ənbəlēvəbəl**.

2. Voiced consonants

The mouth muscles are relaxed to create a voiced sound like **z** or **d**. For unvoiced consonants, such as **s** or **t**, they are sharp and tense. Relaxing your muscles will simultaneously reduce your vowels and voice your consonants. Think of *voiced consonants* as *reduced consonants*. Both reduced consonants and reduced vowels are unconsciously preferred by a native speaker of American English. This explains why **T** so frequently becomes **D** and **S** becomes **Z**: *Get it is to ...* **gedidizdə**.

3. Like sound with like sound

It's not easy to change horses midstream, so when you have a voiced consonant; let the consonant that follows it be voiced as well. In the verb *used*, **yuzd**, for example, the **S** is really a **Z**, so it is followed by **D**. The phrase *used to*, **yus tu**, on the other hand, has a real **S**, so it is followed by **T**. Vowels are, by definition, voiced. So when one is followed by a common, reducible word, it will change that word's first sound—like the preposition *to*, which will change to **də**.

> The only way to get it is to practice all of the time.
> They only wei•də•geddidiz•də•practice all of the time.

Again, this will take time. In the beginning, work on recognizing these patterns when you hear them. When you are confident that you understand the structure beneath these sounds and you can intuit where they belong, you can start to try them out. It's not advisable to memorize one reduced word and stick it into an otherwise overpronounced sentence. It would sound strange.

4. R'læææææææææx

You've probably noticed that the preceding three conditions, as well as other areas that we've covered, such as liaisons and the schwa, have one thing in common—the idea that *it's physically easier this way.* This is one of the most remarkable characteristics of American English. You need to relax your mouth and throat muscles (except for **æ**, **ä**, and other tense vowels) and let the sounds flow smoothly out. If you find yourself tensing up, pursing your lips, or tightening your throat, you are going to strangle and lose the sound you are pursuing. Relax, relax, relax.

Chapter 15

> The tongue doesn't touch anywhere.
> Growl out the **R** in the throat.

The American R

CD 4 Track 17

American English, today—although continually changing—is made up of the sounds of the various people who have come to settle here from many countries. All of them have put in their linguistic two cents, the end result being that the easiest way to pronounce things has almost always been adopted as the most American. **R** is an exception, along with **L** and the sounds of **æ** and **th**, and is one of the most troublesome sounds for people to acquire. Not only is it difficult for adults learning the language but also for American children, who pronounce it like a **W** or skip over it altogether and only pick it up after they've learned all the other sounds. (See also Chapters 1, 3, and the Nationality Guides.)

The Invisible R

The trouble is that you can't see an **R** from the outside. With a **P**, for instance, you can see when people put their lips together and pop out a little puff. With **R**, however, everything takes place behind almost closed lips—back down in the throat—and who can tell what the tongue is doing? It is really hard to tell what's going on if, when someone speaks, you can only hear the *err* sound, especially if you're used to making an **R** by touching your tongue to the ridge behind your teeth. So, what should your tongue be doing? This technique can help you visualize the correct tongue movements in pronouncing the **R**.

1. Hold your hand out flat, with the palm up, slightly dropping the back end of it. That's basically the position your tongue is in when you say *ah*, **ä**, so your flat hand will represent this sound.
2. Now, to go from *ah* to the *er,* take your fingers and curl them into a tight fist. Again, your tongue should follow that action. The sides of your tongue should come up a bit, too. When the air passes over that hollow in the middle of your tongue, that's what creates the *er* sound.

Try it using both your hand and tongue simultaneously. Say *ah,* with your throat open (and your hand flat), then curl your tongue up (and your fingers) and say *errr.* The tip of the tongue should be aimed at a middle position in the mouth, but never touching, and your throat should relax and expand. **R**, like **L**, has a slight schwa in it. This is what pulls the *er* down so far back in your throat.

Another way to get to *er* is to put a spoon on your tongue, and go from the *ee* sound and slide your tongue straight back like a collapsing accordion, letting the two sides of your tongue touch the insides of your molars; the tip of the tongue, however, again, should not touch anything. Now from *ee,* pull your tongue back toward the center of your throat, and pull the sound down into your throat:

> ee ▶ ee ▶ eeeer

Since the **R** is produced in the throat, let's link it with other throat sounds.

Exercise 15-1: R Location Practice · CD 4 Track 18

Repeat after me.

g, gr, greek, green, grass, grow, crow, core, cork, coral, cur, curl, girl, gorilla, her, erg, error, mirror, were, war, gore, wrong, wringer, church, pearl

While you're perfecting your **R**, you might want to rush to it, and in doing so, neglect the preceding vowel. There are certain vowels that you can neglect, but there are others that demand their full sound. We're going to practice the ones that require you to keep that clear sound before you add an **R**.

Exercise 15-2: Double Vowel with R · CD 4 Track 19

Refer to the subsequent lists of sounds and words as you work through each of the directions that follow them. Repeat each sound, first the vowel and then the ɚr, and each word in columns 1 to 3. We will read all the way across.

1	2	3
ä + er	hä•ərd	hard
e + ər	he•ər	here
ɛ + ər	shɛ•ər	share
o + ər	mo•ər	more
ər + ər	wər•ər	were

hä
ərd

We will next read column 3 only. Try to keep that doubled sound, but let the vowel flow smoothly into the **ər**; imagine a double stairstep that cannot be avoided. Don't make them two staccato sounds, though, like **ha•rd**. Instead, flow them smoothly over the double stairstep: *Hääärrrrd.*

Of course, they're not *that* long; this is an exaggeration, and you're going to shorten them up once you get better at the sound. When you say the first one, *hard,* to get your jaw open for the **hä**, imagine that you are getting ready to bite into an apple: **hä**. Then for the *er* sound, you would bite into it: **hä•erd**, *hard.*

▸ Pause the CD to practice five times on your own.

From a spelling standpoint, the American **R** can be a little difficult to figure out. With words like *where*, **wɛər** and *were*, **wər**, it's confusing to know which one has two different vowel sounds *(where)* and which one has just the **ər** *(were).* When there is a full vowel, you must make sure to give it its complete sound, and not chop it short, **wɛ + ər**.

For words with only the schwa + **R ər**, don't try to introduce another vowel sound before the **ər**, *regardless of spelling.* The following words, for example, do not have any other vowel sounds in them.

Looks like	Sounds like
word	wərd
hurt	hərt
girl	gərl
pearl	pərl

The following exercise will further clarify this for you.

Exercise 15-3: How to Pronounce Troublesome Rs CD 4 Track 20

*The following seven **R** sounds, which are represented by the ten words, give people a lot of trouble, so we're going to work with them and make them easy for you. Repeat.*

1.	were	wər•ər
2.	word/whirred	wər•ərd
3.	whirl	wərrul
4.	world/whirled	were rolled
5.	wore/war	woər
6.	whorl	worul
7.	where/wear	wɛər

1. *Were* is pronounced with a doubled **ər**: **wər•ər**
2. *Word* is also doubled, but after the second **ər**, you're going to put your tongue in place for the **D** and hold it there, keeping all the air in your mouth, opening your throat to give it that full-voiced quality (imagine yourself puffing your throat out like a bullfrog): **wərərd**, *word*. Not **wərd**, which is too short. Not **wərdə**, which is too strong at the end. But **wər•ər**[d], *word*.
3. In *whirl* the **R** is followed by **L**. The **R** is in the throat and the back of the tongue stays down because, as we've practiced, **L** starts with the schwa, but the tip of the tongue comes up for the **L**: **wər•rə•lə**, *whirl*.
4. *World/whirled* has two spellings (and two different meanings, of course). You're going to do the same thing as for *whirl*, but you're going to add that voiced **D** at the end, holding the air in: **wər•rəl**[d], *world/whirled*. It should sound almost like two words: *wére rolled*.
5. Here, you have an **o** sound in either spelling before the **ər**: **wo•ər**, *wore/war*.
6. For *whorl*, you're going to do the same thing as in 5, but you're going to add a schwa + **L** at the end: **wo•ərəl**, *whorl*.
7. This sound is similar to 5, but you have **ɛ** before the **ər**: **wɛ•ər**, *where/wear*.

The following words are typical in that they are spelled one way and pronounced in another way. The *ar* combination frequently sounds like **ɛr**, as in *embarrass*, **embɛrəs**. This sound is particularly clear on the West Coast. On the East Coast, you may hear **embæɾəs**.

Exercise 15-4: Zbigniew's Epsilon List	CD 4 Track 22

Repeat after me.

			Common Combinations
embarrass	stationary	Larry	
vocabulary	care	Sarah	
parent	carry	narrate	
parallel	carriage	guarantee	ar
paragraph	marriage	larynx	par
para-	maritime	laryngitis	bar
parrot	barrier	necessary	mar
apparent	baritone	itinerary	lar
parish	Barron's	said	kar
Paris	library	says	war
area	character	transparency	har
aware	Karen	dictionary	sar
compare	Harry	many	nar
imaginary	Mary	any	gar
			rar

Exercise 15-5: R Combinations	CD 4 Track 23

Don't think about spelling here. Just pronounce each column of words as the heading indicates.

	ər	ɑr	ɛr	or	eer	æwr
1.	earn	art	air	or	ear	hour
2.	hurt	heart	hair	horse	here	how 're
3.	heard	hard	haired	horde	here's	■
4.	pert	part	pair	pour	peer	power
5.	word	■	where	war	we're	■
6.	a word	■	aware	award	a weird	■
7.	work	■	wear	warm	weird	■
8.	first	far	fair	four	fear	flower
9.	firm	farm	fairy	form	fierce	■
10.	rather	cathartic	there	Thor	theory	11th hour
11.	murky	mar	mare	more	mere	■
12.	spur	spar	spare	sport	spear	■
13.	sure	sharp	share	shore	shear	shower
14.	churn	char	chair	chore	cheer	chowder

15.	gird	guard	scared	gored	geared	Gower
16.	cur	car	care	core	kir	cower
17.	turtle	tar	tear	tore	tear	tower
18.	dirt	dark	dare	door	dear	dour
19.	stir	star	stair	store	steer	▬
20.	sir	sorry	Sarah	sore	seer	sour
21.	burn	barn	bear	born	beer	bower

Exercise 15-6: The Mirror Store — CD 4 Track 24

Repeat after me.

The Hurly Burly Mirror Store at Vermont and Beverly featured hundreds of first-rate mirrors. There were several mirrors on the chest of drawers*, and the largest one was turned toward the door in order to make the room look bigger. One of the girls who worked there was concerned that a bird might get hurt by hurtling into its own reflection. She learned by trial and error** how to preserve both the mirrors and the birds. Her earnings were proportionately increased at the mirror store to reflect her contribution to the greater good. *chesta drorz **tryla nerr'r

✖ Pause the CD to practice reading out loud three times on your own.

Exercise 15-7: Finding the R Sound — CD 4 Track 25

*Pause the CD and go through our familiar paragraph and find all the **R** sounds. The first one is marked for you.*

Hello, **my** name is_____. I'm taking American **Accent** Training. There's a **lot** to **learn**, but I **hope** to make it as **enjoyable** as possible. I should pick **up** on the American **intonation** pattern pretty **easily**, although the **only** way to **get** it is to **practice** all of the time. I use the **up** and down, or **peaks** and valleys, **intonation** more than I **used** to. I've been paying attention to **pitch, too**. It's like **walking** down a **stair**case. I've been **talking** to a lot of **Americans** lately, and they tell me that I'm **easier** to unde**rstand**. **Any**way, I could go **on** and on, but the **important** thing is to **listen** well and sound **good. Well**, what do you **think**? **Do** I?

▸ Check the Answer Key, beginning on page 210.

One of the best ways to get the **R** is to literally growl. Say **grrrr** as if you were a wild animal growling in the woods.

Chapter 16

> The tongue tip touches the ridge,
> even at the end of a word.

This chapter discusses the sound of **L** (not to be confused with that of the American **R**, which was covered in the last chapter). We'll approach this sound first by touching on the difficulties it presents to foreign speakers of English, and next by comparing **L** to the related sounds of **T**, **D**, and **N**. (See also Chapter 21, and for related sounds see Chapters 14 and 24.)

L and Foreign Speakers of English

The English **L** is usually no problem at the beginning or in the middle of a word. The native language of some people, however, causes them to make their English **L** much too short. At the end of a word, the **L** is especially noticeable if it is either missing (Chinese) or too short (Spanish). In addition, most people consider the **L** as a simple consonant. This can also cause a lot of trouble. Thus, two things are at work here: location of language sounds in the mouth, and the complexity of the **L** sound.

Location of Language in the Mouth

The sounds of many Romance languages are generally located far forward in the mouth. My French teacher told me that if I couldn't see my lips when I spoke French—it wasn't French! Spanish is sometimes even called the smiling language. Chinese, on the other hand, is similar to American English in that it is mostly produced far back in the mouth. The principal difference is that English also requires clear use of the tongue's tip, a large component of the sound of **L**.

The Compound Sound of L

The **L** is not a simple consonant; it is a compound made up of a vowel and a consonant. Like the **æ** sound discussed in Chapter 12, the sound of **L** is a combination of *ə* and *L*. The *ə*, being a reduced vowel sound, is created in the throat, but the *L* part requires a clear movement of the tongue. First, the tip must touch behind the teeth. (This part is simple enough.) But then, the back of the tongue must then drop down and back for the continuing schwa sound. Especially at the end of a word, Spanish-speaking people tend to leave out the schwa and shorten the **L**, and Chinese speakers usually leave it off entirely.

One way to avoid the pronunciation difficulty of a final **L**, as in *call,* is to make a liaison when the next word begins with a vowel. For example, if you want to say *I have to call on my friend,* let the liaison do your work for you; say *I have to kälän my friend.*

L Compared with T, D, and N   CD 4 Track 27

When you learn to pronounce the **L** correctly, you will feel its similarity with **T**, **D**, and **N**. Actually, the tongue is positioned in the same place in the mouth for all four sounds—behind the teeth. The difference is in how and where the air comes out. (See the drawings in Example 16-1.)

T and D

The sound of both **T** and **D** is produced by allowing a puff of air to come out over the tip of the tongue.

N

The sound of **N** is nasal. The tongue completely blocks all air from leaving through the mouth, allowing it to come out only through the nose. You should be able to feel the edges of your tongue touching your teeth when you say *nnn*.

L

With **L**, the tip of the tongue is securely touching the roof of the mouth behind the teeth, but the sides of the tongue are dropped down and tensed. This is where **L** is different from **N**. With **N**, the tongue is relaxed and covers the entire area around the back of the teeth so that no air can come out. With **L**, the tongue is very tense, and the air comes out around its sides.

At the beginning it's helpful to exaggerate the position of the tongue. Look at yourself in the mirror as you stick out the tip of your tongue between your front teeth. With your tongue in this position say *el* several times. Then, try saying it with your tongue behind your teeth. This sounds complicated, but it is easier to do than to describe. You can practice this again later with Exercise 16-3. Our first exercise, however, must focus on differentiating the sounds.

Exercise 16-1: Sounds comparing L with T, D, and N   CD 4 Track 28

For this exercise, concentrate on the different ways in which the air comes out of the mouth when producing each sound of L, T, D, and N. Look at the drawings, included here, to see the correct position of the tongue. Instructions for reading the groups of words listed next are given after the words.

T/D Plosive

A puff of air comes out over the tip of the tongue.

The tongue is somewhat tense.

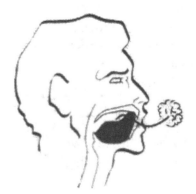

Exercise 16-1: Sounds Comparing L with T, D and N *continued*　　　CD 4 Track 28

N
Nasal

Air comes out through the nose.

The tongue is completely relaxed.

L
Lateral

Air flows around the sides of the tongue.
The tongue is very tense.

The lips are *not* rounded!

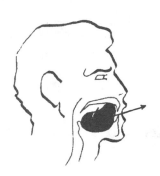

Exercise 16-2: Sounds Comparing L with T, D, and N　　　CD 4 Track 29

Repeat after me, first down and then across.

1.	At the beginning of a word		
law	gnaw	taw	daw
low	know	toe	dough
lee	knee	tea	D
2.	**In the middle of a word**		
belly	Benny		Betty
caller	Conner		cotter
alley	Annie's		at ease
3.	**At the end of a word**		
A hole	hold	hone	hoed
call	called	con	cod
B fill	full	fool	fail
fell	feel	fuel	furl

▶ Look at group 3, B. This exercise has three functions:

1. Practice final *els.*
2. Review vowel sounds.
3. Review the same words with the staircase.

Note *Notice that each word has a tiny schwa after the* **el**. *This is to encourage your tongue to be in the right position to give your words a "finished" sound. Exaggerate the final* **el** *and its otherwise inaudible schwa.*

▶ Repeat the last group of words.

Once you are comfortable with your tongue in this position, let it just languish there while you continue vocalizing, which is what a native speaker does.

▶ Repeat again: fillll, fullll, foollll, faillll, feellll, fuellll, furllll.

What Are All Those Extra Sounds I'm Hearing?   CD 4 Track 30

I hope that you're asking a question like this about now. Putting all of those short little words on a staircase will reveal exactly how many extra sounds you have to put in to make it "sound right." For example, if you were to pronounce *fail* as **fāl**, the sound is too abbreviated for the American ear—we need to hear the full **fāyəlᵊ**.

Exercise 16-3: Final El with Schwa	CD 4 Track 31

Repeat after me.

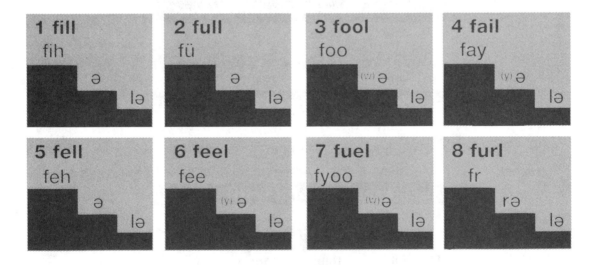

Exercise 16-4: Many Final Els

*This time, simply hold the **L** sound extra long. Repeat after me.*

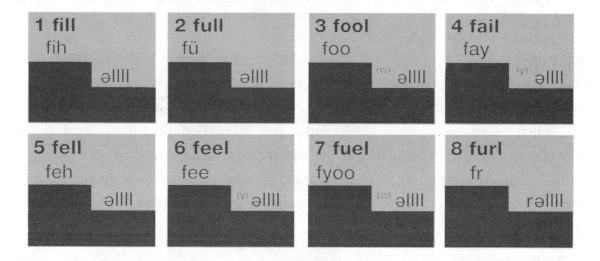

1 fill	2 full	3 fool	4 fail
fih əllll	fü əllll	foo (w) əllll	fay (y) əllll

5 fell	6 feel	7 fuel	8 furl
feh əllll	fee (y) əllll	fyoo (w) əllll	fr rəllll

Exercise 16-5: Liaise the Ls

*As you work with the following exercise, here are two points you should keep in mind. When a word ends with an **L** sound, either (a) connect it to the next word if you can, or (b) add a slight schwa for an exaggerated **lə** sound. For example:*

> (a) enjoyable as   enjoyəbələz
> (b) possible   pasəbələ

Note *Although (a) is really the way you want to say it, (b) is an interim measure to help you put your tongue in the right place. It would sound strange if you were to always add the slight schwa. Once you can feel where you want your tongue to be, hold it there while you continue to make the **L** sound. Here are three examples:*

Call		
caw	kä	(incorrect)
call	cälə	(understandable)
call	källl	(correct)

*You can do the same thing to stop an **N** from becoming an **NG**.*

Con		
cong	käng	(incorrect)
con	känə	(understandable)
con	kännn	(correct)

Exercise 16-6: Finding L Sounds
CD 4 Track 34

*Pause the CD, and find and mark all the **L** sounds in the familiar paragraph below; the first one is marked for you. There are seventeen of them; **five are silent**. Check the Answer Key, beginning on page 210.*

He__l__o, **my** name is_____. I'm taking American **Accent** Training. There's a **lot** to **learn**, but I **hope** to make it as **enjoyable** as possible. I should pick **up** on the American **intonation** pattern pretty **easily**, although the **only** way to **get** it is to **practice** all of the time. **I use** the **up** and down, or **peaks** and valleys, **intonation** more than I **used** to. I've been paying attention to **pitch**, **too**. It's like **walking** down a **stair**case. I've been **talking** to a lot of **Americans** lately, and they tell me that I'm **easier** to under**stand**. **Any**way, I could go **on** and on, but the **important** thing is to **listen** well and sound **good**. **Well**, what do you **think**? **Do** I?

Exercise 16-7: Silent Ls
CD 4 Track 35

*Once you've found all the **L** sounds, the good news is that very often you don't even have to pronounce them. Read the following list of words after me.*

1.	would	could	should
2.	chalk	talk	walk
3.	calm	palm	psalm
4.	already	alright	almond
5.	although	almost	always
6.	salmon	alms	Albany
7.	folk	caulk	polka
8.	half	calf	behalf
9.	yolk	colonel	Lincoln

CD 4 Track 36

Before reading about **Little Lola** in the next exercise, I'm going to get off the specific subject of **L** for the moment to talk about learning in general. Frequently, when you have some difficult task to do, you either avoid it or do it with dread. I'd like you to take the opposite point of view. For this exercise, you're going to completely focus on the thing that's most difficult: leaving your tongue attached to the top of your mouth. And rather than saying, "Oh, here comes an **L**, I'd better do something with my tongue," just leave your tongue attached *all through the entire paragraph!*

Remember our clenched-teeth reading of *What Must the Sun Above Wonder About?*, in Chapter 12? Well, it's time for us to make weird sounds again.

Exercise 16-8: Hold Your Tongue

*You and I are going to read with our tongues firmly held at the roofs of our mouths. If you want, hold a clean dime there with the tongue's tip; the dime will let you know when you have dropped your tongue because it will fall out. (Do not use candy; it will hold itself there since wet candy is sticky.) If you prefer, you can read with your tongue between your teeth instead of the standard behind-the-teeth position, and use a small mirror. Remember that with this technique you can actually see your tongue disappear as you hear your **L** sounds drop off.*

It's going to sound ridiculous, of course, and nobody would ever intentionally sound like this, but no one will hear you practice. You don't want to sound like this: llllllllll. Force your tongue to make all the various vowels in spite of its position. Let's go.

Leave a little for **Lola**!

Exercise 16-9: Little Lola

*Now that we've done this, instead of **L** being a hard letter to pronounce, it's the easiest one because the tongue is stuck in that position. Pause the CD to practice the reading on your own, again, with your tongue stuck to the top of your mouth. Read the following paragraph after me with your tongue in the normal position. Use good, strong intonation. Follow my lead as I start dropping **h**'s here.*

Little Lola felt left out in life. She told herself that luck controlled her and she truly believed that only by loyally following an exalted leader could she be delivered from her solitude. Unfortunately, she learned a little late that her life was her own to deal with. When she realized it, she was already eligible for Social Security, and she had lent her lifelong earnings to a lowlife in Long Beach. She lay on her linoleum and slid along the floor in anguish. A little later, she leapt up and laughed. She no longer longed for a leader to tell her how to live her life. Little Lola was finally all well.

In our next paragraph about *Thirty Little Turtles*, we deal with another aspect of **L**, namely, consonant clusters. When you have a *dl* combination, you need to apply what you learned about liaisons and the American **T** as well as the **L**.

Since the two sounds are located in a similar position in the mouth, you know that they are going to be connected, right? You also know that all of these middle **T**s are going to be pronounced **D**, and that you're going to leave the tongue stuck to the top of your mouth. That may leave you wondering: Where is the air to escape? The **L** sound is what determines that. For the **D**, you hold the air in, the same as for a final **D**; then for the **L**, you release it around the sides of the tongue. Let's go through the steps before proceeding to our next exercise.

Exercise 16-10: Dull versus -dle

CD 4 Track 40

Repeat after me.

laid   Don't pop the final **D** sound.

ladle   Segue gently from the **D** to the **L**, with a small schwa in between. Leave your tongue touching behind the teeth and just drop the sides to let the air pass out.

lay dull Here, your tongue can drop between the **D** and the **L**.

*To hear the difference between **dəl** and **dəᵊl**, contrast the sentences, **Don't lay dull tiles** and **Don't ladle tiles**.*

Exercise 16-11: Final L Practice

CD 4 Track 41

Repeat the following lists.

	üll	äll	æwl	ell	ale	oll	eel	dl
1.	bull	ball	bowel	bell	bale	bowl	Beal	bottle
2.	▮	hall	howl	hell	hail	hole	heel	huddle
3.	▮	hauled	howled	held	hailed	hold	healed	hurtle
4.	pull	pall	Powell	pell	pail	pole	peel	poodle
5.	wool	wall	▮	well	whale	whole	wheel	wheedle
6.	full	fall	foul	fell	fail	foal	feel	fetal
7.	Schultz	shawl	▮	shell	shale	shoal	she'll	shuttle
8.	tulle	tall	towel	tell	tale	toll	teal	turtle
9.	▮	vault	vowel	veldt	veil	vole	veal	vital
10.	you'll	yawl	yowl	yell	Yale	▮	yield	yodel
11.	▮	call	cowl	Kelly	kale	cold	keel	coddle

Exercise 16-12: Thirty Little Turtles in a Bottle of Bottled Water · CD 4 Track 42

Repeat the following paragraph, focusing on the consonant + ²l combinations. (This paragraph was quoted in The New York Times *by Pulitzer-Prize winning journalist, Thomas Friedman.)*

Thrdee Liddəl Terdəl Zinə Bäddələ Bäddəl Dwäder

A bottle of bottled water held 30 little turtles. It didn't matter that each turtle had to rattle a metal ladle in order to get a little bit of noodles, a total turtle delicacy. The problem was that there were many turtle battles for the less than oodles of noodles. The littlest turtles always lost, because every time they thought about grappling with the haggler turtles, their little turtle minds boggled and they only caught a little bit of noodles.

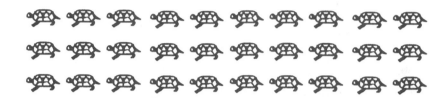

Exercise 16-13: Speed-reading · CD 4 Track 43

We've already practiced strong intonation, so now we'll just pick up the speed. First I'm going to read our familiar paragraph, as fast as I can. Subsequently, you'll practice on your own, and then we'll go over it together, sentence by sentence, to let you practice reading very fast, right after me. By then you will have more or less mastered the idea, so record yourself reading really fast and with very strong intonation. Listen back to see if you sound more fluent. Listen as I read.

Hello, **my** name is_____. I'm taking American **Accent** Training. There's a **lot** to **learn**, but I **hope** to make it as **enjoyable** as possible. I should pick **up** on the American **intonation** pattern pretty **easily**, although the **only** way to **get** it is to **practice** all of the time. I use the **up** and down, or **peaks** and valleys, **intonation** more than I **used** to. I've been paying attention to **pitch**, **too**. It's like **walking** down a **stair**case. I've been **talking** to a lot of **Americans** lately, and they tell me that I'm **easier** to under**stand**. **Any**way, I could go **on** and on, but the **important** thing is to **listen** well and sound **good**. **Well**, what do you **think**? **Do** I?

▸ Pause the CD and practice speed-reading on your own five times.
▸ Repeat each sentence after me.
▸ Record yourself speed-reading with strong intonation.

Exercise 16-14: Tandem Reading · CD 4 Track 44

The last reading that I'd like you to do is one along with me. Up to now, I have read first and you have repeated in the pause that followed. Now, however, I would like you to read along at exactly the same time that I read, so that we sound like one person reading. Read along with me.

S is hissed, **Z** is buzzed.
Most **S**'s are **Z**'s.

CD 4 Track 45

The sound of the letter **S** is **s** only if it follows an unvoiced consonant. Otherwise, it becomes a **Z** in disguise. When an **S** follows a vowel, a voiced consonant, or another **S**, it turns into a **z**. The following exercise will let you hear and practice **S** with its dual sound. There are many more **Z** sounds in English than **S** sounds. (See also Chapters 13 and 21 for related sounds.)

Exercise 17-1: When S Becomes Z
CD 4 Track 46

Under Contrast, in the list that follows, notice how the voiced word is drawn out and then repeat the word after me. Both voiced and unvoiced diphthongs have the underlying structure of the tone shift, or the double stair step, but the shift is much larger for the voiced ones.

prä ̄ äis   prä ̄ äiz

Contrast

	S	**Z**			
1.	price	prize	**nouns**	books	waxes
2.	peace	peas		maps	pencils
3.	place	plays		months	dogs
4.	ice	eyes		hats	trains
5.	hiss	his		pops	oranges
6.	close	to close		bats	clothes
7.	use	to use		bikes	windows
8.	rice	rise	**verbs**	laughs	washes
9.	pace	pays		thanks	arrives
10.	lacey	lazy		eats	comes
11.	thirsty	Thursday		takes	goes
12.	bus	buzz		speaks	lunches
13.	dust	does	**contractions**	it's	there's
14.	face	phase		what's	he's
15.	Sue	zoo		that's	she's
16.	loose	lose	**possessives**	a cat's eye	a dog's ear

Exercise 17-2: A Surly Sergeant Socked an Insolent Sailor — CD 4 Track 47

Repeat the S sounds in the paragraph below.

Sam, a surly sergeant from Cisco, Texas, saw a sailor sit silently on a small seat reserved for youngsters. He stayed for several minutes, while tots swarmed around. Sam asked the sailor to cease and desist, but he sneered in his face. Sam was so incensed that he considered it sufficient incentive to sock the sailor. The sailor stood there for a second, astonished, and then strolled away. Sam was perplexed, but satisfied, and the tots scampered like ants over to the see saw.

Exercise 17-3: Allz Well That Endz Well — CD 4 Track 48

Repeat the Z sounds in the paragraph below.

A lazy Thursday at the zoo found the zebras grazing on zinnias, posing for pictures, and teasing the zookeeper, whose nose was bronzed by the sun. The biggest zebra's name was Zachary, but his friends called him Zack. Zack was a confusing zebra whose zeal for reason caused his cousins, who were naturally unreasoning, to pause in their conversations. While they browsed, he philosophized. As they grazed, he practiced zen. Because they were Zack's cousins, the zebras said nothing, but they wished he would muzzle himself at times.

CD 4 Track 49

As mentioned (page 108), like sounds follow naturally. If one consonant is voiced, chances are, the following plural S will be voiced as well (**dogz**). If it's unvoiced, the following sound will be as well (**cats**). In the past tense, S can be both voiced z and unvoiced s in some cases.

Exercise 17-4: Voiced and Unvoiced Endings in the Past Tense — CD 4 Track 50

The following will explain the differences between four expressions that are similar in appearance but different in both meaning and pronunciation.

	Meaning	Example	Pronunciation
S	Past action	I used to eat rice.	yūst tu
	To be accustomed to	I am used to eating rice.	yūs tu
Z	Present passive verb	Chopsticks are used to eat rice.	yūzd tu
	Simple past	I used chopsticks to eat rice.	yūzd

Used to, depending on its position in a sentence, will take either a tense **ū** or a schwa. At the end of a sentence, you need to say, ... *more than I used tooo;* in the middle of a sentence you can say, *He usta live there.*

Exercise 17-5: Finding S and Z Sounds | CD 4 Track 51

*Go through the paragraph and underline all of the **s** sounds. The first, **æksent** is marked for you. Next, circle all of the **z** sounds, no matter how the word is written (is = iz, as = æz, and so on).*

Hello, **my** name iz _____. I'm taking American **æksent** Training. There's a **lot** to **learn**, but I **hope** to make it as **enjoyable** as possible. I should pick **up** on the American **intonation** pattern pretty **easily**, although the **only** way to **get** it is to **practice** all of the time. I use the **up** and down, or **peaks** and valleys, intonation more than I **used** to. I've been paying attention to **pitch**, **too**. It's like **walking** down a **stair**case. I've been **talking** to a lot of **Americans** lately, and they tell me that I'm **easier** to under**stand**. **Any**way, I could go **on** and on, but the **important** thing is to **listen** well and sound **good**. **Well,** what do you **think**? **Do** I?

▸ Practice reading the paragraph three times on your own, concentrating on strong **Z**s.

Exercise 17-6: Application Steps with S and Z | CD 4 Track 52

Build up the following sentence, adding each aspect one at a time.

Always be a little kinder than necessary.

1. Intonation
Always be a little **kinder** than **necessary**.

2. Word Groups
Always be a little kinder(pause) than necessary.

3. Liaisons
Always be(y)a little kinder tha(n)necessary.

4. æ, ä, ə
äweez be ə littəl kinder thən nesəssary.

5. The American T
Always be a liddle kinder than necessary.

6. The American R
Always be a little kindər than necessɛry.

7. Combination of concepts 1 through 6
äweez be(y)ə liddəl kindər(pause) thə(n)necəssɛry.

Exercise 17-7: Your Own Application Steps with S and Z CD 4 Track 53

Write your own sentence, and then build it up, adding each aspect one at a time.

1. **Intonation**

2. **Word Groups**

3. **Liaisons**

4. **æ, a, ə**

5. **The American T**

6. **The American R**

7. **Combination of concepts 1 through 6**

I wanted to be sure and win the pun contest, so I submitted ten of them.

Unfortunately, no pun in ten did.

Telephone Tutoring
Mid-Point Diagnostic Analysis CD 4 Track 54

After three to six months, you're ready for the follow-up analysis. If you are studying on your own, contact toll-free **1 (800) 457-4255** or go to **AmericanAccent.com** for a referral to a qualified telephone analyst. The diagnostic analysis is designed to evaluate your current speech patterns to let you know where your accent is standard and nonstandard.

Think the United Auto Workers can beat Caterpillar, Inc. in their bitter contract battle? Before placing your bets, talk to Paul Branan, who can't wait to cross the picket line at Caterpillar's factory in East Peoria. Branan, recently laid off by a rubber-parts plant where he earned base pay of $6.30 an hour, lives one block from a heavily picketed gate at the Cat complex. Now he's applying to replace one of the 12,600 workers who have been on strike for the past five months. "Seventeen dollars an hour and they don't want to work?" asks Branan. "I don't want to take another guy's job, but I'm hurting, too."

1. saw, lost, cough
2. can, Dan, last
3. same, say, rail
4. yet, says, Paris
5. shine, time, my
6. sit, silk, been
7. seat, see, bean
8. word, girl, first
9. some, dull, possible
10. tooth, two, blue
11. look, bull, should
12. don't, so, whole
13. how, down, around
14. appoint, avoid, boil

A	B	C	D	E	F
1. parry	1. bury	1. apple	1. able	1. mop	1. mob
2. ferry	2. very	2. afraid	2. avoid	2. off	2. of
3. stew	3. zoo	3. races	3. raises	3. face	3. phase
4. sheer	4. girl	4. pressure	4. pleasure	4. crush	4. garage
5. two	5. do	5. petal	5. pedal	5. not	5. nod
6. choke	6. joke	6. gaucho	6. gouger	6. rich	6. ridge
7. think	7. that	7. ether	7. either	7. tooth	7. smooth
8. come	8. gum	8. bicker	8. bigger	8. pick	8. pig
9. yes	9. rate	9. accent	9. exit	9. tax	9. tags
10. wool	10. grow	10. player	10. correct	10. day	10. tower
11. his	11. me	11. shower	11. carry	11. now	11. neater
12. late	12. next	12. ahead	12. swimmer	12. towel	12. same
13. bleed		13. collect	13. connect	13. needle	13. man
		14. Kelly	14. finger		14. ring

1. Who opened it?
2. We opened it.
3. Put it away.
4. Bob ate an orange.
5. Can it be done?

1. Who⁽ʷ⁾oup'n did?
2. We⁽ʸ⁾oup'n dit.
3. Pü di də way.
4. Bä bei d' nornj.
5. C'n't be dən?

1. Write a letter to Betty.

2. Ride a ledder d' Beddy.

3. tatter	tattoo
4. platter	platoon
5. pattern	perturb
6. critic	critique
7. let	led
8. written	ridden

Review and Expansion

CD 4 Track 55

In the first seventeen chapters of the American Accent Training program, we covered the concepts that form the basis of American speech—intonation, word groups, the staircase, and liaisons, or word connections. We also discussed some key sounds, such as **æ**, **ä**, and **ə** (Cat? Caught? Cut?), the **El**, the American **T**, and the American **R**. Let's briefly review each item.

Intonation

You've learned some of the reasons for changing the pitch (or saying a word louder or even streeetching it out) of some words in a sentence.

1. To introduce new information (nouns)
2. To offer an opinion
3. To contrast two or more elements
4. To indicate the use of the negative contraction *can't*

For example:

New information	**Opinion**
He bought a **car**.	It **feels** like mink, but I think it's **rabbit**.
Contrast	**Can't**
Timing is more important than **technique**.	He **can't do** it.

You've also learned how to change meaning by shifting intonation, without changing any of the actual words in a sentence.

I applied for the job (not **you**!).
I **applied** for the job (but I don't think I'll **get** it).
I applied **for** the job (not I applied myself **to** the job).
I applied for **the** job (the **one** I've been dreaming about for **years**!)
I applied for the **job** (not the **life**style!).

Miscellaneous Reminders of Intonation

When you have a verb/preposition combination, the stress usually goes on the preposition: *pick **up**, put **down**, fall **in**,* and so on. Otherwise, prepositions are placed in the valleys of your intonation: *It's f'r **you**., They're fr'm **LA**.*

When you have initials, the stress goes on the last letter: IB**M**, P**O** Box, ASA**P**, IO**U**, and so on. (See also Chapters 4 and 6.)

Liaisons and Glides

Through liaisons, you learned about *voiced* and *unvoiced consonants*—where they are located in the mouth and which sounds are likely to attach to a following one. You were also introduced to glides. (See also Chapter 7.)

1.	**Consonant and Vowel**	Put it *on*.	Pu•di•dan.
2.	**Consonant and Consonant**	*race*track	ray•stræk
3.	**Vowel and Vowel**	No *other*	No⁽ʷ⁾other
4.	**T and Y**	Put you *on*	Puchü⁽ʷ⁾än
	D and Y	*Had* you?	Hæjoo?
	S and Y	*Yes*, you do.	Yeshu do.
	Z and Y	Is your *cat*?	Izher cat?

Cat? Caught? Cut?

This lesson was an introduction to pronunciation, especially those highly characteristic sounds, æ, ä, and ə. (See also Chapter 12.)

æ   The jaw moves down and back while the back of the tongue pushes forward and the tip touches the back of the bottom teeth. Sometimes it almost sounds like there's a Y in there: *cat*, **kyæt**.

ä   Relax the tongue, open the throat like you're letting the doctor see all the way to your toes: *aah*.

ə   This sound is the sound that would come out if you were pushed (lightly) in the stomach: *uh*. You don't need to put your mouth in any particular position at all. The sound is created when the air is forced out of the diaphragm and past the vocal cords.

The American T

T is **T**, a clear popped sound, when it is at the **top** of the staircase,

- at the the beginning of a word, *table*
- in a stressed syllable, *intend*
- in **ST**, **TS**, **TR**, **CT** clusters, *instruct*
- replaces **D** after unvoiced consonants, *hoped*, **hopt**

T is **D**, a softer sound, when it is in the **middle** of the staircase

- in an unstressed position between vowels, *cattle*, **caddle**

T and **D** are held (*not* pronounced with a sharp burst of air) when they are at the **bottom** of the staircase.

- at the end of a word, *bought*, **bä⁽ᵗ⁾**

T is held before **N**.

- unstressed and followed by *-ten* or *-tain, written*, **wri(tt)en**

T is swallowed by **N**.

- *interview*, **innerview**

(See also Chapter 14.)

The El

The **El** is closely connected with the schwa. Your tongue drops down in back as if it were going to say *uh*, but the tip curls up and attaches to the top of the mouth, which requires a strong movement of the tip of the tongue. The air comes out around the sides of the tongue, and the sound is held for slightly longer than you'd think. (See also Chapter 16.)

The American R

The main difference between a consonant and a vowel is that with a consonant there is contact at some point in your mouth. It might be the lips, **P**; the tongue tip, **N**; or the throat, **G**. Like a vowel, however, the **R** doesn't touch anywhere. It is similar to a schwa, but your tongue curls back in a retroflex movement and produces a sound deep in the throat. *The tongue doesn't touch the top of the mouth.* Another way to approach it is to put your tongue in position for *ee*, and then slide straight back to *eeer*. Some people are more comfortable collapsing their tongue back, like an accordion instead of curling it. It doesn't make any difference in the sound, so do whichever you prefer. (See also Chapter 15.)

Application Exercises

Now you need to use the exercises you've learned so far to make the transference to your everyday speech. In the beginning, the process is very slow and analytical, but as you do it over and over again, it becomes natural and unconscious. The exercises presented here will show you how. For example, take any phrase that may catch your ear during a conversation—because it is unfamiliar, or for whatever other reason—and work it through the practice sequence used in Review Exercise 1.

Review Exercise 1: To have a friend, be a friend.   CD 4 Track 56

Take the repeated phrase in the following application steps. Apply each concept indicated there, one at a time and in the sequence given. Read the sentence out loud two or three times, concentrating only on the one concept. This means that when you are working on liaisons, for instance, you don't have to pay much attention to intonation, just for that short time. First, read the phrase with no preparation and record yourself doing it.

To have a friend, be a friend.

Review Exercise 2: To have a friend, be a friend.   CD 4 Track 57

Pause the CD and go through each step using the following explanation as a guide.

1. Intonation

You want to figure out where the intonation belongs when you first encounter a phrase. In this example, **friend** is repeated, so a good reason for intonation would be the contrast that lies in the verbs *have* and *be*:

To **have** a friend, **be** a friend.

2. Word groups

The pause in this case is easy because it's a short sentence with a comma, so we put one there. With your own phrases, look for a logical break, or other hints, as when you have the verb *to be,* you usually pause very slightly just before it, because it means that you're introducing a definition:

A [(pause)] is **B**.

Cows[(pause)] are **ruminants**.

To **have** a friend,[(pause)] **be** a friend.

3. Liaisons

Figure out which words you want to run together. Look for words that start with vowels and connect them to the previous word:

To hava friend, be[(y)]a friend.

4. æ, ä, ə

Label these common sounds in the sentence:

Tə hævə friend, be ə friend.

5. The American T

Work with it, making it into a **D** or **CH**, holding it back or getting rid of it altogether, as appropriate. In this phrase, there are no **T**s, but the **D** is held:

To have a frien[(d)], be a frien[(d)].

6. The American R

Mark all the **R**s.

To have a friend, be a friend.

7. Combination of concepts 1–6

Tə **hæ**və frɛn[(d)],[(pause)] **be**[(y)]ə frɛnd[(d)].

▸ Practice the sequence of steps a couple of times and then record yourself again; place your second recording right after the first one on your tape. Play them both back and see if you hear a strong difference.

Review Exercise 3: Get a Better Water Heater! CD 4 Track 58

Pause the CD and go through the same steps with "Get a better water heater!"

1.	Intonation	**Get** a better **water** heater!
2.	Word groups	Get a better water heater! (pause)
3.	Liaisons	Geta better water heater!
4.	æ, ä, ə	Getə better wäter heater!
5.	The American T	Gedda bedder wadder heeder!
6.	The American R	Get a better**rr** water**rr** heater**rr**!
7.	Combination of Concepts 1–6	**G**ɛdə bɛddrrr **wä**drrr heedrrr!

Review Exercise 4: Your Own Sentence CD 4 Track 59

Pause the CD and apply the steps to your own sentences.

1.	Intonation
2.	Word groups
3.	Liaisons
4.	æ, ä, ə
5.	The American T
6.	The American R
7.	Combination of Concepts 1–6

CD 4 Track 60

Are you shy? Does doing this embarrass you? Are you thinking that people will notice your new accent and criticize you for it? In the beginning, you may feel a little strange with these new sounds that you are using, but don't worry, it's like a new pair of shoes—they take awhile to break in and make comfortable. Nevertheless, I hope that you are enjoying this program. Adopting a new accent can become too personal and too emotional an issue, so don't take it too seriously. Relax. Have a good time. Play with the sounds that you are making. Whenever a word or phrase strikes your fancy, go somewhere private and comfortable and try out a couple of different approaches, styles, and attitudes with it—as you are going to do in the next exercise. If possible, record yourself on tape so you can decide which one suits you best.

Review Exercise 5: Varying Emotions CD 4 Track 61

Repeat the following statement and response expressing the various feelings or tone indicated in parentheses.

anger	I told you it wouldn't work!!	I thought it would!
excitement	I told you it wouldn't work!!	I thought it would!
disbelief	I told you it wouldn't work?	And I thought it would?
smugness	I told you it wouldn't work.	I thought it would. *(I-told-you-so attitude)*

humor	I told you it wouldn't work.	I thought it would.
sadness	I told you it wouldn't work.	I thought it would.
relief	I told you it wouldn't work.	Whew! I thought it would.
resignation	I told you it wouldn't work.	I thought it would.

▸ Pause the CD and repeat the statement using three other tones that you'd like to try.

Your choice	I told you it wouldn't work.	I thought it would.
Your choice	I told you it wouldn't work.	I thought it would.
Your choice	I told you it wouldn't work.	I thought it would.

Now that you've run through a couple of emotions and practiced speaking with both meaning and feeling, try having some two-word conversations. These are pretty common in day-to-day situations.

Review Exercise 6: Really? Maybe!   CD 4 Track 62

Repeat the following statements and responses expressing the various feelings.

1.	Really?	(general curiosity)	Maybe.	(general potential)
2.	Really?	(avid curiosity)	Maybe.	(suggestive possibility)
3.	Really?	(boredom)	Maybe	(equal boredom)
4.	Really?	(laughing with disbelief)	Maybe.	(slight possibility)
5.	Really?	(sarcasm)	Maybe.	(self-justification)
6.	Really?	(sadness)	Maybe.	(equal sadness)
7.	Really?	(relief)	Maybe.	(hope)
8.	Really?	(coy interrogation)	Maybe.	(coy confirmation)
9.	Really?	(seeking confirmation)	Rilly!	(confirmation)

✗ *Pause the CD and try three on your own.*

10.	Really? (your choice) Maybe. (your choice)
11.	Really? (your choice) Maybe. (your choice)
12.	Really? (your choice) Maybe. (your choice)

Review Exercise 7: Who Did It? I Don't Know!   CD 4 Track 63

Repeat the following statements and responses expressing the various feelings.

1.	Who did it? (curiosity)	I don't know. (ignorance)
2.	Who did it? (interrogation)	I don't know. (self-protection)
3.	Who did it? (anger)	I don't know. (insistence)

Review Exercise 7: Who Did It? I Don't Know! *continued*   CD 4 Track 63

4.	Who did it? (repeating)	I don't know. (strong denial)
5.	Who did it? (sarcasm)	I don't know. (self-justification)
6.	Who did it? (sadness)	I don't know. (despair)
7.	Who did it? (relief)	I sure don't know. (blithe ignorance)
8.	Whooo did it? (coy interrogation)	I don't know. (singsong)
9.	Who did it? (annoyance)	I don't know. (equal annoyance)
10.	Who did it? (laughing with disbelief)	I don't know. (laughing ignorance)
11.	Who did it? (surprise)	I dunno. (sullenness)
12.	Who did it? (your choice)	I don't know. (your choice)

Review Exercise 8: Russian Rebellion   CD 4 Track 64

Rəshəz əfensəv əgɛnst rebəlz in thə brɛikəway reejənəv Chechnyə iz entering ə nyu fɛiz. än thə wən hænd, Rəshən forsəzr teiking fül kəntrol əv thə Rəshən kæpədəl Gräzny, ənd Mäskæo sez thə wor seemz tə be trning in its feivr. än thee əthr hænd, thə rebəlz küd be reetreeding Gräzny jəst tə fight ənəthr day—enshring ə läng grrilə wor. Thə for-mənth känflikt täpt thee əjendə tədäy during Sɛkrətəry əv State Mædəlin älbräit's täks with ækting Rəshən prezəd'nt Vlædəmir Putin, älbräit then left fr Kro⁽ʷ⁾ɛishə, əbæot which we will hear more shortly. Bət frst, we trn tə thə Wrldz Nenet Shevek in Mäskæo.

"olbräit ɛn Pu-tin met feu l'nger thɛn plennd tədäy—feu nillee three äwɛz. äftə theə t'ks, olbrait k'ld thɛ meeting intens, bət plɛznt, ɛn 'feud this ɛsɛsmɛnt ɛf Rəshəz ɛkting prezidɛnt."

"I fæond him ə very wellin formd persən. Heez äveeəslee ə Rəshən paytreeət ən älso səmwən who seeks a norməl pəzishən fr Rəshə within thə West—ən he strəck me əzə präbləm sälvr."

Russia's offensive against rebels in the breakaway region of Chechnya is entering a new phase. On the one hand, Russian forces are taking full control of the Russian capital Grozny, and Moscow says the war seems to be turning in its favor. On the other hand, the rebels could be retreating Grozny just to fight another day—ensuring a long guerilla war. The four-month conflict topped the agenda today during Secretary of State Madeline Albright's talks with acting Russian president Vladimir Putin. Albright then left for Croatia, about which we'll hear more shortly. But first, we turn to the World's Nennet Shevek in Moscow.

"Albright and Putin met for longer than planned today—for nearly three hours. After the talks, Albright called the meeting intense, but pleasant, and offered this assessment of Russia's acting president."

"I found him a very well-informed person. He's obviously a Russian patriot and also someone who seeks a normal position for Russia within the West—and he struck me as a problem solver."

Two-Word Phrases

Review Exercise A: Contrasting Descriptive and Set Phrases   CD 4 Track 65

*Here we are reprising the exercise from Exercises 6-1 to 6-14. To review, an adjective and a noun make a **descriptive phrase**, and the second word is stressed. Two nouns make a compound noun, or **set phrase**, and the first word is stressed. Repeat the following sentences. Copy your descriptive phrases and set phrases (Exercise 6-8). You will continue using these word combinations throughout this series of exercises. (See also Chapter 6.)*

	Descriptive Phrase	Set Phrase
1.	It's a short **nail**.	It's a **finger**nail.
2.	It's a chocolate **cake**.	It's a **pan**cake.
3.	It's a hot **bath**.	It's a **hot** tub.
4.	It's a long **drive**.	It's a **hard** drive.
5.	It's the back **door**.	It's the **back**bone.
6.	There are four **cards**.	It's a **card** trick.
7.	It's a small **spot**.	It's a **spot**light.
8.	It's a good **book**.	It's a **phone** book.
9.	It's a _____	It's a _____
10.	It's a _____	It's a _____
11.	It's a _____	It's a _____

Review Exercise B: Intonation Review Test   CD 4 Track 66

Pause the CD and put an accent mark over the word that should be stressed. Check the Answer Key, beginning on page 210.

1.	They live in **Los Angeles**.	11.	We like **everything**.
2.	Give me a **paper bag**.	12.	It's a **moving van**.
3.	Is that your **lunch bag**?	13.	It's a **new paper**.
4.	7-11 is a **convenience store**.	14.	It's the **newspaper**.
5.	Lucky's is a **convenient store**.	15.	The doll has **glass eyes**.
6.	Do your **homework**!	16.	The doll has **eyeglasses**.
7.	He's a **good writer**.	17.	It's a **high chair**.
8.	It's an **apple pie**.	18.	It's a **high chair**. *(for babies)*
9.	It's a **pineapple**.	19.	It's a **baseball**.
10.	We like **all things**.	20.	It's a **blue ball**.

Three-Word Phrases

*When you modify a **descriptive phrase** by adding an adjective or adverb, you maintain the original intonation pattern and simply add an additional stress point.*

Descriptive Phrase	Modified Descriptive Phrase
1. It's a short **nail**.	It's a **really** short **nail**.
2. It's a chocolate **cake**.	It's a **tasty** chocolate **cake**.
3. I took a hot **bath**.	I took a **long**, hot **bath**.
4. It's a hard **drive**.	It's a **long**, hard **drive**.
5. It's the **back door**.	It's the **only** back **door**.
6. There **are** four **cards**.	There **are four** slick **cards**.
7. It's a little **spot**.	It's a **little** black **spot**.
8. It's a good **book**.	It's a **really** good **book**.
9. It's a _____	It's a _____
10. It's a _____	It's a _____
11. It's a _____	It's a _____

*When you modify a **set phrase**, you maintain the same pattern, leaving the new adjective unstressed.*

Set Phrase	Modified Set Phrase
1. It's a **finger**nail.	It's a short **finger**nail.
2. It's a **pan**cake.	It's a delicious **pan**cake.
3. It's a **hot** tub.	It's a leaky **hot** tub.
4. It's a **hard** drive.	It's an expensive **hard** drive.
5. It's the **back**bone.	It's a long **back**bone.
6. It's a **card** trick.	It's a clever **card** trick.
7. It's a **spot**light.	It's a bright **spot**light.
8. It's a **phone** book.	It's the new **phone** book.
9. It's a _____	It's a _____
10. It's a _____	It's a _____
11. It's a _____	It's a _____

Review Exercise E: Two- and Three-Word Set Phrases

CD 4 Track 69

*You should be pretty familiar with the idea of a set phrase by now. The next step is when you have more components that link together to form a new thing—a three-word set phrase. Combine **three things**: finger + nail + clipper. Leave the stress on the first word: **finger**nail clipper. Although you are now using three words, they still mean **one new thing**. Write your own sentences, using the word combinations from the previous exercises.*

Two-Word Set Phrase	Three-Word Set Phrase
1. It's a **finger**nail.	It's a **finger**nail clipper.
2. It's a **pan**cake.	It's a **pan**cake shop.
3. It's a **hot** tub.	It's a **hot** tub maker.
4. It's a **hard** drive.	It's a **hard** drive holder.
5. It's the **back**bone.	It's a **back**bone massage.
6. It's a **playing** card.	It's a **playing** card rack.
7. It's a **spot**light.	It's a **spot**light stand.
8. It's a **phone** book.	It's a **phone** book listing.
9. It's a _____	It's a _____
10. It's a _____	It's a _____
11. It's a _____	It's a _____

Review Exercise F: Three-Word Phrase Summary

CD 4 Track 70

Repeat the following sentences. Write your own sentences at the bottom, carrying over the same examples you used in the previous exercise.

Modified Description	Modified Set Phrase	3-Word Set Phrase
1. a **really** short **nail**	a long **finger**nail	a **finger**nail clipper
2. a **big** chocolate **cake**	a thin **pan**cake	a **pan**cake shop
3. a **long**, hot **bath**	a leaky **hot** tub	a **hot** tub maker
4. a **long**, boring **drive**	a new **hard** drive	a **hard** drive holder
5. a **broken** back **door**	a long **back**bone	a **back**bone massage
6. **four** slick **cards**	a new **playing** card	a **playing** card rack
7. a **small** black **spot**	a bright **spot**light	a **spot**light stand
8. a **well**-written **book**	an open **phone** book	a **phone** book listing
9.	a blind **sales**man	a **blind** salesman
	(He can't see.)	(He sells blinds.)
10.	a light **house**keeper	a **light**house keeper
	(She cleans the house.)	(She lives in a lighthouse.)
11.	a green **house**plant	a **green**house plant
	(It's a healthy houseplant.)	(It's from a greenhouse.)

12. It's a _____ . It's a _____ . It's a _____ .
13. It's a _____ . It's a _____ . It's a _____ .
14. It's a _____ . It's a _____ . It's a _____ .

Review Exercise G: Three-Word Phrase—Three Little Pigs CD 4 Track 71

*Notice where there are patterns, where the words change, but the rhythm stays the same (**straw**-cutting tools, **wood**cutting tools, **brick**laying tools). Read the story aloud.*

Once upon a time, there were *three little pigs.* They lived with their *kind old mother* near a *large, dark forest.* One day, they decided to build *their own houses. The first little pig* used straw. He took his *straw-cutting tools* and his *new lawn mower* and built a *little straw house.* The *second little pig* used sticks. He took his *woodcutting tools* and some *old paintbrushes* and built a *small wooden house.* The *third little pig,* who was a *very hard worker,* used bricks. He took his *bricklaying tools,* an *expensive mortarboard,* and built a *large brick house.* In the forest, lived a *big bad wolf.* He wanted to eat the *three little pigs,* so he went to *the flimsy straw abode* and tried to blow it down. "Not by the hair of my *chinny chin chin*!" cried the *three little porkers.* But the house was *not very strong,* and the *big bad beast* blew it down. The *three little pigs* ran to the *rickety wooden structure,* but the *big bad wolf* blew *it* down, *too.* Quickly, the *three little piggies* ran to the *sturdy brick dwelling* and hid inside. The *big bad wolf* huffed and he puffed, but he couldn't blow the *strong brick house* down. The *three little pigs* laughed and danced and sang.

Review Exercise H: Sentence Balance—Goldilocks CD 4 Track 72

*One of the most fascinating things about spoken English is how the intonation prepares the listener for what is coming. As you know, the main job of intonation is to announce new information. However, there is a secondary function, and that is to alert the listener of changes down the road. Certain shifts will be dictated for the sake of **sentence balance**. Set phrases and contrast don't change, but the intonation of a **descriptive phrase** will move from the second word to the first, **without changing the meaning**. The stress change indicates that it's not the end of the sentence, but rather, there is more to come. This is why it is particularly important to speak in phrases, instead of word by word.*

When we practiced Goldilocks and the Three Bears *the first time (**page 60**), we had very short sentences so we didn't need sentence balance. All of the blue descriptive phrases would otherwise be stressed on the second word, if the shift weren't needed.*

There is a *little girl* called *Goldilocks.* She is *walking* through a *sunny forest* and sees a *small house.* She *knocks* on the door, but *no one* answers. She *goes* inside to see what's **there.** There are *three* chairs in the *large room. Goldilocks* sits on the *biggest* chair. It's *too high* for her to *sit on.* She sits on the *middle-sized* one, but it's is *too low.* She sits on the *small chair* and it is *just right.* On the table, there are *three* bowls of *porridge.* She tries the *first one,* but it is *too hot* to *swallow.* The *second* one is *too cold,* and the *third one* is *just right,* so she eats it all. *After that,* she *goes* upstairs to *look around.* There are *three* beds in the *bedroom.*

She *sits* down on the **biggest** one. It's *too* hard to **sleep** on. The **middle**-sized bed is *too* **soft**. The **little** one is *just* **right**, so she *lies* down and *falls* **asleep**.

In the *meantime*, the family of *three* **bears** comes home—the **Papa** *bear*, the **Mama** *bear*, and the **Baby** *bear*. They **look** around and **say**, "Who's been sitting in our chairs and eating our porridge?" Then they **run** upstairs and **say**, "Who's been sleeping in our beds?" **Goldi**locks **wakes** up when she hears all the **noise** and is **so** scared that she **runs** out of the house and never *comes* **back**.

Four-Word Phrases

When you continue to modify a set phrase, you maintain the original intonation pattern and simply add an additional stress point.

	Modified Set Phrase	**Remodified Set Phrase**
1.	It's a short **finger**nail.	It's a **really** short **finger**nail.
2.	It's a banana **pan**cake.	It's a **tasty** banana **pan**cake.
3.	It's a leaky **hot** tub.	It's a **leaky** old **hot** tub.
4.	It's a new **hard** drive.	It's a **brand**-new **hard** drive.
5.	It's a long **back**bone.	It's a **long**, hard **back**bone.
6.	It's a wrinkled **playing** card.	It's a **wrinkled**, old **playing** card.
7.	It's a bright **spot**light.	It's a **bright** white **spot**light.
8.	It's the new **phone** book.	It's a **new**-age **phone** book.
9.	It's a _____	It's a _____
10.	It's a _____	It's a _____
11.	It's a _____	It's a _____

In short phrases (#1 and #2), -teen can be thought of as a separate word in terms of intonation. In longer phrases, the number + -teen becomes one word. Repeat after me.

1. How **old** is he?	2. How long has it **been**?	3. How **old** is he?
He's four**teen**. (for**téen**)	**Four**teen **years**.	He's **fourteen** years **old**.
He's **for**ty. (**fór**dy)	Forty **years**.	He's **forty** years **old**.

Review Exercise K: Modifying Three-Word Set Phrases CD 5 Track 2

When you continue to modify a set phrase, you maintain the original intonation pattern and simply add an unstressed modifier.

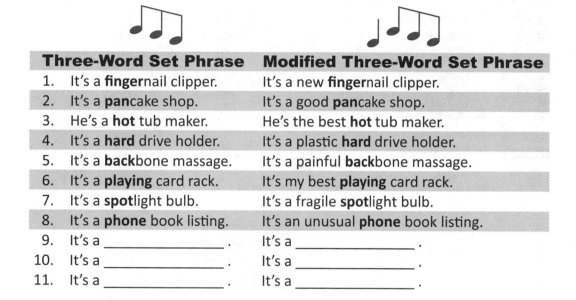

	Three-Word Set Phrase	Modified Three-Word Set Phrase
1.	It's a **finger**nail clipper.	It's a new **finger**nail clipper.
2.	It's a **pan**cake shop.	It's a good **pan**cake shop.
3.	He's a **hot** tub maker.	He's the best **hot** tub maker.
4.	It's a **hard** drive holder.	It's a plastic **hard** drive holder.
5.	It's a **back**bone massage.	It's a painful **back**bone massage.
6.	It's a **playing** card rack.	It's my best **playing** card rack.
7.	It's a **spot**light bulb.	It's a fragile **spot**light bulb.
8.	It's a **phone** book listing.	It's an unusual **phone** book listing.
9.	It's a _____ .	It's a _____ .
10.	It's a _____ .	It's a _____ .
11.	It's a _____ .	It's a _____ .

Rev. Exercise L: Four-Word Phrase Story – Little Red Riding Hood CD 5 Track 3

Repeat after me.

Once upon a time, there was a *cute little redhead* named *Little Red Riding Hood*. One day, she told her mother that she wanted to take a *well-stocked picnic basket* to her *dear old grandmother* on the other side of the *dark, scary Black Forest*. Her mother warned her not to talk to strangers—especially the *dangerous big bad wolf*. *Little Red Riding Hood* said she would be careful, and left. Halfway there, she saw a *mild-mannered hitchhiker*. She pulled over in her *bright red sports car* and offered him a ride. Just before they got to the *freeway turnoff* for her *old grandmother's house*, the *heavily bearded young man* jumped out and ran away. (Was he the wolf?) He hurried ahead to the *waiting grandmother's house*, let himself in, ate her, and jumped into her bed to wait for *Little Red Riding Hood*. When *Little Red Riding Hood* got to the house, she was surprised, "Grandmother, what big *eyes* you have!" The wolf replied, "The better to *see* you with, my dear..." "But Grandmother, what big *ears* you have!" "The better to *hear* you with, my dear..." "Oh, Grandmother, what big *teeth* you have!" "The better to *eat* you with!" And the wolf jumped out of the bed to eat *Little Red Riding Hood*. Fortunately for her, she was a *recently paid-up member* of the infamous *National Rifle Association* so she pulled out her *brand-new shotgun* and shot the wolf dead.

Review Exercise M: Building Up to Five-Word Phrases   CD 5 Track 4

Repeat after me, then pause the CD and write your own phrases, using the same order and form.

1. It's a **pot**.	*noun*
2. It's **new**.	*adjective*
3. It's a new **pot**.	*descriptive phrase (noun)*
4. It's brand-**new**.	*descriptive phrase (adjective)*
5. It's a **brand**-new **pot**.	*modified descriptive phrase*
6. It's a **tea**pot.	*two-word set phrase*
7. It's a new **tea**pot.	*modified set phrase*
8. It's a **brand**-new **tea**pot.	*modified set phrase*
9. It's a **tea**pot lid.	*three-word set phrase*
10. It's a new **tea**pot lid.	*modified three-word set phrase*
11. It's a **brand**-new **tea**pot lid.	*modified three-word set phrase*

1. _____	*noun*
2. _____	*adjective*
3. _____	*descriptive phrase (noun)*
4. _____	*descriptive phrase (adjective)*
5. _____	*modified descriptive phrase*
6. _____	*two-word set phrase*
7. _____	*modified set phrase*
8. _____	*modified set phrase*
9. _____	*three-word set phrase*
10. _____	*modified three-word set phrase*
11. _____	*modified three-word set phrase*

CD 5 Track 5

Since so many people are familiar with the binary system, let's do a quick review of how complex intonation can be viewed with zeroes and ones.

pot	1
new	1
new **pot**	01
brand-**new**	01
brand-new **pot**	101
teapot	10
new **tea**pot	010
brand-new **tea**pot	1010
teapot lid	100
new **tea**pot lid	0100
brand-new **tea**pot lid	10100

Do a global **Search All** and **Replace** for these patterns.

Review Exercise 9: Ignorance on Parade CD 5 Track 6

Now, let's dissect a standard paragraph, including its title, as we did in Review Exercise 1. **First**—*in the boxes in the first paragraph, decide which is a descriptive phrase, which is a set phrase, and where any additional stress might fall. Remember, descriptive phrases are stressed on the second word and set phrases on the first. Use one of your colored markers to indicate the stressed words.* **Second**—*go through the paragraph and mark the remaining stressed words.* **Third**—*put slash marks where you think a short pause is appropriate. Listen as I read the paragraph. (See also Chapters 4 and 11.)*

✖ Pause the CD and do the written exercises including intonation; word groups; liaisons; æ, ä, ə; and the American **T**.

1. *Two-word phrases, intonation, and phrasing*
Ignorance on Parade

You say you don't know a proton from a crouton? Well, you're not the only one. A recent nationwide survey funded by the National Science Foundation shows that fewer than 6 percent of American adults can be called scientifically literate. The rest think that DNA is a food additive, Chernobyl is a ski resort, and radioactive milk can be made safe by boiling. *Judith Stone / 2109 Discover Publications*

2. *Word connections*
Ignoran sän Parade

You say you don't know a proton from a crouton? Well, you're not the only one. A recent nationwide survey funded by the National Science Foundation shows that fewer than 6 percent of American adults can be called scientifically literate. The rest think that DNA is a food additive, Chernobyl is a ski resort, and radioactive milk can be made safe by boiling.

3. *æ, ä, ə*
Ignərənce än Pərade

You say you don't know a proton from a crouton? Well, you're not the only one. A recent nationwide survey funded by the National Science Foundation shows that fewer than 6 percent of American adults can be called scientifically literate. The rest think that DNA is a food additive, Chernobyl is a ski resort, and radioactive milk can be made safe by boiling.

4. *The American T*
Ignorants on Parade

You say you don't know a proton from a crouton? Well, you're not the only one. A recent nationwide survey funded by the National Science Foundation shows that fewer than 6 percent of American adults can be called scientifically literate. The rest think that DNA is a food additive, Chernobyl is a ski resort, and radioactive milk can be made safe by boiling.

Review Exercise 10: Ignorance on Parade Explanations

Here, go over each topic, point by point.

1. **Two-word phrases, intonation, and phrasing**

   a **proton** from a **crouton**? *(contrast)*
   Well, **you're** not the **only** one. *(contrast)*
   A **recent** nationwide **survey** *(modified descriptive phrase)*
   National **Science** Foundation *(modified set phrase)*
   6 percent of American **adults** *(descriptive phrase with sentence balance)*
   scientifically **literate** *(descriptive phrase)*
   The **rest** think *(contrast)*
   DNA *(acronym)*
   food additive *(set phrase)*
   ski resort *(set phrase)*
   radioactive **milk** *(descriptive phrase)*

   Ignorance on Pa**rade**(stop)
   You say you don't know a **pro**ton from a **crou**ton? (pause) **Well,**(pause) **you're** not the **only** one.(pause) A **recent** nationwide **survey** (pause) funded by the National **Science** Foundation (pause) shows that fewer than **6** percent of American **adults** (pause) can be called scientifically **literate**.(stop) The **rest** think(pause) that DNA is a **food** additive,(pause) Cher**no**byl is a **ski** resort,(pause) and radioactive **milk**(pause) can be made **safe** by **boiling**.

2. **Word connections**

   Ignoran sän Parade

   You sa(y)you don(t)knowa **pro**ton froma **crou**ton? **Well**, you're no(t)the(y)**only** one. A **re**cen(t)nationwide**sur**vey funded by the National**Sci**(y)ence Foundation showzthat fewer than**six** percen'v'merica na**dults** can be calledscientifically **lit**erate. The **ress**think that Dee(y)εNA(y)iza **foo** daddtive, Cher**no**byliza **ski** resort, and radi(y)o(w) active **milk** can be made**safe** by boiling.

3. **æ, ä, ə**

   Ignərənce än Pərade

   You say you dont know ə **pro**tän frəm ə **croo**tän? Well, yer nät thee(y)**only** wən. ə **res**ənt nashənwide **srvey** fəndəd by thə Næshənəl **Sci**(y)əns Fæondashən showz thət fewər thən **6** pr senəv əmerəcən **ədəlts** cən be cälld sci(y)əntifəklee **lid**erət. Thə **rest** think thət Dee Yeh **Nay**(y)izə **food** æddətv, Chr**no**bl izə **skee** rəzort, ən radee(y)o(w) æctəv **milk** cən be made **safe** by **boil**ing.

4. The American T

Ignorants on Parade

You say you don[t] know a **pro**Ton from a **crou**Ton? Well, you're nä[t] the **only** one. A **recen**[t] nationwide **sur**vey funded by the National **Sci**ence Foundation shows tha[t] fewer than **6** percen of American a**dulT**s can be called scienTifically **lid**erə[t]. The **ress** think tha[t] DNA is a **food** addidive, Chernobyl is a **ski** resor[t], and radioakdiv **milk** can be made **safe** by **boil**ing.

5. Combined

Ignərən sän Pə**rade**

You sa[(y)]you don[t]no wə **pro**tän frəmə **croo**tän?[(stop)]Well,[(pause)]yer nät thee[(y)]**only** wən. [(pause)]ə **rees**ən[t]nāshənwide **srvey**[(pause)]fəndəd by thə Næshənəl **Sci**[(y)]əns Fæondāshən[(pause)]shoz thə[t] fewər thən **6** prcenə vəmerəcə nə**dəlts**[(pause)]cən be cälld sci[(y)]əntifəklee **lid**erət.[(stop)]Thə **ress** think[(pause)]thə[t] Dee Yeh **Nay**[(y)]izə **foo** dæddədv,[(pause)] Chr**no**bə lizə **skee** rəzort,[(pause)]ən raydee[(y)]o[(w)]æctəv **milk**[(pause)]cən be made **sāfe** by **boil**ing.

Chapter 18

More Reduced Sounds

CD 5 Track 7

There are two sounds that look similar but sound quite different. One is the tense vowel **u**, pronounced *ooh,* and the other is the soft vowel **ü**, whose pronunciation is a combination of *ih* and *uh.* The **u** sound is located far forward in the mouth and requires you to round your lips. The **ü** is one of the four reduced vowel sounds that are made in the throat: the most tense, and highest in the throat is **ɛ**, next, slightly more relaxed is **i**, then **ü**, and deepest and most relaxed is the neutral schwa **ə**. For the reduced semivowel *schwa + R,* the throat is relaxed, but the tongue is tense. (See also Chapters 3, 12, 15, and 20.)

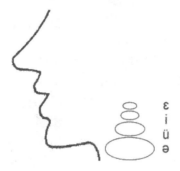

Exercise 18-1: Comparing u and ü

CD 5 Track 8

*Look at the chart that follows and repeat each word. We are contrasting the sound **u** (first and third columns)—a strong, nonreducible sound, **ooh**, that is made far forward in the mouth, with the lips fully rounded—with the reduced **ü** sound in the second and fourth columns.*

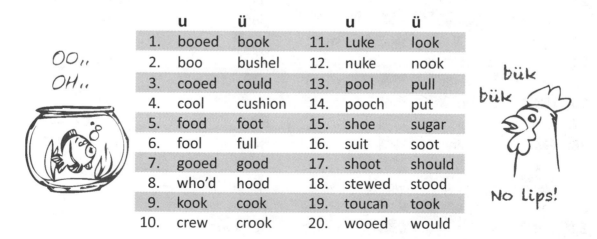

	u	ü		u	ü
1.	booed	book	11.	Luke	look
2.	boo	bushel	12.	nuke	nook
3.	cooed	could	13.	pool	pull
4.	cool	cushion	14.	pooch	put
5.	food	foot	15.	shoe	sugar
6.	fool	full	16.	suit	soot
7.	gooed	good	17.	shoot	should
8.	who'd	hood	18.	stewed	stood
9.	kook	cook	19.	toucan	took
10.	crew	crook	20.	wooed	would

For the **ooh** sound, round your lips like a fish. For the **ü** sound, think of a chicken. Chickens don't have lips, so they certainly can't round them. You have to say **ü** down in the back of your throat.

Exercise 18-2: Lax Vowels CD 5 Track 9

The lax vowels are produced in the throat and are actually quite similar to each other. Let's practice some lax vowels. See also Chapter 20 to contrast with tense vowels. Remember to double the vowel when the word ends in a voiced consonant.

	e	i	ü	ə	ər
1.	end	it	■	un–	earn
2.	bet	bit	book	but	burn
3.	kept	kid	could	cut	curt
4.	check	chick	■	chuck	church
5.	debt	did	■	does	dirt
6.	fence	fit	foot	fun	first
7.	fell	fill	full	■	furl
8.	get	guilt	good	gut	girl
9.	help	hit	hook	hut	hurt
10.	held	hill	hood	hull	hurl
11.	gel	Jill	■	jump	jerk
12.	ked	kid	cook	cud	curd
13.	crest	crypt	crook	crumb	■
14.	let	little	look	lump	lurk
15.	men	milk	■	muck	murmur
16.	net	knit	nook	nut	nerd
17.	pet	pit	put	putt	pert
18.	pell	pill	pull	■	pearl
19.	red	rid	root	rut	rural
20.	said	sit	soot	such	search
21.	shed	shin	should	shut	sure
22.	sled	slim	■	slug	slur
23.	stead	still	stood	stuff	stir
24.	It's stewed.	It'd stick.	It stood.	It's done.	It's dirt.
25.	stretch	string	■	struck	■
26.	tell	tip	took	ton	turn
27.	then	this	■	thus	■
28.	■	thing	■	thug	third
29.	vex	vim	■	vug	verb
30.	wet	wind	would	was	word
31.	yet	yin	■	young	yearn
32.	zen	Zinfandel	■	result	deserve

Tense Vowels

Sound	Symbol	Spelling
ɛi	bāt	bait
ee	bēt	beat
äi	bīt	bite
ou	bōᵘt	boat
ooh	būt	boot
ah	bät	bought
ä + ɛ	bæt	bat
æ + o	bæot	bout

Lax Vowels

Sound	Symbol	Spelling
eh	bɛt	bet
ih	bit	bit
ih + uh	püt	put
uh	bət	but
er	bərt	Bert

Eh (Lax)

Eee (Tense)

Exercise 18-3: Bit or Beat? CD 5 Track 10

*We've discussed intonation in terms of new information, contrast, opinion, and negatives. As you heard on page 25, Americans tend to stretch out certain one-syllable words ... but which ones? The answer is simple—when a single syllable word ends in an unvoiced consonant, the vowel is on a **single** stairstep— short and sharp. When the word ends in a voiced consonant, or a vowel, the vowel is on a **double** stairstep. (For an explanation of voiced and unvoiced consonants, see page 85.) You can also think of this in terms of musical notes.*

*Here you are going to compare the four words **bit**, **bid**, **beat**, and **bead**. Once you can distinguish these four, all of the rest are easy. Repeat.*

	single	double
tense	beat	bead
lax	bit	bid

Note *You may hear* **tense vowels** *called* **long vowels***, but this can cause confusion when you are talking about the long, or doubled, vowel before a voiced consonant. Use the rubber band to distinguish: make a short, sharp snap for the single-note words (beat, bit) and a longer, stretched-out loop for the double-note words (bead, bid).*

Exercise 18-4: Bit or Beat? Bid or Bead? CD 5 Track 11

Read each column down. Next, contrast the single and double tense vowels with each other and the single and double lax vowels with each other.

	Tense Vowels		Lax Vowels	
1.	beat	bead	bit	bid
2.	seat	seed	sit	Sid
3.	heat	he'd	hit	hid
4.	Pete	impede	pit	rapid
5.	feet	feed	fit	fin
6.	niece	knees	miss	Ms.
7.	geese	he's	hiss	his
8.	deep	deed	disk	did
9.	neat	need	knit	(nid)
10.	leaf	leave	lift	live

CD 5 Track 12

Finally, read all four across.

Note *Bear in mind that the single/double intonation pattern is the same for all final voiced and unvoiced consonants, not just **T** and **D**.*

Exercise 18-5: Tense and Lax Vowel Exercise CD 5 Track 13

*Let's practice tense and lax vowels in context. The intonation is marked for you. When in doubt, try to leave out the lax vowel rather than run the risk of overpronouncing it: **l'p** in place of **lip**, so it doesn't sound like **leap**. Repeat.*

	Tense	Lax	
1.	eat	it	I **eat** it.
2.	beat	bit	The **beat** is a bit strong.
3.	keys	kiss	Give me a **kiss** for the keys.
4.	cheek	chick	The chick's **cheek** is soft.
5.	deed	did	He **did** the **deed**.
6.	feet	fit	These **shoes** fit my **feet**.
7.	feel	fill	Do you feel that we should **fill** it?
8.	green	grin	The Martian's **grin** was **green**.
9.	heat	hit	Last **summer**, the **heat** hit **hard**.
10.	heel	hill	Put your **heel** on the **hill**.
11.	jeep	Jill	Jill's **jeep** is here.
12.	creep	crypt	Let's **creep** near the **crypt**.
13.	leap	lip	He bumped his **lip** when he **leaped**.
14.	meal	mill	She had a **meal** at the **mill**.
15.	neat	knit	He can **knit neatly**.
16.	peel	pill	Don't **peel** that **pill**!
17.	reed	rid	Get rid of the **reed**.
18.	seek	sick	We seek the **sixth** sick sheik's **sheep**.
19.	sheep	ship	There are **sheep** on the **ship**.
20.	sleep	slip	The girl **sleeps** in a **slip**.
21.	steal	still	He still **steals**.
22.	Streep	strip	Meryl **Streep** is in a **comic** strip.
23.	team	Tim	**Tim** is on the **team**.
24.	these	this	**These** are better than **this** one.
25.	thief	thing	The **thief** took my **thing**.
26.	weep	whip	Who **weeps** from the **whips**?

CD 5 Track 14

In the time you have taken to reach this point in the program, you will have made a lot of decisions about your own individual speech style. Pronunciation of reduced sounds is more subjective and depends on how quickly you speak, how you prefer to express yourself, the range of your intonation, how much you want to reduce certain vowels, and so on.

Exercise 18-6: The Middle "I" List

The letter I in the unstressed position devolves consistently into a schwa. Repeat.

-ity	ədee
-ify	əfái
-ited	əd'd
-ible	əbᵊl
-ical	əcᵊl
-imal	əmᵊl
-ization	əzāsh'n
-ication	əcāsh'n
-ination	ənāsh'n
-ifaction	əfæksh'n
-itation	ətāsh'n

	chemistry	hostility	opportunity
	chronological	humanity	organization
	clarity	humidity	partiality
	commodity	humility	physical
	community	identity	pitiful
	communication	imitation	politics
	complexity	immaturity	positive
	confident	immigration	possible
	confidentiality	immunity	possibility
	contribution	incident	president
	creativity	individuality	principle
	credit	infinity	priority
ability	critical	insecurity	psychological
accident	cubicle	instability	publicity
accountability	curiosity	institute	qualify
activity	difficult	investigation	quality
adversity	dignity	invisible	quantity
America	disparity	invitation	radical
analytical	diversity	janitor	reality
animal	Edison	Jennifer	rectify
applicant	editor	legalization	resident
application	electricity	liability	responsibility
article	eligibility	Madison	sacrifice
astronomical	eliminated	maturity	sanity
audible	engineer	medicine	security
auditor	episode	mentality	seminar
authority	equality	majority	seniority
availability	evidence	maximum	severity
beautiful	experiment	Michigan	sensitivity
brutality	facility	minimum	similar
calamity	familiarity	minority	skeptical
California	feasibility	modify	superiority
candidate	flexibility	Monica	technical
capacity	Florida	monitor	testify
celebrity	foreigner	municipality	typical
charity	formality	nationality	uniform
Christianity	fraternity	naturalization	unity
clinical	gravity	necessity	university
clerical	heredity	negative	validity
chemical	hospitality	nomination	visitor

Exercise 18-7: Reduction Options   CD 5 Track 16

In the following example, you will see how you can fully sound out a word (such as to), reduce it slightly, or do away with it altogether.

1. ... easier tū⁽ʷ⁾ənderstand.
2. ... easier tü⁽ʷ⁾ənderstand.
3. ... easier tə ənderstand.
4. ... easier tənderstand.
5. ... easier dənderstand.

Each of the preceding examples is correct and appropriate when said well. If you have a good understanding of intonation, you might be best understood if you used the last example.

     How would this work with the rest of our familiar paragraph, you ask? Let's see.

Exercise 18-8: Finding Reduced Sounds   CD 5 Track 17

*Go through the paragraph that follows and find the three **ü**'s and the five to seven **u**'s. Remember that your own speech style can increase the possibilities. With "**to**" before a vowel, you have a choice of a strong **u**, a soft **ü**, a schwa, or to telescope the two words and eliminate the vowel entirely. Pause the CD to mark the **ü** and **u** sounds. The first one is marked for you. Remember to check the Answer Key, beginning on page 210.*

Hello, **my** name is_____. I'm taking American **Accent** Training. There's a **lot** to **learn**, but I **hope** to make it as **enjoyable** as possible. I shüd pick **up** on the American **intonation** pattern pretty **easily**, although the **only** way to **get** it is to **practice** all of the time. I ūse the **up** and down, or **peaks** and valleys, **intonation** more than I **used** to. I've been paying attention to **pitch**, **too**. It's like **walking** down a **stair**case. I've been **talking** to a lot of **Americans** lately, and they tell me that I'm **easier** to under**stand**. **Any**way, I could go **on** and on, but the **important** thing is to **listen** well and sound **good**. **Well**, what do you **think**? **Do** I?

     CD 5 Track 18

All Prefixes Have a Schwa

a-	avert	attend	appellate	attract	apportion	adduce
con/com-	convert	contend	compel	contract	comport	conduct
di/dis/de-	divert	distend	dispel	distract	deport	deduct/deduce
e/ex-	evert	extend	expel	extract	export	educate
in/im-	invert	intend	impel	intractable	import	induce
pro/pre/per-	pervert	pretend	propel	protract	proportion	produce
re-	revert	retain	repel	retract	report	reduce

Exercise 18-9: How Much Wood Would a Woodchuck Chuck?

CD 5 Track 19

How fast can you say:

How much wood	hæo məch wüd
would a woodchuck chuck,	wüdə wüdchək chək
if a woodchuck	ifə wüdchəck
could chuck	cüd chək
wood?	wüd

How many cookies	hæo meny cükeez
could a good cook cook,	cüdə güd cük cük
if a good cook	ifə güd cük
could cook	cüd cük
cookies?	cükeez

In the following two exercises, we will practice the two vowel sounds separately.

Exercise 18-10: Büker Wülsey's Cükbük

CD 5 Track 20

Repeat after me.

Booker Woolsey was a good cook. One day, he took a good look at his full schedule and decided that he could write a good cookbook. He knew that he could and thought that he should, but he wasn't sure that he ever would. Once he had made up his mind, he stood up, pulled up a table, took a cushion, and put it on a bushel basket of sugar in the kitchen nook. He shook out his writing hand and put his mind to creating a good, good cookbook.

bük
bük

No lips!

Exercise 18-11: A True Fool

CD 5 Track 21

Repeat after me.

OO,,
OH,,

A true fool will choose to drool in a pool to stay cool. Who knew that such fools were in the schools, used tools, and flew balloons? Lou knew and now you do, too.

CD 5 Track 22

People often ask if **Tuesday** and **newspaper** are pronounced **Tiuzday** and **niuzpaper** or **Toozday** and **noozpaper**. Most Americans tend toward the latter, but you can go either way. On some words, however, you cannot add that extra **i** sound, as with **shoes** or **cool**.

Chapter 19

"V" as in Victory

CD 5 Track 23

When pronounced correctly, **V** shouldn't stand out too much. Its sound, although noticeable, is small. As a result, people, depending on their native language, sometimes confuse **V** with **B** (Spanish, Japanese), with **F** (German), or with **W** (Chinese, Hindi). These four sounds are not at all interchangeable.

The **W** is a semivowel, and there is no friction or contact. The **B**, like **P**, uses both lips and has a slight pop. Americans tend to have a strong, popping **P**. You can check your pronunciation by holding a match, a sheet of paper, or just your hand in front of your mouth. If the flame goes out, the paper wavers, or you feel a distinct puff of air on your hand, you've said **P** not **B**. **B** is the voiced pair of **P**.

Although **F** and **V** are in exactly the same position, **F** is a hiss and **V** is a buzz. The **V** is the voiced pair of **F**, as you saw in Chapter 11 (pages 85–86). When you say **F**, it is as if you are *whispering*. So, for **V**, say **F** and simply add some voice to it, which is the whole difference between *fairy* and *very*, as you will hear in our next exercise. (The **F**, too, presents problems to Japanese, who say **H**. To pronounce **F**, the lower lip raises up and the inside of the lip very lightly touches the outside of the upper teeth and you make a slight hissing sound. *Don't* bite the outside of your lip at all.)

Note In speaking, *of* is reduced to **əv**.

Exercise 19-1: Mind Your Vees

CD 5 Track 24

Repeat the following words and sounds after me.

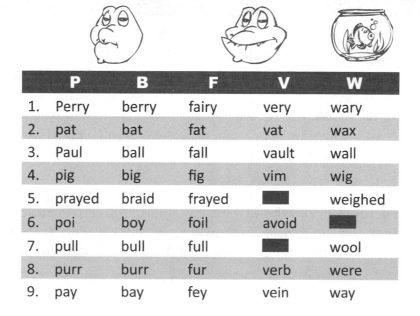

	P	B	F	V	W
1.	Perry	berry	fairy	very	wary
2.	pat	bat	fat	vat	wax
3.	Paul	ball	fall	vault	wall
4.	pig	big	fig	vim	wig
5.	prayed	braid	frayed	▬	weighed
6.	poi	boy	foil	avoid	▬
7.	pull	bull	full	▬	wool
8.	purr	burr	fur	verb	were
9.	pay	bay	fey	vein	way

Exercise 19-2: The Vile VIP
CD 5 Track 25

*Repeat after me, focusing on V and W. Of is pronounced **uv**.*

When revising his visitor's version of a plan for a very well-paved avenue, the VIP was advised to reveal none of his motives. Eventually, however, the hapless visitor discovered his knavish views and confided that it was vital to review the plans together to avoid a conflict. The VIP was not convinced and averred that he would have it vetoed by the vice president. This quite vexed the visitor, who then vowed to invent an indestructible paving compound in order to avenge his good name. The VIP found himself on the verge of a civil war with a visitor with whom he had previously conversed easily. It was only due to his insufferable vanity that the inevitable division arrived as soon as it did. Never again did the visitor converse with the vain VIP and they remained divided forever.

Exercise 19-3: Finding V Sounds
CD 5 Track 26

Underline the five V sounds in this paragraph. The first one is marked for you. Don't forget "of."

Hello, **my** name is_____. I'm taking American **Accent** Training. There's a **lot** to **learn**, but I **hope** to make it as **enjoyable** as possible. I should pick **up** on the American **intonation** pattern pretty **easily**, although the **only** way to **get** it is to **practice** all o_f the time. I use the **up** and down, or **peaks** and valleys, **intonation** more than I **used** to. I've been paying attention to **pitch**, **too**. It's like **walking** down a **stair**case. I've been **talking** to a lot of **Americans** lately, and they tell me that I'm **easier** to under**stand**. **Any**way, I could go **on** and on, but the **important** thing is to **listen** well and sound **good**. **Well**, what do you **think**? **Do** I?

Exercise 19-4: W, V & F
CD 5 Track 27

*Repeat the following sentences, focusing on the targeted sounds. Notice that **one** starts with a W sound and **of** ends with a V sound.*

Where were we in World War One? On one wonderful Wednesday, we were wandering in Westwood with a wonderful woman from Wisconsin, whose name was Wanda Wilkerson. We had been with Wanda for weeks, and we were wondering when we would wear out our welcome. "Don't worry," warbled Wanda, waving wildly, "I've been waiting since winter!"

CD 5 Track 28

Victor Vickerson voted to review the very vilest version of the veto to avoid a controversy. Even Evan reviewed Virginia's available provisions for the vacation as inevitably devoid of value. Evan eventually arrived at the village and saved the day with vast amounts of venison and veal.

CD 5 Track 29

Fred fried five flat fish on Friday afternoon at four.

CD 5 — Track 30

	A	B	C	D	E	F	G	H	I	J	K	L	M	N	O
	æ	æo	u	i	ee	ü	ε	a	ə	ä	r	är	o	i	oi
1.	back	bow	booed	Bic	beak	book	beck	bake	buck	Bach	Burke	bark	boat	bite	point
2.	black	blouse	blued	bliss	bleed	books	bled	blade	blood	block	blurred	blarney	bloat	blight	boy
3.	brad	browse	brood	brick	breed	brook	bread	break	brother	brought	fir	far	broke	bright	broil
4.	pat	about	boot	pit	peak	put	pet	paid	putt	pot	pert	part	post	pike	boil
5.	cat	couch	coot	kit	parakeet	cookie	kept	Kate	cut	caught	curt	cart	coat	kite	coin
6.	cad	cowed	cooed	kid	keyed	could	Keds	okayed	cud	cod	curd	card	code	cried	coil
7.	fat	found	food	fit	feet	foot	fed	fade	fun	fog	first	farm	phone	fight	Foyt
8.	flack	flower	fluke	flick	fleet	put	fleck	flake	flood	father	flurry	far	flow	flight	Floyd
9.	fragile	frown	fruit	frill	free	fructose	French	afraid	from	frog	further	farther	fro	fright	Freud
10.	fallow	foul	fool	fill	feel	full	fell	fail	fuss	fall	furl	Carl	photo	file	foil
11.	gas	gout	gooed	give	geek	good	get	gate	gun	gone	gird	guard	goad	guide	goiter
12.	catch	couch	cool	kick	key	cook	ketch	cake	come	calm	Kirk	carp	coal	kind	coy
13.	lack	loud	Luke	lick	leak	look	lecture	lake	luck	lock	lurk	lark	local	like	lawyer
14.	mallet	mound	mood	mill	meal	wooden	men	main	mother	mom	murmur	march	mobile	mile	Des Moines
15.	pal	Powell	pool	pill	peel	pull	pell	pail	puck	pock	pearl	park	pole	pile	poison
16.	sand	sound	soon	sin	seen	soot	send	same	some	sawn	sir	sorry	sewn	sign	soil
17.	satin	mountain	gluten	mitten	eaten	wouldn't	retina	latent	button	gotten	certain	carton	potent	tighten	ointment
18.	shad	shout	shoed	Schick	sheet	should	shed	shade	shun	shop	insured	sharp	show	shy	■
19.	shack	shower	shooed	shiver	chic	shook	chef	shake	shuck	shock	shirt	shark	shows	shyster	■
20.	shallow	showers	shoot	shift	sheep	sugar	shell	shale	shut	shot	sure	shard	shown	shine	■
21.	chance	chowder	choose	chin	cheek	■	chest	change	chuck	chalk	churn	charge	chose	child	choice
22.	tack	towel	two	tick	teak	took	tech	take	tuck	talk	turkey	tarp	toke	tyke	toy
23.	that	thousand	through	this	these	■	then	they	the	thought	third	cathartic	though	thigh	thyroid
24.	had	how'd	who'd	hid	he'd	hood	hen	hate	hug	hod	heard	hard	hoed	hide	hoi polloi
25.	hat	about	hoot	hit	heat	foot	heck	Hague	hut	hot	hurt	heart	hotel	height	Hoyle
26.	value	vow	review	villain	reveal	■	vegetable	vague	vug	von	verve	varnish	vote	vile	avoid
27.	whack	wow	wooed	wick	weak	would	wed	weighed	what	walk	word	harm	woke	white	woi

Chapter 20

> Move your lips for tense vowels.
> Don't move your lips for lax vowels.

CD 5 Track 31

In this chapter, we tackle tense and lax vowels. This is the difference between ā, *tense* and ε, *lax;* ē, *tense* and i, *lax.* We will start with tense vowels. (See also Chapters 3, 12, and 18.)

Exercise 20-1: Tense Vowels
CD 5 Track 32

*Don't pay attention to spelling or meaning. Just remember, if you are in the ä column, they all have the same **ah** sound. Repeat.*

	æ	æo	ä	i	ā	ē	ū	ōū
1.	at	out	ought	I'd	ate	eat	ooze	own
2.	bat	about	bought	bite	bait	beat	boot	boat
3.	cat	couch	caught	kite	cane	keys	cool	coat
4.	chat	chowder	chalk	child	chair	cheer	choose	chose
5.	dad	doubt	dot	dial	date	deed	do	don't
6.	fat	found	fought	fight	fate	feet	food	phone
7.	fallow	fountain	fall	file	fail	feel	fool	foal
8.	gas	gown	got	kite	gate	gear	ghoul	go
9.	hat	how	hot	height	hate	heat	hoot	hope
10.	Hal	howl	hall	heil	hail	heel	who'll	hole
11.	Jack	jowl	jock	giant	jail	jeep	jewel	Joel
12.	crab	crowd	crawl	crime	crate	creep	cruel	crow
13.	last	loud	lost	line	late	Lee	Lou	low
14.	mat	mountain	mop	might	mate	mean	moon	moan
15.	gnat	now	not	night	Nate	neat	noon	note
16.	pal	pound	Paul	pile	pail	peel	pool	pole
17.	rat	round	rot	right	rate	real	rule	role
18.	sat	sound	soft	sight	sale	seal	Sue	soul
19.	shall	shower	shawl	shine	shade	she	shoe	show
20.	slap	slouch	slop	slide	slade	sleep	slew	slow
21.	stag	stout	stop	style	stale	steal	stool	stole
22.	strap	Stroud	straw	stride	straight	stream	strew	stroll
23.	tap	town	top	type	tape	team	tool	told
24.	that	thou	thar	thine	they	these	▆	though
25.	thang	thousand	thought	thigh	thane	thief	▆	throw
26.	van	vow	volume	viper	vain	veal	voodoo	vote
27.	wax	Wow!	wash	wipe	wane	wheel	woo	woe
28.	yank	Yow!	yawn	yikes	Yale	year	you	yo
29.	zap	Zowie!	zombie	xylophone	zany	zebra	zoo	Zoe

Exercise 20-2: Tense Vowels Practice Paragraph   CD 5 Track 33

*Go through the subsequent paragraph and mark all the tense vowels, starting with ā (there are 12 here). The first one is **name** (nεim, not nεm). The first ē sound (15) is **the American**. The same five æ sounds can be found as in Exercise 12-2 on page 96, plus the æo of **sound** and **down**. Pause the CD to do the marking. Check Answer Key, beginning on page 210.*

Hello, **my** nāme is_____. I'm taking American **æccent** Training. There's a **lot** to **learn**, but I **hope** to make it as **enjoyable** as possible. I should pick **up** on thē American **intonation** pattern pretty **easily**, although the **only** way to **get** it is to **practice** all of the time. I use the **up** and down, or **peaks** and valleys, **intonation** more than I **used** to. I've been paying attention to **pitch, too**. It's like **walking** down a **stair**case. I've been **talking** to a lot of **Americans** lately, and they tell me that I'm **easier** to under**stand**. **Any**way, I could go **on** and on, but the **important** thing is to **listen** well and sound **good. Well**, what do you **think**? **Do** I?

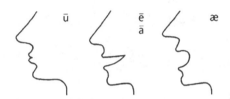

Tense vowels use the lips and jaw muscles.

Exercise 20-3: Lax Vowels   CD 5 Track 34

As we saw in Chapter 18, these are the lax vowels.

	e	i	ü	ə	ər
1.	end	it	▮	un-	earn
2.	bet	bit	book	but	burn
3.	kept	kiss	could	cut	curt
4.	check	chick	▮	chuck	church
5.	debt	did	▮	does	dirt
6.	fence	fit	foot	fun	first
7.	fell	fill	full	▮	furl
8.	get	gill	good	gut	girl
9.	help	hit	hook	hut	hurt
10.	held	hill	hood	hull	hurl

Soft vowels are subtle variations of sound using the throat muscles.

e slightly tense: **bet**
i more relaxed: **bit**
ü even more relaxed: **put**
ə throat is completely relaxed: **but**

Exercise 20-4: Lax Vowels Practice Paragraph

CD 5 Track 35

Again, go over this paragraph and mark the lax vowels, starting with ɛ. The first one (of about 12 possible) is in hello or American. The first i sound (of 9 to 22) may be found in is. (The numbers are approximations because you may have already reduced the ɛ of hello and the i of is into schwas.) Pause the CD to do the marking. Check your answer in the Answer Key, beginning on page 210.

Hello, **my** name is_____. I'm taking American **Accent** Training. There's a **lot** to learn, but I **hope** to make it as **enjoyable** as possible. I should pick **up** on the American **intonation** pattern pretty **easily**, although the **only** way to **get** it is to **practice** all of the time. I use the **up** and down, or **peaks** and valleys, **intonation** more than I **used** to. I've been paying attention to **pitch**, **too**. It's like **walking** down a **stair**case. I've been **talking** to a lot of **Americans** lately, and they tell me that I'm **easier** to under**stand**. **Any**way, I could go **on** and on, but the **important** thing is to **listen** well and sound **good**. **Well**, what do you **think**? **Do** I?

Exercise 20-5: Take a High-Tech Tack

CD 5 Track 36

Repeat the following paragraph and words after me.

Sāy, Rāy, tāke a tack. A high-tack tack? No, Rāy, a high-tech tack, **ei**ght high-tech tacks, tāke them. Then find a wāy to māke a plāce for the tacks on the dāy bed. H**ey**, you lāy the tacks on the pāper plāce mat on the tāble, not on the dāy bed, Rāy. At your āge, why do you always māke the sāme mistākes?

CD 5 Track 37

late	lack	let	tāke	tack	tech	mate	mat	met
hāil	Hal	hell	fāte	fat	fetch	cane	can	Ken

Exercise 20-6: Pick a Peak

CD 5 Track 38

Repeat the following paragraph and words after me. Boldfaced elements represent the ē sound. The i is only marked with underscoring.

People who p**i**ck **pea**ks **wee**kly **seem** to **need** to app**ear** **deep** **i**n order to b**e** d**i**stinguished from m**ere** p**ea** p**i**ckers. **Pe**ter, a champ**io**n **pea**k p**i**cker, thought h**e**'d b**e** **e**ven **nea**ter **i**f h**e** were the **dee**pest **pea**k p**i**cker **i**n **Pe**oria, Ph**oe**nix, and New Zealand. On his **pea**k **pea**k-p**i**cking **wee**k, though, **Pe**ter, a **pea**k p**i**cker's **pea**k p**i**cker, r**ea**lized that h**e** was not **deep**. Th**i**s **i**s not **ea**sy for a **pea**k p**i**cker to adm**i**t, and **i**t p**i**tched **Pe**ter **i**nto a p**i**t of **pea**k-p**i**cking d**e**spair. H**e** was p**i**tiful for three **wee**ks and then l**i**fted h**i**mself to h**i**therto unrev**ea**led personal **pea**ks.

CD 5 Track 39

eat / it	sheep / ship	seat / sit	neat / nit	feet / fit	sleep / slip

> The tongue tip touches the ridge in a variety of ways.

Those Bumps at the Top of Your Mouth   CD 5 Track 40

Those bumps at the top of your mouth form the alveolar ridge, and it's the location of a lot of activity, including **S, Z, T, D, N, L, Sh, Zh, Ch** and **J**! (See also the Nationality Guides.)

Exercise 21-1: It's So Sad   CD 5 Track 41

Repeat the following paragraph.

It's so sad, Sally stole Sammy's snakeskin suit and sold it to a salesman from Sonoma. Sid, the salesman, suggested that Sally stop stealing, but Sally simply said, "So!" Sid sighed sadly and stomped off to search for a more suitable subject.

Exercise 21-2: Allz Well That Endz Well   CD 5 Track 42

Repeat the following paragraph.

Zero Zippers is a zillion-dollar organization near the Osgood zoo in Zimbabwe. It zigzagged through an embezzlement scandal and zipped past all reasonable expectations. Zero was in the most desirable zip code in the business zone, but the end result was zilch. As the founder's motto was "Easy come, easy go!", no one resented the bizarre disaster.

CD 5 Track 43

Make your **T**s crisper (when they are **T**s and not the middle **D**). If the tip of your tongue is even a bit too far forward, it flattens the rest of the tongue. Make sure it's planted right there on the alveolar ridge and that it's clearly popped.

Exercise 21-3: Ted Took Ten Tasty Tacos   CD 5 Track 44

Repeat the following paragraph. Put your hand in front of your mouth when you say the following. You should feel distinct puffs of air against your palm.

Ted took ten tasty tacos from the tidy taco truck on Tuesday at two. It's a tried-and-true test of temperament to try resisting tasty tacos. Take the taco-tasting test ten times to determine your type.

Exercise 21-4: Trudy Tried to Trill in Trinidad CD 5 Track 45

*Repeat the following paragraph. Once you've got your tongue tapping on the alveolar ridge, for this next one, you're going to drop away from the ridge. Remember, in American English, the **R** acts more like a vowel because no two points of the mouth come into contact. With your **T** tensely poised on the ridge, it's going to release plosively from there, and the back of your tongue will form the **R**. You'll still feel the puffs of air.*

Trudy **tr**ied to **tr**ill on **Tr**evor's **Tr**ail in **Tr**inidad, but **tr**ipped up and got off **tr**ack.

Exercise 21-5: Eddie Oughtta Wait a Little Longer CD 5 Track 46

Repeat the following sentence.

E**dd**ie ough**t** to **t**ry **t**o wai**t** a li**tt**le longer. (Eddie oughtta tryda way da little longer.)

Exercise 21-6: Little League in Little Italy CD 5 Track 47

*Repeat the following sentence, focusing on the **L** sounds.*

Little **L**ola p**l**ayed **L**ittle **L**eague with a **l**ittle o**l**d **l**ady in **L**ittle Italy.

Exercise 21-7: No! No! Not Nine! CD 5 Track 48

Repeat the following paragraph.

No! **N**ot **n**ine **n**ew **n**ovels! **N**ine'll **n**ever be e**n**ough!

Exercise 21-8: Chester's Chocolate Cherries CD 5 Track 49

Repeat the following paragraph.

Chuck Ri**ch**ards **ch**arged **Ch**ester a sur**ch**arge on the **ch**ewy **ch**ocolates. **Ch**ester **ch**afed and kvet**ch**ed but fet**ch**ed **Ch**uck a **ch**est of ri**ch**es for his **ch**ocolate **ch**erries.

Exercise 21-9: She Should Share Sherman's Shoes CD 5 Track 50

Repeat the following paragraph.

Shelly and **Sh**erman **sh**are a **sh**adowy passion for **sh**oes. Lu**sh**, plu**sh** **sh**oes in **sh**ocking **sh**ades of **ch**artreuse. Go**sh**, why won't **sh**e **sh**are her **sh**oes with **Sh**erman?

Exercise 21-10: George Judged Jenny's Jewelry CD 5 Track 51

Repeat the following paragraph.

George **j**udged **J**enny's **j**ewelry as **j**ust average. **J**ewelry is **J**enny's life. En**j**oying a**g**eless **g**ems and **j**ewels ca**dg**ed from Ro**g**ers of **J**acksonville, **J**enny ad**j**usted **G**eorge's **j**udgement of her **j**ewelry, as it was not **j**ust average — it was a **g**em **j**ubilee!

Exercise 21-11: Was Your Usual Menage in the Beige Garage?   CD 5 Track 52

Repeat the following paragraph.

It was a beige, beige garage and a vision of precision. The revision of the usual menage's decision was a collision of collusion and illusion.

It was a bei**zh**, bei**zh** gara**zh** and a vi**zh**'n of preci**zh**'n. The revi**zh**'n of the u**zh**ual mena**zh**'s deci**zh**'n was a colli**zh**'n of collu**zh**'n and illu**zh**'n.

CD 5 Track 53

> **Ch** and **J** are almost the same sound. The tongue position is the same, and they both **pop**. There's one little difference. **Ch** is **whispered** and **J** is **spoken**.
>
> **Sh** and **Zh** are almost the same. The tongue position is the same, and they both **slide** out. The difference: **Sh** is **whispered** and **Zh** is **spoken**.

In order to make a clear **Ch**, you need to start with a **T** sound, so it sounds like **tch** not **shhh**. The invisible **T** before the **Ch** blocks the air momentarily, before the rest of the sound comes out. With the **Sh**, the air flows freely. For **J**, start with a **D**, so **judge** sounds like **djudge**.

CD 5 Track 54

Unvoiced	Voiced	Unvoiced	Voiced
Ch	**J**	**Sh**	**Zh**
cheese	jeans	she's	Jaque's
in charge	enjoy	insure	usual
much	judge	mush	garage
watch	lodge	wash	rouge
watcher	lodger	washer	was your
patch	page	bash	beige
patches	pages	bashes	beiges
ritual	vigil	vicious	visual
rich	ridge	wish	menage
hatcher	had your	hasher	has your

Chapter 22

Grammar in a Bigger Nutshell

CD 5 Track 55

In Chapter 9, we studied compound nouns and complex verb tenses. Now, we are going to put them together and practice the intonation of some complicated sentences.

Exercise 22-1: Compound Nouns and Complex Verbs — CD 5 Track 56

No matter how complex the verb gets, remember to follow the basic **Dogs eat bones** *intonation, where you stress the nouns. For the noun intonation, stick with the basic* **set phrase or description** *rule. Let's build up one complex noun for the subject and another one for the object, starting with* **The millionaires were impressed by the equipment.**

Subject	Object
The **millionaires**	the **equipment**.
The elderly **millionaires**	**eaves**dropping equipment.
The **elderly** Texas **millionaires**	electronic **eaves**dropping equipment.
The two **elderly** Texas **millionaires**...**sophisticated** electronic **eaves**dropping equipment.	
The two **elderly** Texas **millionaires** were impressed by the **sophisticated** electronic	**eaves**dropping equipment.

The two elderly Teksəs millyənair zwerim presst by the
səfistəkaydədələktränik ēvzdräppiŋə kwipmənt.

zərim prest **CD 5 Track 57**

1. The two **elderly** Texas **millionaires**'re impressed by the **sophisticated** electronic **eaves**dropping equipment.

zwərim prest

2. The two **elderly** Texas **millionaires** were impressed by the **sophisticated** electronic **eaves**dropping equipment.

zər beeyingim prest

3. At the moment, the two **elderly** Texas **millionaires**'re being impressed by the **sophisticated** electronic **eaves**dropping equipment.

zəl beeyim prest

4. The two **elderly** Texas **millionaires**'ll be impressed by the **sophisticated** electronic **eaves**dropping equipment.

zəd beeyim prest

5. The two **elderly** Texas **millionaires**'d be impressed by the **sophisticated** electronic **eaves**dropping equipment if there were more practical applications for it.

zədəv binim prest

6. The two **elderly** Texas **millionaires**'d've been impressed by the **sophisticated** electronic **eaves**dropping equipment if there had been more practical applications for it.

zədəv bin so im prest

7. The two **elderly** Texas **millionaires** that've been so impressed by the **sophisticated** electronic **eaves**dropping equipment are now researching a new program.

zəv binim prest

8. The two **elderly** Texas **millionaires**'ve been impressed by the **sophisticated** electronic **eaves**dropping equipment for a long time now.

zəd binim prest

9. The two **elderly** Texas **millionaires**'d been impressed by the **sophisticated** electronic **eaves**dropping equipment long before the burglary was thwarted.

zələv bin thərə lee⁽ʸ⁾im prest

10. The two **elderly** Texas **millionaires**'ll've been thoroughly impressed by the **sophisticated** electronic **eaves**dropping equipment by the time I've done my presentation.

zädə bee⁽ʸ⁾im prest

11. The two **elderly** Texas **millionaires** ought to be impressed by the **sophisticated** electronic **eaves**dropping equipment.

shüd bee⁽ʸ⁾im prest

12. The two **elderly** Texas **millionaires** should be impressed by the **sophisticated** electronic **eaves**dropping equipment.

shüd•n beetoo⁽ʷ⁾im prest

13. The two **elderly** Texas **millionaires** shouldn't be too impressed by the **sophisticated** electronic **eaves**dropping equipment.

shüdəv binim prest

14. The two **elderly** Texas **millionaires** should've been impressed by the **sophisticated** electronic **eaves**dropping equipment.

shüdn•nəv bin thæ dim prest

15. Given the circumstances, the two **elderly** Texas **millionaires** shouldn't've been that impressed by the **sophisticated** electronic **eaves**dropping equipment.

cüdee zəlee bee⁽ʸ⁾im prest

16. We think that the two **elderly** Texas **millionaires** could easily be impressed by the **sophisticated** electronic **eaves**dropping equipment.

cüd•n bee⁽ʸ⁾im prest

17. No matter what we did, the two **elderly** Texas **millionaires** couldn't be impressed by even the most **sophisticated** electronic **eaves**dropping equipment.

cüdəv binim prest

18. The two **elderly** Texas **millionaires** could've been impressed by the **sophisticated** electronic **eaves**dropping equipment, but we're not sure.

cüdn•nəv binim prest

19. The two **elderly** Texas **millionaires** couldn't've been impressed by the **sophisticated** electronic **eaves**dropping equipment, because they left after five minutes.

myt bee⁽ʸ⁾im prest

20. The two **elderly** Texas **millionaires** might be impressed by the **sophisticated** electronic **eaves**dropping equipment this time around.

mydəv binim prest

21. The two **elderly** Texas **millionaires** might've been impressed by the **sophisticated** electronic **eaves**dropping equipment, but they gave no indication one way or the other.

Exercise 22-1: Compound Nouns and Complex Verbs *continued*　　　CD 5 Track 57

məss bee⁽ʸ⁾im prest

22. The two **elderly** Texas **millionaires** must be impressed by the **sophisticated** electronic **eaves**dropping equipment because they are considering a huge order.

məsdəv binim prest

23. The two **elderly** Texas **millionaires** must have been impressed by the **sophisticated** electronic **eaves**dropping equipment because they ordered so much of it.

cən bee⁽ʸ⁾im prest

24. The two **elderly** Texas **millionaires** can be impressed by the **sophisticated** electronic **eaves**dropping equipment because they don't know much about surveillance.

cæn⁽ᵗ⁾ bee⁽ʸ⁾im prest

25. The two **elderly** Texas **millionaires** can't be impressed by the **sophisticated** electronic **eaves**dropping equipment because they invented most of the state-of-the-art technology currently available.

Exercise 22-2: Your Own Compound Nouns　　　CD 5 Track 58

Pause the CD and build up your own compound nouns, both subject and object.

Subject	Object
_____	_____
_____	_____
_____	_____
_____	_____
_____	_____
_____	_____
_____	_____
_____	_____

The Verb Map

This is a handy overview of the various verb tenses and verb forms. The **T formation** in each box indicates the more commonly used tenses. The single symbols indicate a completed action, whereas the double symbols indicate two related events. The white symbols are *contrary to fact* and didn't, don't, or won't take place.

Active

	Past	Present	Future
Simple	I did it. ◄	I do it. ●	I will do it. ►
Real Duo	I'd done A before I did B. ◄◄	I've done it. ◄●	I'll have done A before I do B. ►►
Unreal Duo	If I had done A I would've done B. ◄◄	If I did A I would do B. ◁○	If I do A I'll do B. ▷►

To Be

	Past	Present	Future
Simple	I was there. ◄	I am here. ●	I will be there. ►
Real Duo	I'd been there (before then). ◄◄	I've been here (before now). ◄●	I'll have been there for an hour (by then). ►►
Unreal Duo	If I had been there, I'd have done it. ◄◄	If I were there, I would do it. ◁○	If I am there, I'll do it. ►►

Negative

	Past	Present	Future
Simple	I didn't do it.	I don't do it.	I won't do it.
Real Duo	I hadn't done A until I did B.	I haven't done it.	I won't have done A before I do B.
Unreal Duo	If I hadn't done A I wouldn't have done B.	If I didn't do A I wouldn't do B.	If I don't do A I won't do B.

Continuous

	Past	Present	Future
Simple	I was doing it.	I'm doing it.	I'll be doing it.
Real Duo	I had been doing A before I did B.	I've been doing A for a long time.	I'll have been doing A for a while, when I start B.
Unreal Duo	If I'd been doing A, I wouldn've been doing B.	If I were doing A, I'd be doing B,	If I'm doing A I'm doing B.

Questions

	Past	Present	Future
Simple	Did I do it?	Do I do it?	Will I do it?
Real Duo	Had I done A before I did B?	Have I done A?	Will I have done A before I do B?
Unreal Duo	If I had done A would I have done B?	If I did A would I do B?	If I do A will I do B?

Helping Verbs

	Past	Present	Future
Simple	I had to do it.	I have to do it.	I'll have to do it.
Real Duo	I had had to do A before I had to do B.	I've had many times.	I'll have had to do A before I have to do B.
Unreal Duo	If I had had to do A, I would have had to do B.	If I had to do A, I would have to do B.	If I have to do A, I will have to do B.

Causative

	Past	Present	Future
Simple	I had it done.	I have it done.	I will have it done.
Real Duo	I'd had done A before I had B done.	I've had A done many times.	I'll have had A done by the time I have B done.
Unreal Duo	If I had had A done, I would've had B done.	If I had A done, I would have B done.	If I have A done, I'll have B done.

Passive

	Past	Present	Future
Simple	It was done.	It is done.	It will be done.
Real Duo	A had been done before B was done.	A has been done many times.	A will be done before B is done.
Unreal Duo	If A had been done B would have been done.	If A were done B would be done.	If A is done B will be done.

172

Exercise 22-3: Your Compound Nouns and Complex Verbs   CD 5 Track 60

Using your compound nouns from Exercise 22-2, choose a verb and put it through all the changes. Remember that it helps to have a verb that starts with a vowel. Add explanatory words to round out the sentence, complete the thought, and support the verb.

do	1.
did	2.
are doing	3.
will do	4.
would do	5.
would've done	6.
that have done	7.
have done	8.
had done	9.
will've done	10.
ought to do	11.
should do	12.
shouldn't do	13.
should've done	14.
shouldn't have done	15.
could do	16.
couldn't do	17.
could've done	18.
couldn't have done	19.
might do	20.
might've done	21.
must do	22.
must've done	23.
can do	24.
can't do	25.

Practical Application

> Take everything you've learned and use it.

Exercise 23-1: Practical Application – U.S./Japan Trade Friction · CD 5 Track 61

Listen to the following excerpt and compare the two versions.

Forty years after the end of World War II, Japan and the U.S. are again engaged in conflict. Trade frictions, which began as minor irritants in an otherwise smooth relationship in the 1960s, have gradually escalated over the years.

The conflict is more dangerous than it appears because its real nature is partially hidden. It masquerades as a banal and sometimes grubby dispute over widgets with the stakes being whether American or Japanese big business makes more money.

In truth, the issue is strategic and geopolitical in nature. Japan is once again challenging the U.S., only this time the issue is not China or the Pacific but world industrial and technological leadership and the military and economic powers, which have always been its corollaries.

*By permission of *U.S. News and World Report*

Fordee yir **zæf**tr⁽ᵖᵃᵘˢᵉ⁾thee⁽ʸ⁾end'v wrl dwor **too**,⁽ᵖᵃᵘˢᵉ⁾J'**pæn**'n thə yoo⁽ʷ⁾**ess**⁽ᵖᵃᵘˢᵉ⁾ärə **ge**nin gɛij din⁽ᵖᵃᵘˢᵉ⁾**cän**fl'ct.⁽ˢᵗᵒᵖ⁾**Trəid** fr'ksh'nz,⁽ᵖᵃᵘˢᵉ⁾w'ch b'gæn'z mynr **rirrət**'nts⁽ᵖᵃᵘˢᵉ⁾in'n ətherwise⁽ᵖᵃᵘˢᵉ⁾ smooth r'**lɛi**sh'nship in the näinteen **siks**deez⁽ᵖᵃᵘˢᵉ⁾h'v græjəlee⁽ʸ⁾**ɛsc**ələdəd⁽ᵖᵃᵘˢᵉ⁾dover thə **yirz**.

Thə **kän**fl'k d'z mor **dɛin**jer's thəni də**pirz** b'kəzəts **ree**⁽ʸ⁾əl nɛichyr'z pärshəlee **h'd**d'n. It mæske**rɛid** zəzə bə**nä**lən səmtäimz **gr**əbee d'spyu dover **wij**'ts withthə **stɛiks** be⁽ʸ⁾ing wɛtherə **mɛr**əkənər Jæpə**neez** big **biz**n's mɛiks mor **mən**ee.

In **truth**, thee⁽ʸ⁾**ishu**⁽ʷ⁾iz strə**tee**jəkən jee⁽ʸ⁾**opə**lidəkələn nɛichyer. Jə**pæn**əz wən səgɛn **chæl**ənjing thə you⁽ʷ⁾**ess**, only **this** täim, thee⁽ʸ⁾**ishu**⁽ʷ⁾iz nät **Chäi**nə or thə Pəs'fək bət wr rolld'in **dəss**tree⁽ʸ⁾l'n tɛknə**läj**əkəl **lee**dershipən the **mil**ətɛree⁽ʸ⁾ənɛkə**nä**mək pæwrz, w'ch h'**vä**weez bi n'ts **kor**əlɛreez.

The Letter A
CD 5 Track 62

You've seen many examples of illogical spelling by now, and the letter **A** is a major contributor. **A** can be:

æ cat	ä part	ā make	ə final	ɛ parallel	o war

Note People who speak Chinese frequently pronounce **a**, **æ**, and **ɛ** the same. The common denominator of the three sounds is **ɛ**. When a Chinese speaker says *mate, mat, met,* it can sound like *met, met, met.* If this happens to be your case, in order to say common words like *make* and *man* correctly, first practice putting them on the stairsteps and drawing them out. Don't be afraid to exaggerate. You can even draw them out with a final unvoiced consonant.

may eek   mæ æn

make   **man**

Exercise 23-2: Presidential Candidates' Debate   CD 5 Track 63

Thə prezədənt təmärrou näidiz əxpectədiniz stɛidəv thə yoonyən mesəj tə prəpouz fedrəl səbzədeez tə help lou⁽ʷ⁾inkəm fæmleez ouvrkəm thə sou-käld dijədəl dəväid. Izidə nəpropree⁽ʸ⁾ət yusəv gəvrmnt fənz tə hændæot kəmpyudrz ən prəväid Innernet æksɛs tə thouz hu cæn⁽ᵈ⁾əford it; ənd if nät, why nät? Will bəgin with Mr. Keez.

    "I think this iz ənəthər keis whɛer pälətishənz try də jəmpän thə bændwægən əv səmthing thæťs going än in thee⁽ʸ⁾əcänəmee, sou evreebədeez gənnə think thət they ækchəlee hæv səmthing tə do with thə rəzəlt when they dont. Thɛrz nou need fr this. Wiräl reddy seeing æot thɛr prəpouzəlz fr thə distrəbyushən əv free PeeCees, nät beis dän səm pälətishən meiking ə judgment ən spending tæxpeiyer mənee, bət beis dän thə self-intrst əv thouz hu⁽ʷ⁾är involvd inə nyu world, ə nyu world ən which p'rtisəpeishən iz thə kee də präfit—ənd in which thɛr iz ækchəlee ə sträng insentiv əməng thouz hu prtisəpɛidin thə präivət sektər tə giv æksɛss tə indəvijəls sou thæt they c'n impruv their əpərtyunədeez fr präfit, fr infərmeishn shɛring. Thæts whəts älredee bin going än—it will kəntinyu. Thɛr iz nou need fr thə gəvərmənt tə prətend thæt it needs tə teik leedership hir. I think thæts jəst pəlidəkəl päsjuring."

Senədər Mə⁽ᵏ⁾kein.

I bəleev th't wee du hæv ə präbləm. æn thædiz thət thɛrizə growing gæp bətween thə hævz ənd hæv-näts in əmerəkə, thouz thədr ɛibl də tɛik pärdin this infərmeishn teknäləjee ən thouz th't hævnt. Wee took ə mɛijər step forwərd when wee dəsaidəd də wäi⁽ʸ⁾r evree skool ən lybrɛree in əmerəkə tə thee⁽ʸ⁾Innərnet. Thætsə güd prougrəm. Wee hæf tə hæv step tu, three, ən for, which meenz güd əkwipmənt, güd teechərz, ənd güd clæssroomz. No, I wüdn du⁽ʷ⁾it d'rektlee. Bət thɛrz läts əv weiz th'chyu kən inkerəj korpəreishnz, who in their own self-intrest, wüd wänt tə prəvaid... wüd rəseev tæks benəfits, wüd rəseev kredit, ənd mɛny əthər weiz fr beeing invölvd in thə skoolz, in əpgreiding thə kwälədee əv əkwipmənt th't thei hæv, thə kwälədee əv thə styudənts ənd thɛrby prəvaiding ə məch-needed well-treind wərkfors.

Thæng kyu. Mr. Forbz.

The president tomorrow night is expected in his State of the Union message to propose federal subsidies to help low-income families overcome the so-called digital divide. Is it an appropriate use of government funds to hand out computers and provide Internet access to those who can't afford it, and if not, why not? We'll begin with Mr. Keyes.

    "I think this is another case where politicians try to jump on the bandwagon of something that's going on in the economy, so everybody's gonna think that they actually have something to do with the result when they don't. There's no need for this. We're already seeing out there proposals for the distribution of free PCs, not based on some politician making a judgment and spending taxpayer money, but based on the self-interest of those who are involved in a new world, a new world in which participation is the key to profit—and in which there is actually a strong incentive among those who participate in the private sector to give access to individuals so that they can improve their opportunities for profit, for information sharing. That's what's already been going on—it will continue. There is no need for the government to pretend that it needs to take leadership here. I think that's just political posturing."

Senator McCain.

"I believe that we do have a problem. And that is that there is a growing gap between the *haves* and *have-nots* in America, those that are able to take part in this information technology and those that haven't. We took a major step forward when we decided to wire every school and library in America to the Internet. That's a good program. We have to have step two, three, and four, which means good equipment, good teachers, and good classrooms. No, I wouldn't do it directly. But there's lots of ways that you can encourage corporations, who in their own self-interest, would want to provide ... would receive tax benefits, would receive credit, and many other ways for being involved in the schools, in upgrading the quality of equipment that they have, the quality of the students, and thereby providing a much-needed well-trained workforce."

Thank you. Mr. Forbes.

An Australlian tourist steps into the road and a traffic cop yells at him, "Did you come here to die?!"

"Nah, mate. I came here yesterdie!"

Chapter 24

Block the air with your tongue
and release it through your nose.

Nasal Consonants

CD 5 Track 64

We now turn to the three consonants whose sound comes out through the nose—**M**, **N**, and the **NG** combination. They each have one thing in common—their sound is blocked in the mouth in one of three locations. Two of them, **N** and **NG**, you can't even see, as with **R**, so they're hard to pick up on. (See also Chapters 3, 16, 21, and the Nationality Guides.)

m is the easiest and most obvious. Like **b**, the lips come together; the air can't get out, so it has to come out through the nose.

n is in a position similar to **t**, but it can't be at all tense. It has to be completely relaxed, filling the whole mouth, touching the insides of all the teeth, leaving no room for the air to escape, except by the nose.

ng is back in the throat with **g**. The back of the tongue presses back, and again, the air comes out through the nose.

Exercise 24-1: Nasal Consonants CD 5 Track 65

We are going to contrast nasals with regular consonant sounds. Repeat after me.

	Initial		**Middle**		**Final**	
m/b	me	bee	llama	lobber	ROM	rob
n/d	knees	deals	Lana	lauder	Ron	rod
ng/g	long eels	geese	longer	logger	wrong	log

Exercise 24-2: Ending Nasal Consonants CD 5 Track 66

Here we will focus on the final sounds. Repeat after me.

M	**N**	**NG**
rum^{ə}	run^{ə}	rung^{ə}
sum/some	sun/son	sung
bum	bun	bung
turn	ton	tongue
dumb	done	dung
psalm	sawn	song

Exercise 24-3: Reading Nasal Consonant Sounds CD 5 Track 67

We will read the following paragraph. Repeat after me.

The young King Kong can sing along on anything in the kingdom, as long as he can bring a strong ringing to the changing songs. He can only train on June mornings when there is a full moon, but June lends itself to singing like nothing else. Ding Dong, on the other hand, is not a singer; he cannot sing for anything. He is a man often seen on the green lawn on the Boston Open, where no one ever, ever sings.

Exercise 24-4: Finding n and ng Sounds CD 5 Track 68

*Find and mark the final **n** and **ng** sounds.*

Hello, **my** name is_____. I'm taking American **Accent** Training. There's a **lot** to **learn**, but I **hope** to make it as **enjoyable** as possible. I should pick **up** on the American **intonation** pattern pretty **easily**, although the **only** way to **get** it is to **practice** all of the time. I use the **up** and down, or **peaks** and valleys, **intonation** more than I **used** to. I've been paying attention to **pitch, too**. It's like **walking** down a **stair**case. I've been **talking** to a lot of **Americans** lately, and they tell me that I'm **easier** to under**stand**. **Any**way, I could go **on** and on, but the **important** thing is to **listen** well and sound **good**. **Well**, what do you **think**? **Do** I?

Chapter 25

Throaty Consonants

CD 5 Track 69

There are five consonant sounds that are produced in the throat: **h**, **k**, **g**, **ng**, **er**. Because **R** can be considered a consonant, its sound is included here. For pronunciation purposes, however, elsewhere this book treats it as a semivowel. (See also Chapters 15, 24, and the Nationality Guides.)

Exercise 25-1: Throaty Consonants

CD 5 Track 70

Here we will read across the lists of initial, middle, and final consonants.

	Initial	Middle	Final
h	haw	reheat	
	hood	in half	
	he'll	unhinge	
	hat	unheard of	
k	caw	accident	rink
	could	accent	rack
	keel	include	cork
	cat	actor	block
g	gaw	regale	rug
	good	ingrate	hog
	geese	agree	big
	gat	organ	log
ng	Long Island	Bronx	wrong
	a long wait	inky	daring
	Dang you!	larynx	averaging
	being honest	English	clung
r	raw	error	rare
	roof	arrow	air
	real	mirror	injure
	rat	carbon	prefer

Exercise 25-2: The Letter X   CD 5 Track 71

*The letter **X** can sound like either **KS** or **GZ**, depending on the letter that follows the **X** and where the stress falls.*

ks	excite	**ɛks**äit
	extra	**ɛks**trə
Followed by	exercise	**ɛks**ersiz
*the letter **C** or*	experience	ɛks**pir**ee⁽ʸ⁾əns
*other **unvoiced***	except	ək**sɛpt**
consonants	execute	**ɛks**ekyut
	excellent	**ɛks**ələnt
gz	example	əg**zæm**pᵊl
	exist	əg**zist**
Followed by a	exam	əg**zæm**
***vowel** and usually*	exert	əg**zrt**
stressed on the	examine	əg**zæm**ən
second syllable	executive	əg**zɛ**kyudəv
	exit	**ɛg**zit
	exactly	əg**zæk**lee

Exercise 25-3: Reading the H, K, G, NG, and R Sounds   CD 5 Track 72

Repeat after me.

H

"Help!" hissed the harried intern. "We have to hurry! The half-wit who was hired to help her home hit her hard with the Honda. She didn't have a helmet on her head to protect her, so she has to have a checkup ahead of the others."

CD 5 Track 73

K

The computer cursor careened across the screen, erasing key characters as it scrolled past. The technician was equally confused by the computer technology and the complicated keyboard, so he clicked off the computer, cleaned off his desk, accepted his paycheck, and caught a taxicab for the airport, destination Caracas.

CD 5 Track 74

G

The Wizard of Og

There was a man named...	Og
Who was his best friend?	Dog
Where did he live?	Bog
What was his house made of?	Log
Who was his neighbor?	Frog
What did he drink?	Eggnog
What did he do for fun?	Jog
What is the weather in his swamp?	Fog

CD 5 Track 75

NG

The stunning woman would not have a fling with the strong young flamingo trainer until she had a ring on her finger. He was angry because he longed for her. She inquired if he were hungry, but he hung his head in a funk. The flamingo trainer banged his fist on the fish tank and sang out, "Dang it, I'm sunk without you, Punkin!" She took in a long, slow lungful of air and sighed.

CD 5 Track 76

R

War is horrible. During any war, terrible things occur. The result is painful memories and disfiguring scars for the very people needed to rebuild a war-torn country. The leaders of every country must learn that wars are never won, lives are always lost, and history is doomed to repeat itself unless we all decide to live in harmony with our brothers and sisters.

Exercise 25-4: Glottal Consonant Practice Paragraph CD 5 Track 77

*Pause the CD and go through the paragraph and mark the **h**, **k**, **g**, **ng**, and **r** sounds.*

He**l**lo, **my** name is_____. I'm taking American **Accent** Training. There's a **lot** to **learn**, but I **hope** to make it as **enjoyable** as possible. I should pick **up** on the American **intonation** pattern pretty **easily**, although the **only** way to **get** it is to **practice** all of the time. I use the **up** and down, or **peaks** and valleys, **intonation** more than I **used** to. I've been paying attention to **pitch, too**. It's like **walking** down a **stair**case. I've been **talking** to a lot of **Americans** lately, and they tell me that I'm **easier** to under**stand**. **Any**way, I could go **on** and on, but the **important** thing is to **listen** well and sound **good**. **Well**, what do you **think**? **Do** I?

Telephone Tutoring
Final Diagnostic Analysis

CD 5 Track 78

After a year, you're ready for the final analysis. If you're studying on your own, contact toll-free **1 (800) 457-4255** or go to **AmericanAccent.com** for a referral to a qualified telephone analyst. The diagnostic analysis is designed to evaluate your current speech patterns to let you know where your accent is standard and nonstandard.

The Nasdaq composite index on Monday suffered its biggest loss in three weeks after a wave of selling slammed Internet and other tech shares in Asia and Europe overnight—suggesting many investors are increasingly nervous about tech shares' current heights. The Nasdaq index ended down 141.38 points, or 2.8%, at 4,907.24, though it recovered from a morning sell-off that took it down as much as 209 points from Friday's record high. Biotechnology stocks were particularly hard hit. The broader market was also lower, though the Dow Jones industrial average managed to inch up 18.31 points to 9,37.13.

1. law, job, collar	5. China, dime, fly	9. won, color, Florida	13. about, now, down
2. class, chance, last	6. if, is, been	10. new, blue, through	14. joy, royal, deploy
3. name, date, way	7. eve, ease, bean	11. good, put, could	
4. ten, many, says	8. worm, third, hard	12. won't, know, go	

A	B	C	D	E	F
1. pat	1. bat	1. apparition	1. abolition	1. lap	1. lab
2. fat	2. vat	2. a rifle	2. arrival	2. life	2. live
3. stink	3. zinc	3. graces	3. grazes	3. dice	3. dies
4. sheer	4. girl	4. mesher	4. measure	4. dish	4. deluge
5. ten	5. den	5. latter	5. ladder	5. ought	5. odd
6. cheer	6. jeer	6. nature	6. major	6. etch	6. edge
7. thing	7. the	7. author	7. other	7. breath	7. breathe
8. core	8. gore	8. lacking	8. lagging	8. snack	8. snag
9. yet	9. rice	9. access	9. example	9. box	9. bogs
10. wolf	10. prance	10. association	10. refract	10. way	10. bar
11. her	11. my	11. actual	11. arrive	11. down	11. mutter
12. lice	12. not	12. behind	12. climber	12. ball	12. name
13. plants		13. reflect	13. innate	13. muddle	13. ran
		14. alive	14. singer		14. wrong

1. Sue arranged it.
2. She organized her office.
3. Get your report done.
4. Where did you put it?
5. She's your usual television star.

1. Get a better water heater.

2. Gedda bedder wädr heedr.

1. Soo⁽ʷ⁾ərɛinj dit.
2. Shee⁽ʸ⁾orgənizdr räfəs.
3. Gɛcher r'port dən.
4. Wɛrjə püd't?
5. Shezhier yuzhəwəl tɛləvizhən stär.

3. alter	later
4. intern	enter
5. data	deter
6. metal	metallic

7. bet	bed

Nationality Guides

No matter what language you speak, you will have different sounds and rhythms from a native speaker of American English. These Nationality Guides will give you a head start on what to listen for in American English from the perspective of your own native language. In order to specifically identify what you need to work on, this section can be used in conjunction with the *diagnostic analysis.* The analysis provides an objective rendering of the sounds and rhythms based on how you currently speak, as well as specific guidelines for how to standardize your English; call (800) 457-4255 for a private consultation. (See also Chapter 3.)

• Intonation
• Liaisons
• Word endings
• Pronunciation
• Location in the mouth
• Particular difficulties

Each section will cover *intonation, word connections, word endings, pronunciation, location of the language in the mouth,* as well as particular difficulties to work through, and solutions to common misperceptions.

Most adult students rely too heavily on spelling. It's now your job to listen for pure sound, and reconcile that to spelling—not the other way around. This is the same path that a native speaker follows.

As you become familiar with the major characteristics and tendencies in American English, you will start using that information in your everyday speech. One of the goals of the diagnostic analysis is to show you what you already know, so you can use the information and skills in English as *transfer skills,* rather than *newly learned skills.* You will learn more readily, more quickly, and more pleasantly—and you will retain the information and use the accent with less resistance.

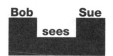

Read all the nationality guides—you never know when you'll pick up something useful for yourself. Although each nationality is addressed individually, there are certain aspects of American English that are difficult for everyone, in this order:

1. Pitch changes and meaning shifts of intonation (See also Chapter 4.)
2. Regressive vocalization with a final voiced consonant *(bit/bid)*
3. Liaisons (See also Chapter 11.)
4. **R & L** (See also Chapters 15 and 16.)
5. **æ, ä, ə** (including the **æo** in *ow*) (See also Chapter 12.)
6. Tense & lax vowels (**i/ē** and **ü/ū**) (See also Chapter 20.)
7. **Th** (See also Chapter 13.)
8. **B & V & W** (See also Chapter 19.)

Nouns generally indicate new information and are stressed.

Ideally, you would have learned intonation before you learned grammar, but since that didn't happen, you can now incorporate the intonation into the grammar that you already know. When you first start listening for intonation, it sounds completely random. It shifts all around even when you use the same words. So, where should you start? In basic sentences with a *noun-verb-noun* pattern, the nouns are usually stressed. Why? Because nouns carry the new information. Naturally, contrast can alter this, but noun stress is the default. Listen to native speakers and you will hear that their pitch goes up on the noun most of the time.

You will, however, also hear verbs stressed. When? The verb is stressed when you replace a noun with a pronoun. Because *nouns are new information* and *pronouns are old information*—and we don't stress old information—the intonation shifts over to the verb. Intonation is the most important part of your accent. Focus on this, and everything else will fall into place with it.

Pronouns indicate old information and are unstressed.

Chinese

Intonation

Important Point

In English, a pitch change indicates the speaker's intention. In Chinese, a pitch change indicates a different word.

There are several immediately evident characteristics of a Chinese accent. The most notable is the lack of speech music, or the musical intonation of English. This is a problem because, in the English language, *intonation* indicates meaning, new information, contrast, or emotion. Another aspect of speech music is *phrasing*, which tells if it is a statement, a question, a yes/no option, a list of items, or where the speaker is in the sentence (introductory phrase, end of the sentence, etc.). In Chinese, however, a change in tone indicates a different vocabulary word. (See also Chapter 4.)

In English, Chinese speakers have a tendency to increase the *volume* on stressed words but otherwise give equal value to each word. This atonal volume increase will sound aggressive, angry, or abrupt to a native speaker. When this is added to the tendency to lop off the end of each word, and almost no word connections at all, the result ranges from choppy to unintelligible.

In spite of this unpromising beginning, Chinese learners have a tremendous advantage. Here is an amazingly effective technique that radically changes how you sound. Given the highly developed tonal qualities of the Chinese language, you are truly a "pitch master." In order for you to appreciate your strength in this area, try the four *ma* tones of Mandarin Chinese. (Cantonese is a little more difficult since it has eight to twelve tones and people aren't as familiar with the differentiation.) These four tones sound identical to Americans—*ma, ma, ma, ma.*

The four "ma" tones of Mandarin Chinese

ma¹ —
ma² ╱
ma³ ╲╱
ma⁴ ╲

Take the first sentence in Exercise 4-5, *It sounds like* **rain**, and replace *rain* with *ma*¹. Say *It sounds like ma*¹. This will sound strangely flat, so then try *It sounds like ma*². This isn't it either, so go on to *It sounds like ma*³ and *It sounds like ma*⁴. One of the last two will sound pretty good, usually *ma*³. You may need to come up with a combination of *ma*³ and *ma*⁴, but once you have the idea of what to listen for, it's really easy. When you have that part clear, put *rain* back in the sentence, keeping the tone:

Chinese Intonation Summary

*1. Say the four **ma**'s.*
2. Write them out with the appropriate arrows.
*3. Replace the stressed word in a sentence with each of the four **ma**'s.*
4. Decide which one sounds best.
5. Put the stressed word back in the sentence, keeping the tone.

It sounds like *ma*³.
It sounds like *rain*³.

If it sounds a little short *(It sounds like ren)*, **double** the sound:

It sounds like

When this exercise is successful, go to the second sentence, *It **sounds** like rain* and do the same thing:

It *ma*³ like rain.
It *sounds*³ like rain.

Then, contrast the two:

It sounds like *rain*³.
It *sounds*³ like rain.

From this point on, you only need to periodically listen for the appropriate *ma*, substituting it in for words or syllables. You don't even need to use the rubber band since your tonal sophistication is so high.

The main point of this exercise is to get you listening for the tone shifts in English, which are very similar to the tone shifts in Chinese. The main difference is that Americans use them to indicate stress, whereas in Chinese, they are fully different words when the tone changes.

A simple way to practice intonation is with the sound that American children use when they make a mistake—***uh**-oh*. This quick note shift is completely typical of the pattern, and once you have mastered this double note, you can go on to more complex patterns. Because Chinese grammar is fairly similar to English grammar, you don't have to worry too much about word order.

Liaisons

All of the advantages that you have from *intonation* are more than counterbalanced by your lack of *word connections*. The reason for this is that Chinese characters (words or parts of words) start with consonants and end with either a vowel or a nasalized consonant, **n** or **ng**. There is no such thing as a final **t**, **l**, or **b** in Chinese. To use an example we've all heard of: *Ma<u>o</u> Ts<u>e</u> Tu<u>ng</u>.* This leads to several difficulties:

- No word endings
- No word connections
- No distinction between final voiced or unvoiced consonants.

It takes time and a great deal of concentration, but the lack of word endings and word connections can be remedied. Rather than force the issue of adding on sounds that will be uncomfortable for you, which will result in overpronunciation, go with your strengths — notice how in *speech,* but not *spelling,* Americans end their words with vowel sounds and start them with consonants, just as in Chinese! It's really a question of rewriting the English script in your head that you read from when you speak. (See also Chapter 11.)

Liaisons or *word connections* will force the final syllable to be pronounced by pushing it over to the beginning of the next word, where Chinese speakers have no trouble — not even with **L**.

Written English	Chinese Accent	American (with Liaisons)
Tell him	teo him	tellim
Pull it out	puw ih aw	pü li dout

Because you are now using a natural and comfortable technique, you will sound smooth and fluid when you speak, instead of that forced, exaggerated speech of people who are doing what they consider unnatural. It takes a lot of correction to get this process to sink in, but it's well worth the effort. Periodically, when you speak, write down the exact sounds that you made, then write it in regular spelling, so you can *see* the Chinese accent and the effect it has on meaning *(puw ih aw* has no meaning in English). Then convert the written English to spoken American *(pull it out* changes to *pü li dout)* to help yourself rewrite your English script.

When you don't use liaisons, you also lose the underlying hum that connects sentences together. This *co-assonance* is like the highway, and the words are the cars that carry the listener along.

The last point of intonation is that Chinese speakers don't differentiate between voiced and unvoiced final consonants — *cap* and *cab* sound exactly the same. For this, you will need to go back to the staircase. When a final consonant is voiced, the vowel is lengthened or doubled. When a final consonant is unvoiced, the vowel is short or single.

Goal
To get you to use your excellent tone control in English.

Chinese characters start with consonants and end with either a vowel or a nasalized consonant (n *or* ng).

Goal
To get you to rewrite your English script and to speak with sound units rather than word units.

Additionally, the long *a* before an *m* is generally shortened to a short ɛ. This is why the words *same* and *name* are particularly difficult, usually being pronounced *sem* and *nem.* You have to add in the second half of the sound. You need *nay + eem* to get *name.* Doubled vowels are explained on page 25.

Pronunciation

Goal
For you to hear the actual vowel and consonant sounds of English, rather than a Chinese perception of them.

The most noticeable nonstandard pronunciation is the lack of final **L**. This can be corrected by either liaisons, or by adding a tiny schwa after it (l^uh or l^ə) in order to position your tongue correctly. This is the same solution for *n* and *ng.* Like most other nationalities, Chinese learners need to work on *th* and *r,* but fortunately, there are no special problems here. The remaining major area is ā, ɛ, and æ, which sound the same. *Mate, met, mat* sound like *met, met, met.* The ɛ is the natural sound for the Chinese, so working from there, you need to concentrate on Chapters 3, 12, and 20. In the word *mate,* you are hearing only the first half of the ɛi combination, so double the vowel with a clear *eet* sound at the end (even before an unvoiced final consonant). Otherwise, you will keep saying *meh-eht* or *may-eht.*

ā It frequently helps to know exactly how something would look in your own language—and in Chinese, this entails characters. The characters on the left are the sounds needed for a Chinese person to say both the long *i* as in *China* and the long ā as in *made* or *same.* Read the character, and then put letters in front and in back of it so you are reading half alphabet, half character. An *m* in front and a *d* in back of the first character will let you read *made.* A *ch* in front and *na* in back of the second character will produce *China.* It's odd, but it works. (See also Chapter 12.)

I A word that ends in *—ail* is particularly difficult for Chinese speakers since it contains both the hard ɛi combination and a final **l** (Chapter 5). It usually sounds something like *feh-o.* You need to *say fail* as if it had three full syllables — *fay-yə-l^ə.* (See also Chapter 16.)

u, v, f, w Another difficulty may be *u, v, f,* and *w.* The point to remember here is that *u* and *w* can both be considered *vowels* (i.e., they don't touch anywhere in the mouth), whereas *v* and *f* are *consonants* (your upper teeth touch your lower lip). ū, as in *too* or *use* should be no problem. Similar to ū, but with a little push of slightly rounded lips is *w,* as in *what* or *white.* The letters *f* and *v* have basically the same sound, but *f* is unvoiced and *v* is voiced. Your lower lip should come up a little to meet your top teeth. You are not biting down on the outside of your lip here; the sound is created using the inside of your lower lip. Leave your mouth in the same position and make the two sounds, both voiced and unvoiced. Practice words such as *fairy, very,* and *wary.* (See also Chapter 19.)

There is another small point that may affect people from southern mainland China who use *l* and *n* interchangeably. This can be corrected by working with *l* words and pinching the nose shut. If you are trying to say *late* and it comes out *Nate,* hold your nose closed and the air will be forced out through your mouth. (See also Chapter 16.)

æ The **æ** sound doesn't exist in Chinese, so it usually comes out as *ä* or *ɛ,* so *last* sounds like *lost* or *name* sounds like *nem.* You need to work on Chapter 12, which drills this distinctively American vowel. (See also Chapters 12, 18, and 20.)

ä	Because of spelling, the *ä* sound can easily be misplaced. The *ä* sound exists in Chinese, but when you see an *o,* you might want to say *ō,* so *hot* sounds like *hōht* instead of *häht*. Remember, most of the time, the letter *o* is pronounced *ah*. This will give you a good reference point for whenever you want to say *ä* instead of *ō: astronomy, cäll, läng, prägress,* etc. (See also Chapters 12, 18, and 20.)
o	Conversely, you may pronounce the letter *o* as *ä* or *ə* when it should be an *o,* as in *only, most, both*. Make sure that the American *o* sounds like *ou: ounly, moust, bouth*. (See also Chapters 12, 18, and 20.)
ə	The schwa is typically overpronounced based on spelling. Work on Chapter 4, American Intonation, and Chapter 12, Cat? Caught? Cut?. If your intonation peaks are strong and clear enough, then your valleys will be sufficiently reduced as well. Concentrate on smoothing out and reducing the valleys and *ignore spelling!* (See also Chapters 12, 18, and 20.)
ü	The ü sound is generally overpronounced to *ooh*. Again, spelling is the culprit. Words such as *smooth, choose,* and *too* are spelled with two *o*'s and are pronounced with a long *ū* sound, but other words such as *took* and *good* are spelled with two *o*'s but are pronounced halfway between *ih* and *uh;* **tük** and **güd**. (See also Chapters 18 and 20.)
i	In most Chinese dictionaries, the distinction between *i* and *ē* is not made. The *ē* is generally indicated by *i:,* which causes problems with final consonants, and the *ih* sound is overpronounced to *eee*. Practice these four sounds, remembering that *tense vowels* indicate that you tense your lips or tongue, while *lax vowels* mean that your lips and tongue are relaxed and the sound is produced in your throat. *Unvoiced* final consonants (*t, s, k, p, ch, f*) mean that the vowel is short and sharp; *voiced* final consonants (*d, z, g, b, j, v*) mean that the vowel is doubled. Work on *Bit or Beat? Bid or Bead?* in Chapter 18. (See also Chapter 20.)
r	Chinese speakers usually pronounce American *r* as *ä* at the end of a word (*car* sounds like *kaaah*) or almost a *w* in the beginning or middle (*grow* sounds like *gwow*). The tongue should be curled back more, and the *r* produced deep in the throat. (See also Chapter 15.)
th	If you pronounce *th* as *t* or *d* (depending if it's voiced or unvoiced), then you should allow your tongue tip to move about a quarter of an inch forward, so the very tip is just barely between your teeth. Then, from this position you make a sound similar to *t* or *d*. (See also Chapter 13.)
n	Chinese will frequently interchange final *n* and *ng*. The solution is to add a little schwa at the end, just like you do with the *el:* **men**ᵊ, **thing**ᵊ, **call**ᵊ. This will make the tongue position more apparent, as you can see on page 117. (See also Chapter 25.)
sh	Some people pronounce the *sh* in a particularly Chinese-sounding way. It seems that the tongue is too curled back, which changes the sound. Make sure that the tongue is flat, the tongue tip is just at the ridge behind the top teeth, and that only a thin stream of air is allowed to escape. (See also Chapter 21.)
t	American English has a peculiar characteristic in that the *t* sound is, in many cases, pronounced as a *d*. (See also Chapter 14.)

Final Consonants One of the defining characteristics of Chinese speech is that the final consonants are left off (*hold* sounds like *ho*). Whenever possible, make a liaison with the following word. For example, *hold* is difficult to say, so try *hold on = hol dän*. Pay particular attention to Chapter 11.

Location of the Language

Chinese, like American English, is located in the *back of the throat*. The major difference between the two languages is that English requires that the speaker use the *tongue tip* a great deal: *l, th,* and final *t, d, n, l*. Chapter 21, The Ridge, will help a great deal with this.

Japanese

Intonation

Although Chinese and Japanese are both Asian languages and share enormously in their written characters, they are opposites in terms of intonation, word-endings, pronunciation, and liaisons. Whereas the Chinese stress every word and can sound aggressive, Japanese speakers give the impression of stressing no words and sounding timid. Both impressions are, of course, frequently entirely at odds with the actual meaning and intention of the words being spoken. Chinese speakers have the advantage of *knowing* that they have a tonal language, so it is simply a question of transferring this skill to English.

Japanese, on the other hand, almost always insist that the Japanese language "has no intonation." Thus, Japanese speakers in English tend to have a picket fence intonation: | | | | | | | | | | . In reality, the Japanese language does express all kinds of information and emotion through intonation, but this is such a prevalent myth that you may need to examine your own beliefs on the matter. Most likely, you need to use the rubber band extensively in order to avoid volume increases rather than on changing the pitch. (See also Chapter 4.)

One of the major differences between English and Japanese is that there is a fixed word order in English—a verb grid—whereas in Japanese, you can move any word to the head of a sentence and add a topic particle *(wa* or *ga).* Following are increasingly complex verbs with adverbs and helping verbs. Notice that the positions are fixed and do *not* change with the additional words.

	auxiliary	negative	perfect auxiliary	adverb	passive	continuous	main verb
Draw!							Draw!
He draws.							
He							draws.
He does draw.							
He	does						draw.
He is drawing.							
He	is						drawing.
He is not drawing.							
He	is	not					drawing.
He is not always drawing.							
He	is	not		always			drawing.
He is not always being drawn.							
He	is	not		always		being	drawn.
He has not always been drawn.							
He	has	not		always	been		drawn.
He has not always been being drawn.							
He	has	not		always	been	being	drawn.
He will not have always been being drawn.							
He	will	not	have	always	been	being	drawn.

Liaisons

Whereas the Chinese drop word endings, Japanese totally overpronounce them. This is because in the katakana syllabary, there are the five vowels sounds and then consonant-vowel combinations. In order to be successful with word connections, you need to think only of the final consonant in a word and connect that to the next word in the sentence. For example, for *What time is it?* instead of *Whato tāimu izu ito?* connect the two **T**s, and let the other consonants move over to connect with the vowels, *w'tāi mi zit?* Start with the held *t* in Chapter 14 and use that concept for the rest of the final consonants. (See also Chapter 11.)

Written English	The only way to get it is to practice all of the time.
American accent	Thee[(y)]only way də geddidiz də præctisälləv th' time.
Japanese accent	Zä ondee weh tsu getto itto izu tsu pudäctees odu obu zä taimu.

Pronunciation

æ   The **æ** doesn't exist in Japanese; it usually comes out as *ä*, so *last* sounds like *lost*. You need to raise the back of your tongue and drop your jaw to produce this sound. Work on Chapter 3, which drills this distinctively American vowel. (See also Chapters 12, 18, and 20.)

ä   The *ä* sound is misplaced. You have the *ä* sound, but when you see an *o*, you want to say *o*, so *hot* sounds like *hohto* instead of *haht*. Here's one way to deal with it. Write the word *stop* in katakana—the four characters for *su + to + hold + pu*, so when you read it, it sounds like *stohppu*. Change the second character from *to* to *ta*: *su + tä + hold + pu*, it will sound like *stop*. This will give you a good reference point for whenever you want to say *ä* instead of *o*: *impossible, call, long, problem,* etc. (See also Chapters 12, 18, and 20.)

o   You may pronounce the letter *o* as *ä* or *ə* when it should be an *o*, as in *only, most, both.* Make sure that the American *o* sounds like *ou: ounly, moust, bouth.* This holds true for the diphthongs as well — *oi* sounds like *ou-ee.*

toun	tone	nout	note	houm	home
ounli	only	coul	coal	jouk	joke

Another way to develop clear strong vowels instead of nonstandard hybrids is to understand the relation between the American English spelling system and the Japanese katakana sounds. For instance, if you're having trouble with the word *hot,* say *ha, hee, hoo, heh, hoh* in Japanese, and then go back to the first one and convert it from *ha* to *hot* by adding the held *t* (Chapter 14). Say *hot* in Japanese, *atsui,* then add an *h* for *hatsui,* and then drop the *-sui* part, which will leave *hot.* (See also Chapters 12, 18, and 20.)

ə   The schwa is typically overpronounced, based on spelling. Concentrate on smoothing out and reducing the valleys and *ignore spelling!* (See also Chapters 12, 18, and 20.)

ü   Distinguishing tense and lax vowels is difficult, and you'll have to forget spelling for *ū* and *ü*. They both can be spelled with *oo* or *ou,* but the lax vowel *ü* should sound much closer to *i* or *uh*. If you say *book* with a tense vowel, it'll sound like *booque*. It should be much closer to *bick* or *buck.* (See also Chapters 18 and 20.)

i   Similarly, you need to distinguish between *e* and *i,* as in *beat* and *bit,* on page 151. Also, tone down the middle *i* in the multisyllabic words on page 153; otherwise, *similar* **sim'lr** will sound like **see-mee-lär**. Most likely, you overpronounce the lax vowel *i* to *eee,* so that *sit* is mispronounced as *seat*. Reduce the lax *i* almost to a schwa; *sit* should sound like *s't*. In most Japanese dictionaries, the distinction between *i* and *ē* is not made. Practice the four sounds— *bit, beat, bid, bead*—remembering that *tense vowels* indicate that you tense your lips or tongue, while *lax vowels* mean that your lips and tongue are relaxed and the sound is produced in your throat. *Unvoiced* final consonants *(t, s, k, p, ch, f)* mean that the vowel is short and sharp; *voiced* final consonants *(d, z, g, b, j, v)* mean that the vowel is doubled. Work on *"Bit or Beat? Bid or Bead?"* in Chapter 18. (See also Chapter 20.)

	single	double
tense	beat	bead
lax	bit	bid

The Japanese R = The American T

ベリ バラ ビラ	Betty bought a bit of	アイ ニーダ ラァダ タイム	I need a lot of time.
アイ バラ バイク	I bought a bike.	マイ マロウ	my motto
クディ ドゥイッ	Could he do it?	ミリン	meeting
ウィ アラ ゴウ	We ought to go.	アイム ナラン タイム	I'm not on time.

The Japanese *r* is a consonant. This means that it touches at some point in the mouth. Japanese speakers usually trill their *rs* (tapping the ridge behind the top teeth), which makes it sound like a *d* to the American ear. The tongue should be curled back, and the *r* produced deep in the throat—*not* touching the top of the mouth. The Japanese pronunciation of *r* is usually just an *ä* at the end of a word (*car* sounds like *caaah*) or a flap in the beginning or middle (*area* sounds like *eddy-ah*).

l   Japanese speakers often confuse the *el* with *r* or *d,* or drop the schwa, leaving the sound incomplete. (See also Chapter 16.)

th   The *th* sound is mispronounced *s* or *z,* depending if it is voiced or unvoiced. (See also Chapter 13.)

v   **v** is mispronounced either as a simple *bee,* or if you have been working on it, it may be a combination such as *buwee.* You need to differentiate between the four sounds of *p/b/f/v.* The plosives *b/p* pop out; the sibilants *f/v* slide out. *b/v* are voiced; *f/p* are unvoiced. *b/v* are the *least* related pair. The root of the problem is that you need a good, strong **v** first. To the American ear, the way the Japanese say *Mount Fuji* sounds like *Mount Hooji.* Push your bottom lip up with your finger so that it is *outside* your top teeth and make a sharp popping sound. (See also Chapter 19.) Practice these sounds:

F	V	B	F	V	B
fat	*vat*	*bat*	*ferry*	*very*	*berry*
face	*vase*	*base*	*effort*	*ever*	*Ebber*
fear	*veer*	*beer*	*foul*	*vowel*	*bowel*

Once you have the *f* in place, simply allow your vocal cords to vibrate and you will then have a *v.*

	whispered	spoken
popped	P	B
hissed	F	V

w   The *w* is erroneously dropped before *ü,* so *would* is shortened to *ood.* Since you can say *wa, wi, wo* with no problem, use that as a starting point; go from *waaaaa, weeeeeeee, woooooo* to *wüüüüü.* It's more a concept problem than a physical one. (See also Chapter 19.)

n   Japanese will frequently interchange final *n* and *ng.* Adding the little schwa at the end will clear this up by making the tongue position obvious, as in Chapter 16. (See also Chapter 25.)

z   *z* at the beginning of a word sounds like *dz* (*zoo* sounds like *dzoo*). For some reason, this is a tough one. In the syllabary, you read *ta, chi, tsu, teh, toh* for unvoiced and *da, ji, dzu, de, do* for voiced. Try going from unvoiced *sssssue* to *zzzzzzzoo,* and don't pop that *d* in at the last second. (See also Chapter 17.)

si   The *si* combination is mispronounced as *shi,* so *six* comes out as *shicks,* and I don't even want to say what *city* sounds like! Again, this is a syllabary problem. You read the *s* row as *sa, shi, su, seh, soh.* You just need to realize that since you already know how to make a hissing *s* sound, you are capable of making it before the *i* sound. (See also Chapter 18.)

Location of the Language

Japanese is *more forward* in the mouth than American English and there is much *less lip movement.*

Spanish

Intonation

Spanish-speaking people (bearing in mind that there are 22 Spanish-speaking countries) tend to have strong intonation, but it's usually toward the end of a phrase or sentence. It is very clear sometimes in Spanish that a person is taking an entire phrase pattern and imposing it on the English words. This can create a subtle shift in meaning, one that the speaker is completely unaware of. For example,

Spanish	English with a Spanish Pattern	Standard English Pattern
Quiero comer *álgo.*	I want to eat *sóme*thing.	I want to *éat* something.

This is a normal stress pattern in Spanish, but it indicates in English that either you are willing to settle for less than usual or you are contrasting it with the possibility of *nothing.*

Spanish has five pure vowels sounds—*ah, ee, ooh, eh, oh*—and Spanish speakers consider it a point of pride that words are clearly pronounced the way they are written. The lack of the concept of schwa or other reduced vowels may make you overpronounce heavily in English. You'll notice that I said the *concept* of schwa—I think that every language has a schwa, whether it officially recognizes it or not. The schwa is just a neutral vowel sound in an unstressed word and at some point in quick speech in any language, vowels are going to be neutralized. (See also Chapter 4.)

Liaisons

In Spanish, there are strong liaisons—*el hombre* sounds like *eh lombre*—but you'll probably need to rewrite a couple of sentences in order to get away from word-by-word pronunciation. Because consonant clusters in Spanish start with an epsilon sound (*español* for *Spanish, estudiante* for *student*), this habit carries over into English. Rewriting expressions to accommodate the difference will help enormously. (See also Chapter 11.)

With Epsilon	Rewritten	With Epsilon	Rewritten
I estudy	ice tudy	excellent espeech	excellence peech
in espanish	ince panish	my especialty	mice pecialty
their eschool	theirss cool	her espelling	herss pelling

Word Endings

In Spanish, words end in a vowel *(o* or *a),* or the consonants *n, s, r, l, d.* Some people switch *n* and *ng (I käng hear you)* for either *I can hear you* or / *I can't hear you.* Another consequence is that final consonants can get dropped in English, as in *short* (shor) *or friend* (fren). (See also Chapters 14 and 24.)

Pronunciation

With most Spanish speakers, the *s* is almost always unvoiced, *r* is trilled, *l* is too short and lacks a schwa, *d* sounds like a voiced *th,* and *b* and *v* are interchangeable. Spanish speakers also substitute the *ä* sound whenever the letter *a* appears, most often for *œ, ä,* and *ə.* Bear in mind that there are six different pronunciations for the letter *a* as in Chapter 12. Knowing these simple facts will help you isolate and work through your difficulties. (See also Chapter 3.)

The Spanish S = The American S, But...

In Spanish, an *s* always sounds like an *s.* (In some countries, it may be slightly voiced before a voiced consonant such as in *mismo.)* In English, a final *-s* sounds like *z* when it follows a voiced consonant or a vowel (*raise,* raz; *runs,* rənz). The most common verbs in English end in the *z* sound—*is, was, does, has,* etc. Double the preceding vowel and allow your vocal cords to vibrate. (See also Chapter 17.)

The Spanish R = The American T

Beˈri baˈra biˈra	Betty bought a bit of	ai niˈra lara taim	I need a lot of time.
¡Ai Caˈracól!	I caught a cold.	mai maˈrou	my motto
Cuˈri du it?	Could he do it?	miˈrin	meeting
ui aˈra gou	We ought to go.	aim naˈran taim	I'm not on time.

In Spanish, *r* is a consonant. This means that it touches at some point in the mouth. Spanish speakers usually roll their *r*s (touching the ridge behind the top teeth), which makes it sound like a *d* to the American ear. The tongue should be curled back, and the *r* produced deep in the throat—*not* touching the top of the mouth. The Spanish pronunciation of *r* is usually the written vowel and a flap *r* at the end of a word (*feeler* is pronounced like *feelehd)* or a flap in the beginning or middle (*throw* sounds like *tdoh)*. In English, the pronunciation of *r* doesn't change if it's spelled *r* or *rr*. (See also Chapter 15.)

The -ed Ending

You may have found yourself wondering how to pronounce *asked* or *hoped*; if you came up with *as-ked* or *ho-ped,* you made a logical and common mistake. There are three ways to pronounce the *-ed* ending in English, depending what the previous letter is. If it's voiced, *-ed* sounds like *d: played*, pleid. If it's unvoiced, *-ed* sounds like *t: laughed*, læft. If the word ends in *t* or *d*, *-ed* sounds like *əd: patted*, pædəd. (See also Chapter 14.)

The Final T

The *t* at the end of a word should not be heavily aspirated. Let your tongue go to the *t* position, and then just stop. It should sound like *hät*, not *hä*, or *häch*, or *häts*. (See also Chapter 14.)

The Spanish D = The American Th (voiced)

The Spanish *d* in the middle and final positions is a fricative *d* (*coda* and *sed*). If you are having trouble with the English *th*, substitute in a Spanish *d.* First, contrast *cara* and *cada* in Spanish, and then note the similarities between *cam* and *caught a,* and *cada* and *father.* (See also Chapters 3 and 13.)

cada	*father*		*beid*	*bathe*

The Spanish of Spain Z or C = The American Th (unvoiced)

The letters *z* and *c* in most Spanish-speaking countries sound like *s* in English (not in Andalusia, however). The *z* and *c* from Spain, on the other hand, are equivalent to the American unvoiced *th*. When you want to say *both* in English, say *bouz* with an accent from Spain. (See also Chapters 3 and 13.)

bouz	*both*	*gracias*	*grathias*	*uiz*	*with*

The Spanish I = The American Y (not j)

In most Spanish-speaking countries, the *y* and *ll* sounds are equivalent to the American *y*, as in *yes* or in liaisons such as *the(y)other one.* (See also Chapter 20.) *Jes, I jelled at jou jesterday* can be heard in some countries such as Argentina for *Yes, I yelled at you yesterday*.

hielo	*yellow (not jello)*	*ies*	*yes*	*iu*	*you*

The Doubled Spanish A Sound = The American O, AL, or AW Spelling

Because of spelling, the *ä* sound can easily be misplaced. The *ä* sound exists in Spanish, but it is represented with the letter *a*. When you see the letter *o,* you pronounce it *o,* so *hot* sounds like *hoht* instead of *haht*. Remember, most of the time, the letter *o* is pronounced *ah*. You can take a sound that already exists in Spanish, such as *jaat* (whether it means anything or not) and say it with your native accent — *jaat* with a Spanish accent more or less equals *hot* in English. This will give you a good reference point for *ä* instead of *o: astronomy, call, long, progress,* etc. Focus on Chapter 12, differentiating æ, ä, ə.

jaat	*hot*	*caal*	*call*	*saa*	*saw*

The Spanish O = The American OU

You may pronounce the letter *o* as *ä* or *ə* when it really should be an *o,* as in *only, most, both.* Make sure that the American *o* sounds like *ou: ounly, moust, bouth.* This holds true for the diphthongs as well — *oi* sounds like *ou-ee.* (See also Chapter 20.)

ounli	*only*	*joup*	*hope*	*nout*	*note*

æ	The **æ** sound doesn't exist in Spanish, so it usually comes out as *ä,* so *last* sounds like *lost.* You need to work on Chapter 12, which drills this distinctively American vowel. (See also Chapters 18 and 20.)
ə	The schwa is typically overpronounced, based on spelling. Work on Chapter 4, American Intonation and Chapter 12, Cat? Caught? Cut?. If your intonation peaks are strong and clear enough, then your valleys will be sufficiently reduced as well. Concentrate on smoothing out and reducing the valleys and *ignore spelling!* (See also Chapters 18 and 20.)
ü	The **ü** sound is generally overpronounced to *ooh.* Again, spelling is the culprit. Words such as *smooth, choose,* and *too* are spelled with two *o*'s and are pronounced with a long *ū* sound, but other words, such as *took* and *good,* are spelled with two *o*'s but are pronounced halfway between *ih* and *uh;* **tük** and **güd.** (See also Chapters 18 and 20.)
i	Spanish speakers overpronounce the lax vowel *i* to *eee,* so *sit* comes out as *seat.* In most Spanish dictionaries, the distinction between *i* and *ē* is not made. Practice the four sounds—*bit, beat, bid, bead*—remembering that *tense vowels* indicate that you tense your lips or tongue, while *lax vowels* mean that your lips and tongue are relaxed and the sound is produced in your throat. *Unvoiced* final consonants *(t, s, k, p, ch, f)* mean that the vowel is short and sharp; *voiced* final consonants *(d, z, g, b, j, v)* mean that the vowel is doubled. Work on *"Bit or Beat? Bid or Bead?"* in Chapter 18. Reduce the soft *i* to a schwa; *sit* should sound like *s't.* (See also Chapter 20.)

	single	**double**
tense	beat	bead
lax	bit	bid

Also, watch out for cognates such as *similar,* pronounced **see-mee-lär** in Spanish, and **si•m'•lr** in American English. Many of them appear in the Middle "I" List on page 153.

I	The Spanish *I* lacks a schwa, leaving the sound short and incomplete to the American ear. Contrast similar words in the two languages and notice the differences. (See also Chapter 16.)

Written	**Pronounced**	**Spanish**
ball	*bä-uhl*	*bal*

v	A Spanish speaker usually pronounces *v* and *b* the same (*I have trouble with my bowels* instead of *I have trouble with my vowels*). You need to differentiate between the four sounds of *p/b/f/v.* The plosives *b/p* pop out; the sibilants *f/v* slide out. *b/v* are voiced; *f/p* are unvoiced; *b/v* are the *least* related pair. Push your bottom lip up with your finger so that it is *outside* your top teeth and make a sharp popping sound. (See also Chapter 19.) Practice these sounds:

F	V	B	F	V	B
fat	*vat*	*bat*	*ferry*	*very*	*berry*
face	*vase*	*base*	*effort*	*ever*	*Ebber*
fear	*veer*	*beer*	*foul*	*vowel*	*bowel*

Once you have the *f* in place, simply allow your vocal cords to vibrate and you will then have a *v*.

	whispered	spoken
popped	P	B
hissed	F	V

n	The final *n* is often mispronounced *ng* — *meng* rather than *men*. Put a tiny schwa at the end to finish off the *n*, **men**ᵊ or **thing**ᵊ, as explained in Chapter 16. (See also Chapter 25.)
w	The *w* sound in Spanish can sound like a *gw (I gwould do it)*. You need to practice *g* in the throat, rounding your lips for *w*. You can also substitute in a Spanish *ū*, as in *will* **uil**. (See also Chapter 19.)
h	The Spanish *h* is silent, as in *hombre*, but Spanish speakers often use a stronger fricative than Americans would. The American *h* is equivalent to the Spanish *j*, but the air coming out shouldn't pass through a constricted throat—it's like you're steaming a mirror—*hat, he, his, her, whole, hen*, etc. In some Spanish-speaking countries, *they* is fricative and in others it is not. Also, there are many words in which the *h* is completely silent, as in *hour, honest, herb*, as well as in liaisons with object pronouns such as *her* and *him (tell her* sounds like *teller)*. (See also Chapter 25.)
ch	In order to make the *ch* sound different from the *sh*, put a *t* in front of the *ch*. Practice the difference between *wash* **wäsh** / *watch* **watch**, or *sharp* **sharp** / *charm* **chärm**. (See also Chapter 21.)
p	The American *p* is more strongly plosive than its Spanish counterpart. Put your hand in front of your mouth — you should feel a strong burst of air. Practice with *Peter picked a peck of pickled peppers*. (See also Chapter 19.)
j	In order to make a clear *j* sound, put a *d* in front of the *j*. Practice *George* **djordj**. (See also Chapter 21.)
sh	There was a woman from Spain who used to say, "Es imposible que se le quite el acento a uno," pronouncing it, "Esh imposhible que se le quite el athento a uno." In her particular accent, *s* sounded like *sh*, which would transfer quite well to standard American English. What it also means is that many people claim it is impossible to change the accent, but as we all know, that is not the case.

Location of the Language

Spanish is very far forward with much stronger use of the lips.

Indian

Intonation

Of the many and varied Indian dialects (Hindi, Telugu, Punjabi, etc.), there is a common intonation transfer to English—sort of a curly, rolling cadence that flows along with little relation to meaning. It is difficult to get the average Indian learner to change pitch. Not that people are unwilling to try or difficult to deal with; on the contrary, in my experience of working with people from India, I find them incredibly pleasant and agreeable. This is part of the problem, however. People agree in concept, in principle, in theory, in every aspect of the matter, yet when they *say* the sentence, the pitch remains unchanged.

I think that what happens is that, in standard American English, we raise the pitch on the beat, Indians drop their pitch on the beat. Also, the typical Indian voice is much higher pitched than Americans are accustomed to hearing. In particular, you should work on the voice quality exercise in Chapter 1.

Of the three options *(volume, length, pitch),* you can raise the volume easily, but it doesn't sound very good. Since volume is truly the least desirable and the most offensive to the listener, and since pitch has to be worked on over time, lengthening the stressed word is a good stopgap measure. Repeating the letter of a stressed word will help a lot toward changing a rolling *odabah odabah odabah* intonation to something resembling peaks and valleys.

The ***oooonly*** way to ***geeeeeee***didiz to ***prœœœœœœœœœœœœek***tis all of the time.

One thing that works for pitch is to work on the little sound that children make when they make a mistake, "uh-oh!" The first sound is on a distinctly higher level than the second one. Because it's a nonsense syllable, it's easier to work with as you're focusing on pure pitch change and not a real word.

Since so much emotion is conveyed through intonation, it's vital to work with the various tone shifts in Chapter 1.

It's necessary to focus on placing the intonation on the correct words (nouns, compound nouns, descriptive phases, etc.), as well as contrasting, negating, listing, questioning, and exclaiming.

Intonation is also important in numbers, which are typically difficult for Indian speakers. There are both intonation and pronunciation between 13 and 30. The number 13 should sound like *thr-**teen**,* while 30 sounds like ***thr-dee;*** 14 is *for-**teen**,* and 40 is ***for-dee**.* (See also Chapter 4.)

Liaisons

Liaisons shouldn't be much of a problem for you once the pattern is pointed out and reinforced. (See also Chapter 11.)

Pronunciation

One way to have an accent is to leave out sounds that should be there, but the other way is to put in sounds that don't exist in that language. Indians bring a rich variety of voiced consonants to English that contribute to the heavy, rolling effect.

t For the initial *t* alone, there are eight varieties, ranging from plosive to almost swallowed. In American English, *t* at the top of a staircase is a sharp *t*, and *t* in the middle is a soft *d*. Indians tend to reverse this, using the popping British *t* in the middle position (**water**) and a *t*-like sound in the beginning. (*I need two* sounds like *I need doo*). The solution is to substitute *your th*— it will sound almost perfect (*I need thoo* sounds just like *I need two*). Another way is to separate the *t* from the rest of the word and whisper it. **T + aim = time**. Bit by bit, you can bring the whispered, sharply popped *t* closer to the body of the word. A third way is to imagine that it is actually *ts,* so you are saying *tsäim,* which will come out sounding like *time*. (See also Chapter 14.)

T	D	T	D
tennis	*Dennis*	*ten*	*den*
time	*dime*	*to*	*do*

The final *t* is typically too plosive and should be held just at the position before the air is expelled.

p This is similar to the initial *t*, in that you probably voice the unvoiced *p* so it sounds like a *b*. Start with the *m*, progress to the *b*, and finally whisper the *p* sound. (See also Chapter 19.)

M	B	P	M	B	P
men	*Ben*	*pen*	*mull*	*bull*	*pull*
mail	*bail*	*pail*	*mossy*	*bossy*	*possible*
met	*bet*	*pet*	*mile*	*bile*	*pile*

æ	The æ sound usually sounds like *ä.* You might refer to *the last class,* but it will sound like *the lost closs.* You should raise the back of your tongue, and make a noise similar to that of a lamb. (See also Chapters 12, 18, and 20.)

Because of spelling, the *ä* sound can easily be misplaced. The *ä* sound exists in the Indian languages, but is represented with the letter *a.* When you see the letter *o,* you pronounce it *o,* so *John* sounds like *Joan* instead of *Jahn.* Remember, most of the time, the letter *o* is pronounced *ah.* You can take a sound that already exists in your language, such as *tak* (whether it means anything or not), and say it with your native accent—*tak* with an Indian accent more or less equals *talk* in English. This will give you a good reference point for whenever you want to say *ä* instead of *o: astronomy, call, long, progress,* etc. Focus on Chapter 12, differentiating *æ, ä, ə.* (See also Chapters 12, 18, and 20.)

ä

h<u>aa</u>t	h<u>o</u>t	c<u>aa</u>l	c<u>a</u>ll	s<u>aa</u> s<u>a</u>w

o	You may pronounce the letter *o* as *ä* or *ə* when it really should be an *ō,* as in *only, most, both.* Make sure that the American *o* sounds like *ou, ounly, moust, bouth.* This holds true for the diphthongs as well—*oi* should sound like *ou-ee.* (See also Chapters 12, 18, and 20.)

<u>ou</u>nli	<u>o</u>nly	h<u>ou</u>p	h<u>o</u>pe	n<u>ou</u>t	n<u>o</u>te

r Indians tend to have a British *r,* which means that it is either a flap at the beginning or middle of a word, or it is reduced to *ä* at the end of a word. You need to understand that the American *r* is not a consonant (i.e., it doesn't touch at any two points in the mouth)—it is much closer to a vowel in that the tongue curls back to shape the air flow. (See also Chapter 15.)

th	The American *th,* both voiced and unvoiced, usually sounds like a *d* when said by an Indian speaker: *thank you* sounds like *dank you.* Also you must distinguish between a voiced and an unvoiced *th.* The voiced ones are the extremely common, everyday sounds—*the, this, that, these, those, them, they, there, then;* unvoiced are less common words—*thing, third, Thursday, thank, thought.* (See also Chapter 13.)

v Indians usually reverse *v/w: These were reversed > Dese ver rewersed.* It should be a simple thing to simply reverse them back, but for some reason, it's more problematic than that. Try substituting in the other word in actual sentences. (See also Chapter 19.)

He vent to the store.	*He closed the went.*
I'll be back in avile.	*It was a while attack.*

Think of the *w,* a "double *u",* or even as a "single *u";* so in place of the *w* in *want,* you'd pronounce it *oo-änt.* There can be NO contact between the teeth and the lips for *w,* as this will turn it into a consonant. Feel the *f/v* consonants, and then put *oo* in place of the *w (oo–ile* for *while).* Conversely, you can substitute *ferry* for *very* so that it won't come out as *wary.* Because of the proximity of the consonants, *f* and *v* are frequently interchanged in English (**belief/believe, wolf/wolves**). Consequently, *It was ferry difficult* is easier to understand than *It was wary difficult.* Practice Exercise 19-1 to distinguish among *p/b, f/v,* and *w.*

F	**V**	**W**		**F**	**V**	**W**
fence	*vent*	*went (oo-ent)*		*first*	*verse*	*worse (oo-rs)*
face	*vase*	*waste (oo-aste)*		*file*	*vile*	*while (oo-ile)*

L	The L is too heavy, too drawn out, and is missing the schwa component. (See also Chapter 16.)

Location of the Language

Far forward and uttered through rounded lips.

Russian

Intonation

Russian intonation seems to start at a midpoint and then cascade down. The consequence is that it sounds very downbeat. You definitely need to add a lilt to your speech—more peaks, as there're already *plenty* of valleys. To the Russian ear, English can have a harsh, almost metallic sound due to the perception of nasal vibrations in some vowels. This gives a clarity to American speech that allows it to be heard over a distance. When Russian speakers try to imitate that "loudness" and clarity, without the American speech music, instead of the intended pronunciation, it can sound aggressive. On the other hand, when Russians do not try to speak "loud and clear," it can end up sounding vaguely depressed. (See also Chapters 1 and 4.)

Liaisons

Word connections should be easy since you have the same fluid word/sound boundaries as in American English. The phrase *dosvedänyə* sounds like *dos vedanya,* whereas you know it as *do svedanya.* It won't be difficult to run your words together once you realize it's the same process in English. (See also Chapter 11.)

Pronunciation

Although you have ten vowels in Russian, there are quite a few other vowels out there waiting for you.

æ The æ sound doesn't exist in Russian, so *last* is demoted to the lax ɛ, *lest.* In the same way, Russian speakers reduce *actually* to *ekchually,* or *matter* to *metter.* Drop your jaw and raise the back of your tongue to make a noise like a goat: æ! Work on Chapter 12, which drills this distinctively American vowel. (See also Chapters 18 and 20.)

ä The ä sound exists in Russian, but is represented with the letter *a.* Bear in mind that there are six different pronunciations of the letter *a,* as you can see on page 175. Because of spelling, the ä sound can easily be misplaced. When you see the letter *o,* you pronounce it *o,* so *job* sounds like *jobe* instead of *jääb.* Remember, most of the time, the letter *o* is pronounced *ah.* Take a sound that already exists in Russian, such as *baab* (whether it means anything or not) and say it with your native accent; *baab* with a Russian accent more or less equals *Bob* in English. This will give you a good reference point for whenever you want to say ä instead of *o: biology, call, long, problem,* etc. Focus on Chapter 13, differentiating æ, ä, ə. (See also Chapters 18 and 20.)

o Conversely, you may pronounce the letter *o* as ä or ə when it really should be an ō, as in *only, most, both* (which are exceptions to the spelling rules). Make sure that the American *o* sounds like **ou**: *ounly, moust, bouth.* This holds true for the diphthongs as well — *oi* should sound like *ou-ee.* (See also Chapters 12, 18, and 20.)

| t<u>ou</u>n | t<u>o</u>ne | n<u>ou</u>t | n<u>o</u>te | h<u>ou</u>m | h<u>o</u>me |
| <u>ou</u>nli | <u>o</u>nly | c<u>ou</u>l | c<u>oa</u>l | OK | <u>ou</u>kei |

ə The schwa is often overpronounced to ä, which is why you might sound a little like Count Dracula when he says, *I vänt to säck your bläd* instead of *I wänt to sək your bləd.* Don't drop your jaw for the neutral schwa sound; it's like the final syllable of *spasiba,* sp'sibə, not sp'sibä. Similarly, in English, the schwa in an unstressed syllable is completely neutral; *famous* is not fay-moos, but rather fay-m's. (See also Chapters 12, 18, and 20.)

ü Distinguishing tense and lax vowels is difficult, and you'll have to forget spelling for *u* and *ü.* They both can be spelled with *oo* or *ou,* but the lax vowel ü should sound much closer to *i* or *uh.* If you say *book* and *could* with a tense vowel, it'll sound like *booque* and *cooled.* It should be much closer to *bick* or *buck.* (See also Chapters 18 and 20.)

i	Similarly, you need to distinguish between *ee* and *i*, as in *beat* and *bit* (Chapter 20), as *his big sister* is mispronounced as *heez beeg seester* or with the extra **y**, *hyiz byig systr*. Frequently, Russian speakers transpose these two sounds, so while the lax vowel in *his big sister* is overpronounced to *heez beeg seester*, the tense vowel in *She sees Lisa* is relaxed to *shi siz lissa*. Also, tone down the middle *i* in the multisyllabic words on page 153; otherwise, *similar*, **sim'lr** will sound like **see-mee-lär**. (See also Chapter 18.)
-y	Russian speakers often mispronounce the final *-y* as a short *-i*, so that *very funny* sounds like *verə funnə*. Extend the final sound out with three *e*'s: *vereee funneee*. (See also Chapter 20.)

The Russian R = The American T

The Cyrillic *r* is a consonant. This means that it touches at some point in the mouth. Russian speakers usually roll their *r*s (touching the ridge behind the top teeth), which makes it sound like a *d* to the American ear. The American *r* is not really a consonant anymore—the tongue should be curled back, and the *r* produced deep in the throat—*not* touching the top of the mouth. The Russian pronunciation of *r* is usually the written vowel and a flap *r* at the end of a word (*feeler* sounds like *feelehd*) or a flap in the beginning or middle (*throw* sounds like *tdoh*). (See also Chapter 14.)

бэри бара бира	Betty bought a bit of	аин ира лара таим	I need a lot of time.
аи бара баик	I bought a bike.	маи мароу	my motto
уэира сэкен	Wait a second.	мирин	meeting
уи ара гоу	We ought to go.	аин наран таим	I'm not on time.
юв гара пэира гэрит	You've got to pay to get it.	бюрафли	beautifully

Another major point with the American *r* is that sometimes the preceding vowel is pronounced, and sometimes it isn't. When you say *wire*, there's a clear vowel plus the *r*—wy•r; however, with *first*, there is simply no preceding vowel. It's *frst*, not *feerst* (Exercises 15-2 and 15-3).

t	At the beginning of a word, the American *t* needs to be more plosive—you should feel that you are "spitting air." At the end of the word, it is held back and not aspirated. (See also Chapter 14.)
eh	One of the most noticeable characteristics of a Russian accent is the little *y* that is slipped in with the *eh* sound. This makes a sentence such as *Kevin has held a cat* sound like *Kyevin hyes hyeld a kyet*. This is because you are using the back of the tongue to "push" the vowel sound out of the throat. In English, you need to just allow the air to pop through directly after the consonant, between the back of the tongue and the soft palate: **k•æ**, not **k•yæ**. (See also Chapters 18 and 20.)
h	Another strong characteristic of Russian speech is a heavily fricative *h*. Rather than closing the back of the throat, let the air flow unimpeded between the soft palate and the back of your tongue. Be sure to keep your tongue flat so you don't push out the little *y* mentioned above. Often, you can simply drop the *h* to avoid the whole problem. For *I have to*, instead of *I hhyef to*, change it to *I y'v to*. (See also Chapter 25.)
v	The **v** is often left unvoiced, so the common word *of* sounds like *oaf*. Allow your vocal cords to vibrate. (See also Chapter 19.)
sh	There are two *sh* sounds in Russian, ш and щ. The second one is closer to the American *sh*, as in щиуз for *shoes*, not шуз. (See also Chapter 21.)
th	You may find yourself replacing the voiced and unvoiced *th* sounds with *t/d* or *s/z*, saying *dä ting* or *zä sing* instead of *the thing*. This means that your tongue tip is about a half inch too far back on the alveolar ridge (the bumps behind the teeth). Press your tongue against the *back* of the teeth and try to say *dat*. Because of the tongue position, it will sound like *that*. (See also Chapter 13.)

-ing	Often the *-ing* ending is not pronounced as a single *ng* sound, but rather as *n* and *g,* or just *n.* There are three nasals, *m* (lips), *n* (tongue tip and alveolar ridge), and *ng* (soft palate and the back of the tongue). It is not a hard consonant like *g,* but rather a soft nasal. (See also Chapter 24.)

French

Intonation

The French are, shall we say, a linguistically proud people. More than working on accent or pronunciation; you need to "believe" first. There is an inordinate amount of psychological resistance here, but the good thing is that, in my experience, you are very outspoken about it. Unlike the Japanese, who will just keep quiet, or Indians, who agree with everything with sometimes no discernible change in their speech patterns, my French students have quite clearly pointed out how difficult, ridiculous, and unnatural American English is. If the American pattern is a stairstep, the Gallic pattern is a fillip at the end of each phrase. (See also Chapter 4.)

Hello, *my* name is Pierre. I live in *Par*is. Al*lo,* my name is *Pierre.* I live in Par*ee.* I ride the sub*way.*

Liaisons

The French either invented liaisons or raised them to an art form. You may not realize, though, that the rules that bind your phrases together, also do in English. Just remember, in French, it is spelled *ce qu'ils disent,* but you've heard it pronounced colloquially a thousand times, *skidiz!* (See also Chapter 11.)

Pronunciation

th	In French, the *tee aitch* is usually mispronounced *s* or *f,* as in *sree or free* for *three.* (See also Chapters 3 and 13.)
r	The French *r* is in the same location as the American one, but it is more like a consonant. For the French *r,* the back of the tongue rasps against the soft palate, but for the American *r,* the throat balloons out, like a bullfrog. (See also Chapter 15.)
æ	The *æ* sound doesn't exist in French, so it usually comes out as *ä* or *ɛ*; consequently, *class* sounds like *closs,* and *cat* sounds like *ket.* The *in-* prefix, however, sounds like a nasalized *æ.* Say *in* in French, and then denasalize it to *æd.* Work on Chapter 12, which drills this distinctively American vowel. (See also Chapters 12, 18, and 20.)
ə	The schwa is typically overpronounced, based on spelling. Work on Chapter 1, for the rhythm patterns that form this sound, and Chapter 12, for its actual pronunciation. If your intonation peaks are strong and clear enough, then your valleys will be sufficiently reduced as well. Concentrate on smoothing out and reducing the valleys and *ignore spelling!* (See also Chapters 18 and 20.)
ü	The *ü* sound is generally overpronounced to *ooh,* which leads to *could* being mispronounced as *cooled.* Again, spelling is the culprit. Words such as *smooth, choose,* and *too* are spelled with two *o*'s and are pronounced with a long *ū* sound, but other words such as *look* and *took* are spelled with two *o*'s but are pronounced halfway between *ih* and *uh*: *lük* and *tük. Leuc* and *queuc* with a French accent are very close. (See also Chapters 18 and 20.)

French speakers overpronounce the lax vowel *i* to *eee,* so *sit* comes out like *seat.* Reduce the soft *i* to a schwa; *sit* should sound like *s't.* In most French dictionaries, the distinction between *i* and *ē* is not made. Practice the four sounds—*bit, beat, bid, bead*—remembering that *tense vowels* indicate that you tense your lips or tongue, while *lax vowels* mean that your lips and tongue are relaxed, and the sound is produced in your throat. *Unvoiced* final consonants (*t, s, k, p, ch, f*) mean that the vowel is short and sharp; *voiced* final consonants (*d, z, g, b, j, v*) mean that the vowel is doubled. Work on *"Bit or Beat? Bid or Bead?"* in Chapter 18.

	single	double
tense	beat	bead
lax	bit	bid

Also, watch out for cognates such as *typique/typical,* pronounced **tee•peek** in French, and **ti•p'•kl** in American English. Many of them appear in the Middle "I" List in Chapter 18. (See also Chapter 20.)

ä Because of spelling, the *ä* sound can easily be misplaced. The *ä* sound exists in French, but is represented with the letter *a.* When you see the letter *o,* you pronounce it *o,* so *lot* sounds like *loht* instead of *laht.* Remember, most of the time, the letter *o* is pronounced *ah.* You can take a sound that already exists in French, such as *laat* (whether it means anything or not) and say it with your native accent — *laat* with a French accent more or less equals *lot* in English. This will give you a good reference point for whenever you want to say *ä* instead of *o*: *astronomy, call, long, progress,* etc. Focus on Chapter 12, differentiating *æ, ä, ə.* (See also Chapters 18 and 20.)

h<u>aa</u>t   *h<u>o</u>t*   *c<u>oa</u>l* *c<u>a</u>ll*   *s<u>aa</u>*   *s<u>aw</u>*

o On the other hand, you may pronounce the letter *o* as *ä* or *ə* when it really should be an *o,* as in *only, most, both.* Make sure that the American *o* sounds like *ou*: *ounly, moust, bouth.* This holds true for the diphthongs as well—*oi* sounds like *o-u-ee.* (See also Chapters 12, 18, and 20.)

<u>ou</u>nli   *<u>o</u>nly*   *l<u>ou</u>n l<u>oa</u>n*   *n<u>ou</u>t*   *n<u>o</u>te*

h French people have the most fascinating floating *h.* Part of the confusion comes from the *hache aspiré,* which is totally different from the American *aitch.* Allow a small breath of air to escape with each *aitch.* (See also Chapter 25.)

in- The nasal combination *in-* and *-en* are often pronounced like *œñ* and *äñ,* so *interesting* **in**tr' sting sounds like *æñteresting,* and enjoy, ɛn**joy** and *attention,* ətɛnshən sound like *äñjoy* and *ätäñseeõn.* (See also Chapters 3, 18, and 20.)

Location in the Mouth
Very far forward, with extensive use of the lips.

German

Intonation
Germans have what Americans consider a stiff, rather choppy accent. The great similarity between the two languages lies in the two-word phrases, where a **hót**dog is food and a *hot* **dóg** is an overheated chihuahua. In German, a *thimble* is called a **fingerhut,** literally a *finger hat,* and a *red* **hat** would be a *rote* **hut,** with the same intonation and meaning shift as in English. (See also Chapter 4.)

Liaisons

German word connections are also quite similar to American ones. Consider how *In einem Augenblick* actually is pronounced *ineine maugenblick.* The same rules apply in both languages. (See also Chapter 11.)

Pronunciation

j	A salient characteristic of German is the unvoicing of *j*, so you might say *I am Cherman* instead of *I am German.* Work with the other voiced pairs (*p/b, s/z, k/g*) and then go on to *ch/j* while working with **J** words such *as just, Jeff, German, enjoy, age,* etc. (See also Chapter 21.)
w	Another difference is the transposing of *v* and *w*. When you say *Volkswagen,* it most likely comes out *Folksvagen.* It works to rewrite the word as *Wolksvagen,* which then will come out as we say *Volkswagen.* A German student was saying that she was a *wisiting scholar,* which didn't make much sense — say *wisiding* with a German accent — it'll sound like *visiting* in American English. (See also Chapter 19.)
th	In German, the *tee aitch* is usually pronounced *t* or *d*. (See also Chapters 13 and 14.)
r	The German *r* is in the same location as the American one, but it is more like a consonant. For the German *r*, the back of the tongue rasps against the soft palate, but for the American *r*, the throat balloons out, like a bullfrog. (See also Chapter 15.)
æ	The æ sound doesn't exist in German, so it usually comes out as *ä* or *ɛ*, so *class* sounds like *closs.* You need to work on Chapter 12, which drills this distinctively American vowel. (See also Chapters 12, 18, and 20.)
ə	The schwa is typically overpronounced, based on spelling. Work on Chapter 4, for the rhythm patterns that form this sound, and Chapter 3, for its actual pronunciation. If your intonation peaks are strong and clear enough, then your valleys will be sufficiently reduced as well. Concentrate on smoothing out and reducing the valleys and *ignore spelling!* (See also Chapters 12, 18, and 20.)
ü	The *ü* sound is generally overpronounced to *ooh*, which leads to *could* being mispronounced as *cooled.* Again, spelling is the culprit. Words such as *smooth, choose,* and *too* are spelled with two *o*'s and are pronounced with a long *u* sound, but other words such as *look* and *took* are spelled with two *o*'s but are pronounced halfway between *ih* and *uh*: *lük* and *tük*. (See also Chapters 18 and 20.)
i	German speakers overpronounce the lax vowel *i* to *eee*, so *sit* comes out like *seat.* Reduce the soft *z* to a schwa; *sit* should sound like *s't*. In most German dictionaries, the distinction between *i* and *ē* is not made. Practice the four sounds—*bit, beat, bid, bead*—remembering that *tense vowels* indicate that you tense your lips or tongue, while *lax vowels* mean that your lips and tongue are relaxed, and the sound is produced in your throat. *Unvoiced* final consonants (*t, s, k, p, ch, f*) mean that the vowel is short and sharp; *voiced* final consonants (*d, z, g, b, j, v*) mean that the vowel is doubled. Work on *"Bit or Beat? Bid or Bead?"* in Chapter 18.

	single	double
tense	beat	bead
lax	bit	bid

Also, watch out for words such as *chemical/Chemikalie*, pronounced **ke•mi•kä•lee•eh** in German, and **kɛmək°l** in American English. Many of them appear in the Middle "I" List in Chapter 18.

ä
Because of spelling, the *ä* sound can easily be misplaced. The *ä* sound exists in German, but is represented with the letter *a*. When you see the letter *o*, you pronounce it *o*, so *lot* sounds like *loht* instead of *laht*. Remember, most of the time, the letter *o* is pronounced *ah*. You can take a sound that already exists in German, such as *laat* (whether it means anything or not), and say it with your native accent — *laat* with a German accent more or less equals *lot* in American English. This will give you a good reference point for whenever you want to say *ä* instead of *o*: *astronomy, call, long, progress,* etc. Focus on Chapter 12, differentiating *æ, ä, ə*. (See also Chapters 12, 18, and 20.)

| *h<u>aa</u>t* | *hot* | *c<u>aa</u>l* | *call* | *s<u>aa</u>* | *saw* |

o
German speakers tend to use the British *o*, which sounds like *ɛo* rather than the American *ou*. Make sure that the American *o*, in *only, most, both,* sounds like *ou, ounly, moust, bouth*. This holds true for the diphthongs as well — *oi* sounds like *o-u-ee*. (See also Chapters 12, 18, and 20.)

| *<u>ou</u>nli* | *only* | *h<u>ou</u>p* | *hope* | *n<u>ou</u>t* | *note* |

Korean

Intonation

While English is a stress-timed language, Korean is a syllable-timed language. Korean is more similar to Japanese than Chinese in that the pitch range of Korean is also narrow, almost flat, and not rhythmical. Many Korean speakers tend to stress the wrong word or syllable, which changes the meaning in English (*They'll sell **fish*** and *They're **sel**fish.*) Korean speakers tend to add a vowel to the final consonant after a long vowel: *b/v (babe/beibu* and *wave/weibu), k/g (make/meiku* and *pig/pigu),* and *d (made/meidu).* Koreans also insert a vowel after *sh/ch/j (wash/washy, church/churchy, bridge/brijy),* and into consonant clusters *(bread/bureau).* It is also a common problem to devoice final voiced consonants, so that *dog* can be mispronounced as either *dogu* or *dock.* All this adversely influences the rhythm patterns of spoken English. The different regional intonation patterns for Korean interrogatives also affect how questions come across in English. In standard Korean, the intonation goes up for both *yes/no* questions and *wh* questions (who?, what?, where?, when?, why?); in the Kyungsang dialect, it drops for both; and in the Julia dialect, it drops and goes up for both. In American English, the intonation goes up for *yes/no* and drops down for *wh* questions. (See also Chapter 4.)

Word Connections

Unlike Japanese or Chinese, word connections are common in Korean. The seven final consonants (*m, n, ng, l, p, t, k*) slide over when the following word begins with a vowel. Although a *t* between two vowels in American English should be voiced (*latter/ladder* sound the same), a frequent mistake Korean speakers make, however, is to also voice *k* or *p* between two vowels, so *back up, check up,* and *weekend* are mispronounced as *bagup, chegup,* and *weegend;* and *cap is* sounds like *cab is.* Another liaison problem occurs with a plosive consonant (*p/b, t/d, k/g*) just before a nasal (*m, n, ng*)—Koreans often nasalize the final consonant, so that *pick me up* and *pop music* sound like *ping me up* and *pom music.* (See also Chapter 11.)

Pronunciation

l/r
At the beginning of a word or in a consonant cluster, *l* and *r* are confused, with both being pronounced like the American *d*, which can be written with the letter *t* (*glass* or *grass* sound like either *gurasu* or *gudasu,* and *light* or *right* sound like *raitu* or *daitu*). The final *r* is usually dropped (*car/kaa*). (See also Chapters 15 and 16.)

f The English *f* does not exist in Korean, so people tend to substitute a *p*. This leads to words such as *difficult* sounding like *typical* to the American ear. When a Korean speaker says a word from the F column, it's likely to be heard by Americans as being from the P column. (See also Chapter 19.)

F	P		F	P		F	P
difficult	typical		coffee	copy		half and	happen
calf	cap		deaf	tape		Steph	step
left	leapt		cough	cop		laugh	lap
often	open		fat	pet		informant	important
stuff	stop		after	apter		fossil	possible
enough	and up		friend	planned		free	pre—

æ The exact **æ** sound doesn't exist in Korean; it's close to ɛ, so *bat* sounds like *bet*. You need to raise the back of your tongue and drop your jaw to produce this sound. Work on Chapter 3, which drills this distinctively American vowel. (See also Chapters 12, 18, and 20.)

ä The *ä* sound is misplaced. You have the *ä* sound when you laugh *hahaha* 하하하, but when you see an *o*, you want to say *ō*, as in *hohoho* 호호호, so *John* sounds like *Joan* instead of *Jähn*. If you're having trouble with the word *hot,* say *ha*핫 in Korean, and then add a very slight *t*. (See also Chapters 12, 18, and 20.)

o You may pronounce the letter *o* as *ä* or *ə* when it really should be an *ō*, as in *only, most, both*. Make sure that the American *o* sounds like *ou: ounly, moust, bouth*. This holds true for the diphthongs as well — *oi* sounds like *ou-ee*. (See also Chapters 12, 18, and 20.)

t<u>ou</u>n	t<u>o</u>ne	n<u>ou</u>t	n<u>o</u>te	h<u>ou</u>m	h<u>o</u>me
<u>ou</u>nli	<u>o</u>nly	c<u>ou</u>l	c<u>oa</u>l	j<u>ou</u>k	j<u>o</u>ke

ə The schwa is typically overpronounced, based on spelling. Concentrate on smoothing out and reducing the valleys and *ignore spelling!* (See also Chapters 12, 18, and 20.)

ü Distinguishing tense and lax vowels is difficult, and you'll have to forget spelling for *u* and *ü*. They both can be spelled with *oo* or *ou*, but the lax vowel *ü* should sound much closer to *i* or *uh*. If you say *book* with a tense vowel, it'll sound like *booque*. It should be much closer to *bick* or *buck*. (See also Chapters 18 and 20.)

i Similarly, you need to distinguish between *e* and *i*, as in *beat* and *bit,* as on page 151. Tone down the middle *i* in multisyllabic words, as in Chapter 18, otherwise, *beautiful,* **byoo•d'•fl** will sound like **byoo-tee-fool**. Most likely, you overpronounce the lax vowel z to *eee,* so *sit* is overpronounced to *seat*. Reduce the soft *i* to a schwa; *sit* should sound like *s't*. In most Korean dictionaries, the distinction between *i* and *ē* is not made. Practice the four sounds—*bit, beat, bid, bead*—remembering that *tense vowels* indicate that you tense your lips or tongue, while *lax vowels* mean that your lips and tongue are relaxed and the sound is produced in your throat. *Unvoiced* final consonants (*t, s, k, p, ch, f*) mean that the vowel is short and sharp; *voiced* final consonants (*d, z, g, b, j, v*) mean that the vowel is doubled. Work on *"Bit or Beat? Bid or Bead?"* in Chapter 18. (See also Chapter 20.)

	single	double
tense	beat	bead
lax	bit	bid

The Korean R = The American T

The Korean *r* is a consonant. This means that it touches at some point in the mouth. Korean speakers usually trill their *r*s (tapping the ridge behind the top teeth), which makes it sound like a *d* to the American ear. The tongue should be curled back, and the *r* produced deep in the throat—*not* touching the top of the mouth. The Korean pronunciation of *r* is usually just an *ä* at the end of a word (*car* sounds like *caaah*) or a flap in the beginning or middle (*area* sounds like *eddy-ah*). (See also Chapter 14.)

베리 바라비라	Betty bought a bit of	아이 니랄라라 타임	I need a lot of time.
아이 카라콜드	I caught a cold.	마이 마로우	my motto
쿠리 두잇	Could he do it?	미링	meeting
위 아라 고우	We ought to go.	아임 나란 타임	I'm not on time.

Arabic

Though there are several dialects in Arabic, from the Levantine dialect of Jordan, Palestine, Lebanon, and Syria, to the dialect specific to the Gulf States, as well as the regional differences in Iraq, Egypt, and Libya, there remains a common accent thread in Arabic speakers. Especially noticable in those who have had little prior exposure to English or other Western languages, the accent is typified by a leaden intonation and the lack of several key consonants and vowels. (See also Chapters 3 and 4.)

Intonation

The overall intonation can be perceived as leaden, as it's rather heavy and nonmusical. Syllable stress is also an issue as nonstandard syllables are stressed, such as in *subséquent* and *dévelopment*. When the Arabic speaker is unaware of the rules of American intonation, there is a tendency to simply guess where intonation goes. As a result, intonation pretty much lands on every other word, greatly confusing the American listener. (See also Chapter 4.)

Liaisons

This is a category that causes confusion for Arabic speakers, resulting in comprehension and pronunciation problems. Because Americans tend to connect all their words, many Arabic speakers are not sure where one word ends and the next begins. Relying on the phonetic transcriptions of phrases and sentences teaches the Arabic speaker the construction of American liaisons. Also, simple rules like *T + Y = CH* are tremendously helpful with high-frequency phrases such as *"Got you,"* pronounced *"Gotcha."* (See also Chapter 11.)

Pronunciation

There is no ambiguity in pronouncing words in Arabic, and because of that, there's a very strong tendency to carry this purely phonetic concept over to the wilds of English where *-ough* can be pronounced *cough, through, enough, though,* and *thought*. Phonetics are the problem; phonetics are the solution. Because the concept of phonetics is so strong in the Arabic psyche, then reliance on the phonetic transcription will be very useful.

Word Endings

Arabic speakers overstress the final consonant. At times it can be surprising to an American listener, as it sounds overly emphatic or emotional. The idea of an "unvoiced" final consonant is new to Arabic speakers. Listening carefully to the exercises dealing with unvoiced final consonants, recording yourself, and repeating, will address this issue. Liaisons will assist with word endings.

The Arabic R

The Arabic *R* is a single trill of the tongue tip on the alveolar ridge, which ends up sounding like a *D* or a middle *T* to the American ear. The final *R* also tends to pick up the preceding vowel, so *her* sounds like *hair*, *verb* like *vairb*, *were* like *where*. To the American ear, the initial *R* is like five *D*s fluttered in a row. Making sure that the tongue has no contact with the rest of the mouth is the start of the process for the American *R*.

The Arabic T

All *T*s are popped, regardless of the position in the word. The *T* at the beginning of a word doesn't typically have the necessary puff of air, and a *tssh* sound should be added.

Conversely, middle *T*s should be changed to *D*, as in *authority* (*authoridy*) or dropped completely as in *twenty* or *identity* (*twenny* and *idenadee*).

بِرِي بارَ برُف بِرَد بَرَرْ	Betty bought a bit of better butter.	آي نِيزَ لارْا تَيْم	I need a lot of time.
آي بارَ بايك	I bought a bike.	مانْ مازْو	my motto
كُرِي ذو وِت؟	Could he do it?	مِيرِنج	meeting
وِي آزْا جُو	We ought to go.	آيْمْ نازِن تَيْمْ	I'm not on time.

In particular, the word *To* should be changed to *duh*, as in *day to day* (*day da day*) or *like to mention* (*like duh mention*). The final *T* should be held in for risk of sounding tense or annoyed. The held *T* before *N* is also usually popped and should be held, instead, as in *important, written, forgotten*.

Although there are two *Th* sounds in Arabic, this often ends up sounding like a *D*. The tongue tip needs to be about a half inch more forward, either against the back of the teeth or on the biting edge, but definitely not on the ridge.

Middle I

Arabic speakers tend to overpronounce this sound, and instead, should reduce it to a schwa.

V

The *V* sound doesn't exist in Arabic, and is often replaced with an *F*.

P

The *P* sound doesn't exist in Arabic, and is often replaced with a *B*, resulting in *brivate, broblem, beeble*. A joke making the rounds is *"Officer, may I blease bark here?" "Sure, you can bark anywhere!"*

F	V	B	F	V	B
fat	vat	bat	ferry	very	berry
face	vase	base	effort	ever	Ebber
fear	veer	beer	foul	vowel	bowel

g The *G* is an interesting and important sound in Arabic, as it's the one dealing with the problematic spelling of Ghaddafi, Khaddafi, Qhaddafi. Given that Arabic is considered a gutteral language, this is a very noticeable sound. Especially the soft *G*, which is hardened, so *bring it* sounds like *bring git*.

The American South

Granted, the American South, the land of the lilting drawl, encompasses a lot of geography, and to the denizens, there are very clear regional distinctions. We are not going to address that here, but rather give some general guidelines on standardizing the accent. Clearly, the predominate characteristic is the duration of the vowels. Clipped Yankee vowel durations can sound snippy, rude, or cold to a Southerner, so there may be a little psychological resistance to shortening them up. To a Northerner, these shortened vowels sound completely neutral.

Intonation

Word stress can be different from standard speech, with emphasis on the first syllable. (See also Chapter 4.)

Southern	Standard	Southern	Standard	Southern	Standard
Détroit	Detróit	´TV	TV´	dísplay	displáy
políce	políce	cément	cemént	béhind	behínd
ínsurance	insúrance	úmbrella	umbrélla	récycle	recy´cle
Thánksgiving	Thanksgíving	guítar	guitár	áddress	addréss

Word Endings

A classic Southernism is the dropped *g* of *ing*. This can be changed in two ways. The standard way is to bring up the back of the tongue until it meets the soft palate. The other way is the Californian *-een*, so *running* sounds like *runneen*. Practice with *Mr. Manning was being confusing as he was running, jumping and singing.* (See also Chapter 11.)

The Final *D* is dropped in *understand*: *unnerstan'*, *friend*: *fren'*, and so on. In terms of vowel duration, the vowels are often lengthened with a lilt, but with final voiced consonants, the last consonant is devoiced, so that *job* sounds more like *jop*, and and *did* like *dit*.

The -ed Ending

When there is a voiced consonant followed by *-ed*, you need vocalize the *D*. Otherwise, it can sound like a *T*, such as *The deer was killt as it crossed the tracks.* (See also Chapter 14.)

Pronunciation

Consonants are similar to standard American, but vowels tend to be doubled or even tripled. If you just change the long *I* from *ah* to *äi*, round off the final *R* and don't add an extra syllable after the æ sound, you'll make a major change in how you sound. (See also Chapter 3.)

The Southern R

The Southern *R* (or lack thereof) is most noticeable at the end of a word, where it sounds more like a schwa than an *R*, as *Put the paypuh upstayuhz.* Use a growly RRRR to finish off these words, so it sounds like *Put the paperrrr upstairrrrrs.* Make sure that *sure* doesn't sound like *shore*. Don't let *hair* and *there* become *hayuh* and *they-uh*. Practice with *Therrrrre arrrre fourrrrr shorrrrrrt hairrrrrrs overrrrr therrrrrre.* Yes, you'll sound a little like a pirate.

You'll also want to make a clear distinction between *card* (cärd) / *cord* (kord), *far* (fär) / *for* (for), *farm* (färm) / *form* (form). (See also Chapter 15.)

æ	Resist adding an extra syllable to *cat* (cayut), *can* (cayan), *pan* (payan). Make sure that *can't* doesn't sound like *cain't* and the *æo* in *about* doesn't come out as *abat*. Practice: *Jack sat back, drank from his glass and laughed about how it sounded.* (See also Chapters 12, 18, and 20.)
Long i	This is a classic sound associated with the south, where *My eye* sounds like *Mah aahh*. What's going on is that the first half of the *äi* sound is elongated and the second half gets dropped off. Practice this sentence: *I'm tired. I'd like a nice slice of lime pie.* (See also Chapters 12, 18, and 20.)
ü	The *ü* sound can either be elongated from *book* to *buuhk*, or turned into an *ih* sound, a *good cook* sounds like a *gid kick*. (See also Chapters 18 and 20.) Practice with this sentence: *I took a good look at the cook book.* A Northerner was driving through the South and heard advertisements on the radio, and was surprised that someone was selling an automobile and four *guitars*. Listening further, he realized of course, that it was a car with four *good tires*.
ih	The *ih* sound can go in three directions. Words like *pin* are often pronounced *pen, again / agin, get / git*. Also, *ih* can sound like *æ*, *thing / thang* and *drink / drank*. For this, try saying it *theeng* and *dreenk*. Third, it can also turn into a lilting *E* sound, with *Bill* sounding like *Beel*. Practice this sentence: *Bill filled his thin pen again.* (See also Chapters 18 and 20.)
ɛ	Resist adding an extra syllable to *bed* (beyed), *pet* (peyet), *next* (nayext). Practice with this sentence: *Jeb gets to help the next pet.* (See also Chapters 12, 18, and 20.)
o	Try not rounding and extending the *ah* sound so much, so *dog* doesn't sound like *dawg*, nor *talk* like *tawk*. Practice this sentence. *Bob talked about John's dog all along the walk with Tom*. This should all have the same *ah* sound in every word: *Bahb tahkt about Jahnz dahg ahl alahng the wahk with Tahm*. Think of a ventriloquist's dummy, where your jaw just clacks up and down. (See also Chapters 12, 18, and 20.)
ee	Make sure that the *ee* sound doesn't relax into the *ih*, so *I feel good* doesn't sound like *I fill good*. (See also Chapter 20.)
ə	As you saw in the *R* section, this neutral vowel is commonly used to replace *-er* and *-or*. Practice saying *favrrr* (favor) instead of *favuh*, and *rathrrrr* (rather) instead of *rathuh*. Practice sentence: *Her cars were over there.* (See also Chapters 12, 18, and 20.)
oi	This should be two full vowels. The Southern *boy* almost sounds like *boa*. Practice with *Joy's boy toy foiled the royal oil ploy*. (See also Chapter 20.)
z	The *Z* sound (spelled with an *S*) turns to a *D* before *N*. *That dudn't make sense. It just idn't right. It's a good bidness, innit? That wadn't what happened.* Practice putting in buzzy Zs: *He duzzzzen know, duzzzzy? It wazzzzen any good, wuzzzzzit?* (See also Chapter 17.)
L	Make sure to pronounce the *L* in *help* and *values* so that it doesn't sound like "Hep yoursef," and "va-yoos".

Vocabulary

Modal stacking is particular to the south. *I used to could do it. You might could send them an email. You might should tell her about it.* Leave either one of them off.

Y'all can be changed to *you guys, everyone, everybody* or just plain *you*. (Make sure to say *everybody*, not *ever'body*).

Fixing to is more readily recognizable as *getting ready to*.

Done can be omitted in *I done told you about it!* or *I done had lunch*.

Make sure to change *doin' good* to *doing well*.

Answer Key

Exercise 1-4: Sounds of Empathy

1. B	4. A	7. C	10. A	13. A	16. B	19. C
2. B	5. B	8. C	11. C	14. C	17. A	20. B
3. B	6. A	9. B	12. A	15. B	18. A	21. B

Exercise 3-5: Regular English

1. Bob lost his job.
2. Scott taught a lot.
3. Don bought a bike.

Exercise 3-7: Rhyme Time

1. No	11. No	21. Yes	31. Yes	41. Yes
2. No	12. No	22. No	32. Yes	42. Yes
3. Yes	13. Yes	23. Yes	33. Yes	43. Yes
4. Yes	14. Yes	24. No	34. No	44. Yes
5. No	15. Yes	25. Yes	35. No	45. Yes
6. Yes	16. No	26. No	36. Yes	46. Yes
7. No	17. Yes	27. No	37. No	47. Yes
8. No	18. No	28. Yes	38. No	48. No
9. No	19. No	29. No	39. Yes	49. Yes
10. No	20. Yes	30. No	40. No	50. Yes

Exercise 4-4: Sentence Intonation Test

1. **Sam** sees **Bill**.
2. She **wants** one.
3. **Betty** likes **English**.
4. They **play** with them.
5. **Children** play with **toys**.
6. **Bob** and I call you and **Bill**.
7. You and **Bill** read the news.
8. It **tells** one.
9. **Bernard** works in a restaurant.
10. He **works** in one.
11. He **sees** him.
12. **Mary** wants a **car**.
13. She **likes** it.
14. They **eat** some.
15. Len and **Joe** eat some **pizza**.
16. We **call** you.
17. You **read** it.
18. The **news** tells a **story**.
19. **Mark** lived in **France**.
20. He **lived** there.

Exercise 4-17: Can or Can't Quiz

1. A	4. D	7. C
2. B	5. A	8. B
3. C	6. D	9. A

Exercise 4-18: Application of Stress

Hello, **my** name is_____. I'm taking American **Accent** Training. There's a **lot** to **learn**, but I **hope** to make it as **enjoyable** as possible. I should pick **up** on the American **intonation** pattern pretty **easily**, although the **only** way to **get** it is to **practice** all of the time. I use the **up** and down, or **peaks** and valleys, intonation more than I **used** to. I've been paying attention to **pitch, too.** It's like **walking** down a **staircase**. I've been **talking** to a lot of **Americans** lately, and they tell me that I'm **easier** to under**stand**. **Any**way, I could go **on** and on, but the **important** thing is to **listen** well and sound **good. Well,** what do you **think**? Do **I**?

Exercise 4-26: Regular Transitions of Adj. and Verbs

1. You need to in**sert** a paragraph here on this newspaper **insert**.
2. How can you ob**ject** to this **object**?
3. I'd like to pre**sent** you with this **present**.
4. Would you care to ela**borate** on his e**labor**'t explanation?
5. The manufacturer couldn't re**call** if there'd been a **recall**.
6. The religious **con**vert wanted to con**vert** the world.
7. The political **rebels** wanted to re**bel** against the world.
8. The mogul wanted to re**cord** a new **record** for his latest artist.
9. If you per**fect** your intonation, your accent will be **per**fect.
10. Due to the drought, the fields didn't pro**duce** much **produce** this year.
11. Unfortunately, City Hall wouldn't per**mit** them to get a **per**mit.
12. Have you heard that your as**soci**'t is known to asso**cieit** with gangsters?
13. How much do you **esti**meit that the **estim**'t will be?
14. The facilitator wanted to **separeit** the general topic into **sepr**'t categories.

Exercise 6-6: Making Set Phrases

1. a **chair**man	8. the **Bullet** train	15. a **dump** truck
2. a **phone** book	9. a **race** car	16. a **jelly**fish
3. a **house** key	10. a **coffee** cup	17. a **love** letter
4. a **base**ball	11. a **wrist**watch	18. a **thumb**tack
5. a **door**bell	12. a **beer** bottle	19. a **lightning** bolt
6. the **White** House	13. a **high** chair	20. a **pad**lock
7. a **movie** star	14. a **hunting** knife	

Exercise 6-12: Contrast of Compound Nouns

1. The **White** House	21. **convenience** store	41. a **door**knob
2. a white **house**	22. convenient **store**	42. a glass **door**
3. a **dark**room	23. to pick **up**	43. a locked **door**
4. a dark **room**	24. a **pick**up truck	44. **ice** cream
5. Fifth **Avenue**	25. six years **old**	45. I **scream.**
6. **Main** Street	26. a **six**-year-old	46. **elem**entary
7. a main **street**	27. six and a **half**	47. a **lémon** tree
8. a hot **dog**	28. a **sugar** bowl	48. **Water**gate
9. a **hot**dog	29. a wooden **bowl**	49. the back **gate**
10. a **baby** blanket	30. a large **bowl**	50. the final **year**
11. a baby's **blanket**	31. a **mixing** bowl	51. a **year**book
12. a baby **bird**	32. a **top** hat	52. United **States**
13. a **black**bird	33. a nice **hat**	53. New **York**
14. a black **bird**	34. a straw **hat**	54. **Long** Beach
15. a **green**house	35. a **chair**person	55. Central **Park**
16. a green **house**	36. Ph.**D.**	56. a raw **deal**
17. a green **thumb**	37. IB**M**	57. a **deal** breaker
18. a **parking** ticket	38. MI**T**	58. the bottom **line**
19. a one-way **ticket**	39. US**A**	59. a **bottom** feeder
20. an unpaid **ticket**	40. ASA**P**	60. a new **low**

Exercise 6-13: Description and Set Phrase Test

1. He's a **nice** guy.
2. He's an **American** guy from San Francisco.
3. The **cheerleader** needs a **rubber band** to hold her **ponytail**.
4. The **executive asst.** needs a **paper clip** for the **final report**.
5. The **law student** took an **English test** in a foreign country.
6. The **policeman** saw a **red car** on the **freeway** in Los Angeles.
7. My **old dog** has **long ears** and a **flea problem**.
8. The **new teacher** broke his **coffee cup** on the **first day.**
9. His **best friend** has a broken **cup** in his **other office.**
10. Let's play **football** on the **weekend** in New **York.**
11. "**Jingle Bells**" is a **nice song.**
12. Where are my **new shoes**?
13. Where are my **tennis shoes**?
14. I have a **headache** from the **heat wave** in South Carolina.
15. The **newlyweds** took a **long walk** in Long Beach.
16. The **little dog** was sitting on the **sidewalk.**
17. The **famous athlete** changed clothes in the **locker room.**
18. The **art exhibit** was held in an **empty room.**
19. There was a **class reunion** at the **high school.**
20. The **headlines** indicated a **new policy.**
21. We got **online** and went to AmericanAccent **dot com.**
22. The **stock options** were listed in the **company directory.**
23. All the **second graders** were out on the **playground.**

Exercise 7-4: Punctuation & Phrasing

1. D 2. A 3. C 4. B

Exercise 7-5: Tag Endings

1. isn't he	8. will you	15. hadn't we	22. did I
2. can't he	9. doesn't he	16. wouldn't we	23. will I
3. does she	10. don't we	17. hasn't it	24. don't you
4. didn't they	11. haven't we	18. could you	25. aren't you
5. do you	12. didn't we	19. won't you	26. didn't you
6. is it	13. didn't we	20. shouldn't he	27. did you
7. aren't I	14. hadn't we	21. shouldn't he	28. isn't it

Exercise 8-3: Extended Listening Practice
1. Take it! tay•kit
2. Thank you. thæng•kiu
3. I need a cup of coffee. äi•nee•də•kə•pə•kä•fee
4. What did he do? wə•di•dee•doo
5. Can we go get it now? kwee•go•geh•dit•næo
6. Where did you learn to speak English so well?
   where•jə•lrrn•də•spee•king•glish•so•well
7. I'm going to have to think about it.
   äi•mə•nə•hæf•tə•thing•kə•bæou•dit
8. I'm a little late. äi•mə•li•də•late
9. Try to get another one. try•də•ge•də•nə•thr•wən
10. Why don't you turn it on? wyn•chə•tr•ni•dän
11. Could/Can you hold on to this for a sec?
    kyu•hol•dän•də•this•frə•sec

Exercise 9-3: Writing Your Own Phonetics
1. bä bry tsa ledder
2. bä bro də ledder
3. bä bi zrydi ngə ledder
4. bä bəl ry də ledder
5. bä bədry də ledderif
6. bä bə də ri(t)n nə ledder
7. thə gäi thə dəz ri(t)n nə ledder
8. bä bə zri(t)n nə ledder
9. bä bə dri(t)n nə ledder
10. bä bə lə vri(t)n nə ledder
11. bä bädə ry də ledder
12. bäb shüdry də ledder
13. bäb shüdn ry də ledder
14. bäb shüdə vri(t)n nə ledder
15. bäb shüdnə vri(t)n nə ledder
16. bäb cüdry də ledder
17. bäb cüdn dry də ledder
18. bäb cüdə vri(t)n nə ledder
19. bäb cüdn nəvri(t)n nə ledder
20. bäb my(t) ry də ledder
21. bäb my də vri(t)n nə ledder
22. bäb məs dry də ledder
23. bäb məs də vri(t)n nə ledder
24. bäb cən ry də ledder
25. bäb cæn(t) ry də ledder

Exercise 11-4: Consonant/Vowel Liaison Practice
1. ree donly
2. fä läff
3. fällo wə pän
4. cə min
5. cä lim
6. se lit
7. ta kout
8. fa də way
9. sik so
10. eh may

Exercise 11-8: Consonant/Consonant Liaison Practice
1. businessteal
2. credi(t)check
3. the topfile
4. sellnine newcars
5. sitdown
6. someplan znee dluck
7. che(ck)cashing
8. let(t)themma(k)conditions
9. hadthe
10. bothdays

Exercise 11-9: Vowel/Vowel Liaison Practice
1. go(w)enywhere
2. so(w)änest
3. through(w)är
4. you(w)är
5. he(y)iz
6. do(w)äi
7. I(y)æskt
8. to(w)open
9. she(y)äweez
10. too(w)äffen

Exercise 11-11: T, D, S, or Z + Y Liaison Practice
1. dijoo
2. hoozhier
3. jesjer
4. jesjer
5. misshue
6. tisshue
7. gächer
8. wherzhier
9. c'ngræjələshunz
10. hæjer

Exercise 11-12: Finding Liaisons and Glides
Hello, **my** name-is _____. I'm taking-American-Accent-Training. There's-a **lot**-to **learn**, but-I **hope** to make-it-as-enjoyable-as possible. I should pick-**up**-on-the(y)American-into**na**tion pattern pretty(y)**ea**sily, although the(y)**only** way-də **get**-it-is-to prac**tice**-all-of the time. I(y)use the(y)**up**-and-down, or **peaks**-and valleys,-intonation more than-I(y)**used**-to. I've-been paying-attention-to **pitch,-too**. It's-like-**walk**ing down-a **stair**case. I've-been-**talk**ing to(w)a lot-of-A**mer**icans-lately, and-they tell me that-I'm-**eas**ier to(w) under**stand**. Anyway,-I could go(w) on-and-on, but-the(y)im**por**tant-thing-is-to **lis**ten-well-and-sound **good**. Well, what-do-you **think**? Do(w)I?

Exercise 12-2: Finding æ, ä, and ə Sounds
Həllo, **my** name is _____. I'm taking əmerəcən **æc**sənt Training. There's ə **lät** tə **learn**, bət I **hope** tə make ət əs ənj**oy**əbələs **päss**əbəl. I should pick əp än the əmerəcən əntənashən pættern pretty **ea**səly, äªlthough the **only** way tə **get** ət əs tə **præc**təss äªll əv thə time. I use the **əp** ənd down, ər **peaks** ənd **væll**eys, intənashən more thən I **used** to. I've-been paying əttenshən tə **pitch, too**. It's like **wälk**ing down ə **stair**case. I've been **talk**ing to ə **lät** əf **əmer**əcəns lately, ənd they tell me thət I'm **eas**ier tə ənder**stænd**. Anyway, I could go **än** ənd än, bət the im**por**tant thing əs tə **lis**sən weªll ənd sound **good**. Weªll, whət də yə **think**? **Do** I?

Exercise 13-1: Targeting the Th Sound
Hello, **my** name is _____. I'm taking American **Ac**cent Training. <u>Th</u>ere's a **lot** to **learn**, but I **hope** to make it as en**joy**able as possible. I should pick **up** on <u>th</u>e American into**na**tion pattern pretty **ea**sily, al<u>th</u>ough <u>th</u>e **only** way to **get** It is to prac**tice** all of <u>th</u>e time. I use <u>th</u>e **up** and down, or **peaks** and valleys, **into**nation more <u>th</u>an I **used** to. I've been paying attention to **pitch, too**. It's like **walk**ing down a **stair**case. I've been **talk**ing to a lot of A**mer**icans lately, and <u>th</u>ey tell me <u>th</u>at I'm **eas**ier to under**stand**. Anyway, I could go **on** and on, but <u>th</u>e im**por**tant <u>th</u>ing is to **lis**ten well and sound **good**. Well, what do you <u>th</u>ink? **Do** I?

Exercise 13-4: Mr. Thingamajig
I was looking randomly through my belongings for the little unnamed object to fix the darned other little thing, but some guy had put it in the unnamed place, as usual! How annoying. Always the same nonsense with that guy. He's such a small insignificant person! If I found it, (sound of cash register), I'd be rich, which would be just great. I'd be totally confused! That unnamed person had misplaced the unnamed thing again, so surprise, surprise! There was something wrong with it. What a confused situation!

I had a hard time getting in touch with some girl to come over and take care of it with her special little contraption, that she keeps in the unspecified location. For the hundredth time, the silly girl said OK, she wouldn't waste time—she'd come over with her mechanical device fixer and everything to do a great job on the whole project. That's right, the whole repair project, no excuses and no nonsense. Yes, but she was a little busy right then, etc. Yes, we usually do have many devices, but with all the activity and excitement, it's all out of control because that big fool is still in the unnamed location, acting like everything's fine.

That's a lot of nonsense! He's such an old fashioned person. The antics of that guy! Well, I wanted to find it on my own, and not be penalized for it—I'm so tired of requests and catches by curious people who are past their prime, and out associating with snobbish people who used to be famous. The truth is that young and old, they're just a group of cheerful lightweights and crabby old people who don't know anything. I looked through the trinkets, decorative objects, cheap and showy ornaments and small worthless objects, there in the back of the unspecified place, but I couldn't find anything at all. Some guy gave me information about the unnamed thing, but I don't know where it is. It's a big problem when you can't even remember where the darned thing is!

Exercise 14-14: Finding American T Sounds

Hello, my name is _____. I'm taking American **Accen**(t) Training. There's a **lo**(t) to **learn**, bud I **hope** to make id as en**joy**able as possible. I should pick **up** on the American intonation paddern priddy **eas**ily, although the **only** way də **ged**didis də **prac**tice all of the time. I use the **up** and down, or **peaks** and valleys, intonation more than I **use**(t)to. I've been paying attention to **pitch, too**. It's like **walk**ing down a **stair**case. I've been **talk**ing to a **läd**dəv Americans la(t)ely, and they tell me the dime **eas**ier də understand. **Any**way, I could go **on** and on, bu(t) the im**por**(t) n(t) thing is də **lis**sen well and sound **good. Well**, wha(d) do you **think? Do** I?

Exercise 15-7: Finding the R Sound

Hello, my name is _____. I'm taking Ame**r**ican **Accent** T**r**aining. The**r**e's a **lot** to **lea**r**n**, but I **hope** to make it as en**joy**able as possible. I should pick **up** on the Ame**r**ican into**na**tion patte**r**n pretty **eas**ily, although the **only** way to **get** it is to **prac**r**tice** all of the time. I use the **up** and down, or **peaks** and valleys, **intona**tion mo**r**e than I **used** to. I've been paying attention to **pitch, too**. It's like **walk**ing down a **stair**case. I've been **talk**ing to a lot of Ame**r**icans **late**ly, and they tell me that I'm **eas**ier to unde**r****stand**. **Any**way, I could go **on** and on, but the im**po**r**t**ant thing is to **lis**ten well and sound **good. Well**, what do you **think? Do** I?

Exercise 16-6: Finding L Sounds

Hel**lo, my** name is _____. I'm taking American **Accent** Training. There's a **l**ot to **l**earn, but I **hope** to make it as en**joy**ab**l**e as possib**l**e. I should pick **up** on the American intonation pattern pretty **eas**i**l**y, a**l**though the on**l**y way to **get** it is to **prac**tice a**ll**of the time. I **use** the **up** and down, or **peaks** and va**ll**eys, **intona**tion more than I **used** to. I've been paying attention to **pitch, too**. It's **l**ike **walk**ing down a **stair**case. I've been **talk**ing to a **l**ot of Americans **late**ly, and they te**ll** me that I'm **eas**ier to understand. **Any**way, I could go **on** and on, but the im**por**tant thing is to **l**isten we**ll** and sound **good. We**ll**, what do you **think? Do** I?

Exercise 17-5: Finding S and Z Sounds

Hello, my name i**z** _____. I'm taking American **Ac**s**ent** Training. There'**z** a **lot** to **learn**, but I **hope** to make it a**z** en**joy**able a**z** po**ss**ible. I should pick **up** on the American intonation pattern pretty ea**z**ily, although the **only** way to **get** it i**z** to **prac**ti**s**e all of the time. I u**z**e the **up** and down, or **peak**s and valle**yz**, intonation more than I **used** to. I've been paying attention to **pitch, too**. It'**s** like **walk**ing down a **stair**ca**s**e. I've been **talk**ing to a lot of American**z** lately, and they tell me that I'm **eas**ier to under**s**tand. **Any**way, I could go **on** and on, but the im**por**tant thing i**z** to **lis**ten well and **s**ound **good. Well**, what do you **think? Do** I?

Review Exercise B: Intonation Review Test

1.	Los **Angeles**	11.	**every**thing
2.	paper **bag**	12.	**moving** van
3.	**lunch** bag	13.	new **paper**
4.	**convenience** store	14.	**news**paper
5.	convenient **store**	15.	glass **eyes**
6.	**home**work	16.	**eye**glasses
7.	good **writer**	17.	high **chair**
8.	apple **pie**	18.	**high**chair
9.	**pine**apple	19.	**base**ball
10.	all **things**	20.	blue **ball**

Exercise 18-8: Finding Reduced Sounds

Hello, my name is _____. I'm taking American **Accent** Training. There's a **lot** to **learn**, but I **hope** to make it as en**joy**able as possible. I **shüd** pick **up** on the American intonation pattern pretty **eas**ily, although the **only** way to **get** it is to practice all of the time. I **üse** the up and down, or **peaks** and valleys, intonation

more than I **used tü**. I've been paying attention to **pitch, tü**. It's like **walk**ing down a **stair**case. I've been **talk**ing **tü** a lot of Americans lately, and they tell me that I'm **easier tü** understand. **Any**way, I **cüd** go **on** and on, but the im**por**tant thing is to **listen** well and sound **güd. Well**, what do you **think? Dü** I?

Exercise 19-3: Finding V Sounds

Hello, my name is _____. I'm taking American **Accent** Training. There's a **lot** to **learn**, but I **hope** to make it as en**joy**able as possible. I should pick **up** on the American intonation pattern pretty **eas**ily, although the **only** way to **get** it is to **prac**tice all o**f** the time. I use the **up** and down, or **peaks** and **v**alleys, intonation more than I **used** to. I'**v**e been paying attention to **pitch, too**. It's like **walk**ing down a **stair**case. I'**v**e been **talk**ing to a lot o**f** Americans lately, and they tell me that I'm **eas**ier to understand. **Any**way, I could go **on** and on, but the im**por**tant thing is to **listen** well and sound **good. Well**, what do you **think? Do** I?

Exercise 20-2: Tense Vowels Practice Paragraph

Hello, my n**a**me is_____. I'm t**a**king American **æk**sent Tr**a**ining. There's a **lot** to learn, but I **hope** to m**a**ke it as en**joy**able as possible. I should pick **up** on th**e** American into**na**tion p**æ**ttern pretty **eas**ily, although th**e** only w**a**y to **get** it is to **præc**tice all of the time. I use th**e** **up** an d**æ**on, or **peaks** and v**æ**ll**e**ys, intona**tion more than I **used** to. I've been p**a**ying attention to **pitch, too**. It's like **walk**ing d**æ**on a **stair**c**a**se. I've been **talk**ing to a lot of Americans l**a**tely, and th**a**y tell m**e** that I'm **eas**ier to underst**æ**nd. **Any**w**a**y, I could go **on** and on, but th**e** **import**'nt thing is to **listen** well and s**æ**ond **good. Well**, what d' you **think? Do** I?

Exercise 20-4: Lax Vowels Practice Paragraph

Hello, my name is_____. I'm taking əmerəcən **Accənt** Training. Th**ɛ**re's ə **lot** tə learn, bət I **hope** tə make it əs **ɛn**joy**əb**ᵊl əs possəbəl. I should pick **əp** on the əmerəcən intənashən pattern pritty **eas**əly, although the only way tə **get**itis tə **prac**təs all əv thə time. I use the **up** ən down, or **peaks** ən valleys, intənashən more than I **used** to. I've bin paying əttenshən tə **pitch, too**. It's like **walk**ing down ə **st**ɛ**rcase. I've bin **talk**ing to ə lot əv **əmɛr**əcəns lately, ənd they tɛll me thət I'm **eas**ier to əndərstand. **ɛn**yway, I could go **on** ənd on, bət the im**port**'nt thing is to **list**ən wɛll ənd sound **good. Wɛll**, whət d' you **think? Do** I?

Exercise 24-4: Finding n and ng Sounds

Hello, my **n**ame is _____. I'm taking America**n** **Accent** Trai**n**i**ng**. There's a **lot** to **lear**n, but I **hope** to make it as e**n**joyable as possible. I should pick **up** o**n** the American i**nto**n**ation** patter**n** pretty **eas**ily, although the **only** way to **get** it is to **prac**tice all of the time. I use the **up** a**n**d dow**n**, or **peaks** a**n**d valleys, i**nto**n**ation** more tha**n** I **used** to. I've bee**n** paying atte**n**tion to **pitch, too**. It's like **walk**ing dow**n** a **stair**case. I've bee**n** **talk**ing to a lot of America**n**s lately, a**n**d they tell me that I'm **eas**ier to u**n**der**sta**n**d**. **Any**way, I could go **on** a**n**d o**n**, but the im**por**ta**n**t thing is to **liste**n well a**n**d sou**n**d **good. Well**, what do you **thi**n**gk? Do** I?

Exercise 25-4: Glottal Consonant Practice Paragraph

Hello, my name is _____. I'm taki**ng** Ameri**k**an A**k**cent Training. There's a **lot** to **lear**n, but I **hope** to make it as en**joy**able as possible. I should pi**ck** **up** on the Ameri**k**an into**na**tion patter**n** pretty **eas**ily, although the **only** way to **get** it is to **prak**tice all of the time. I use the **up** and down, or **peaks** and valleys, intonation more than I **used** to. I've been payi**ng** attention to **pitch, too**. It's like **walk**ing down a **stair**kase. I've been **talk**ing to a lot of Ameri**k**ans lately, and they tell me that I'm **eas**ier to under**stand**. **Any**way, I **k**ould go **on** and on, but the im**por**tant thi**ng** is to **listen** well and sound **good. Well**, what do you **think? Do** I?

Teacher's Guide

This is a very practical, step-by-step guide to working with foreign-born adults. If you go through all the exercises, giving strong feedback, you should have results similar to the one you heard on CD 1.

Chapter 1: The American Sound

Intonation, **voice quality, liaisons** and **pronunciation** are the four pillars of the American Accent Training method. It's the way that children learn their native language, and they are the main elements that are unfortunately missing when adults study a foreign language. Without intonation and voice quality, a student is simply using English words in a non-English format. It is your task to make sure that the voice is properly placed and that the rhythm patterns become ingrained. Voice quality is a combination of vocal placement and cadence, which means a throaty sound and a stairstep intonation. Intonation is the pitch-change patterns used by native speakers. Within a word, a phrase, or a sentence, certain syllables are given more stress (accorded a higher pitch) than others. How this stress changes the meaning of a sentence, how it can move around in a sentence and how it can reflect the speaker's intent—or even personality—is what you need to convey to your students. Use the Nationality Guides to let the students see the correlation between their intonation and pronunciation; where it's similar and where it's different. Also point out that every language has intonation, but it's most likely that they won't have realized that about their own language.

Asking Questions

In America, students are encouraged to ask questions; Asian students are not. Your students need to realize that not only are questions welcomed, they **must** ask them. ESL teachers tend to talk too much. Limit yourself to 10% of the talking, and have your students do the other 90%. This means you only talk for six minutes in a one-hour class. Make the students do the work, not you.

The American Sound

The first step is to get the student to generate his voice from the correct place. It's not up in the head or forward in the mouth, but in the back of the throat with the air projected from the diaphragm. While working on the airflow and sound production, have the student start correlating the phonetic symbols with the actual spelling. One of the main goals is to get visual students oriented to the auditory aspects of English.

As you heard on CD 1 Track 4, Eddie Izzard demonstrates moving his voice back and down to imitate the American sound. This essential throaty quality—*rhoticity*—is that solid R as in **hard** and **far**.

With a slight detour to the general pronunciation introduction in Chapter 3, the first third of this program deals with voice quality and intonation. Even as you work through word connections and pronunciation, you'll find yourself coming back to vocal placement and cadence as the most important determinants of a standard accent.

Most intermediate to advanced students have studied a lot of grammar and have sufficient vocabularies. They need to understand, however, that their accent is actually more important than perfect grammar or an extensive vocabulary—after all, if the listener can't understand, what's the point of a mastery of the pluperfect subjunctive? It's interesting to know that 25% of what we say consists of just nine words: *and, be, have, it, of, the, to, will, you* and they are almost always unstressed. Of the hundreds of thousands of words that exist in English, the daily usage is about 1000. Get your students to focus on high-frequency vocabulary.

Explain the difference between the intonation or rhythm of a sentence—the music or tonality—and the actual sounds of the individual words or pronunciation and demonstrate that rhythm has more to do with "sounding American" than the individual words do. Make the sound that Americans make when they say, **I don't know** (one step beyond **I dunno**) without enunciating the words. In this case, rhythm alone is communication. (See page 27).

Getting Started

During the diagnostic analysis on page x, ask why the student is taking an accent class. You can call us for advice at 800-457-4255. In order to get students into the zone and to find out what they think their potential is, ask what they think they can achieve on a scale of 1 to 10. Make a note of the number. Ask where they think they are now and note that number as well. It's usually pretty accurate.

In order to give them confidence in what you will be doing, explain that they will be recorded at the beginning and at the end of the course, as well as intermittently throughout, and that after they have gone through the steps, they can't help but sound more American. If the students haven't had a diagnostic analysis, mention you will be integrating all four components of the accent (voice quality, intonation, liaisons, pronunciation), and you will be covering it all in detail. Things like **tense** and **lax vowels**, **voiced** and **unvoiced consonants** can all be dealt with as they come up in their respective chapters. If you are asked directly, of course, go ahead and answer. Start right in on the American speech music on page 3 and get the student to have the proper vocal placement. In the second exercise, you'll be approaching the American sound via nonsense syllables. This will circumvent the student's inclination to fall back on old habits and misconceptions. Have the student write down the five syllables, **bä bee bä də bäik**. It doesn't have to be phonetically accurate and don't insist on the symbols. If they write **bah bi bah duh byk**, that's just fine. Have the student say it out loud as a regular sentence and they will get bits and pieces before figuring out, **Bobby bought a bike**. The major take-aways are that the letter **O** sounds like **ah** and that the **T** between vowels turns into a **D**. This is the first step in guiding a student from spelling-based pronunciation to a phonetic understanding of pure sound. Next, have the student work on perfecting a go-to phrase, including vocal placement and facial position, to get into the American zone. Along these same lines, work on active listening, with the student responding to your scenarios with the various options on page 5. This segues directly into the non-verbal intonation exercise and the sounds of empathy. For Exercise 1-4, you can either work from CD 1 Track 18 or, if you're confident, you can create the sounds yourself.

Chapter 2: Psycholinguistics

Have the student listen to the before/after audio on CD 1 Track 21. The purpose of this is to get them in the frame of mind that *it's just an accent*. To find out if your students are all-at-oncers or step-by-steppers, play CD 1 Track 24, **Please call Stella**, and have them mimic the sound. If they sound pretty much like they already do, or fixate on what the actual words are, you've got *steppers*. If they capture the essence of the sound, you've got *oncers*. Follow up on this with Exercise 2-2 to see how they respond. This is actually a quick triage to see who is flexible and who might be more stubborn and resistant to change. Follow up on the Stella mimicry by having the student imitate you saying, **There was a time when people really had a way with words**. Their mimicry should include the vocal quality, rhythm, and as much pronunciation as possible. (These words were chosen because they are very high frequency.) Circling back to pure sound in Exercise 2-4, have the student read **gäddit**. Make sure the **ä** is clear and open and that it's a quick, flicked **D** in the middle. Stress the first syllable. Have the student repeat at least ten times or until it sounds just right. As you correlate in Exercise 2-5, you may notice some backsliding with the **O** in **got** rounding up a little. In that case, go back to the phonetics and make sure that the vowel is nice and open and the lips aren't at all rounded. The next step is super important, particularly for the empiricists in your class. They need to actually go out and use this phrase with actual Americans. They can use it as either a statement: **Got it**, an exclamation: **Got it**! or a query: **Got it?** Have them bring back the real-life experience of how it turned out. This is an important discussion and will lead to a better understanding of how to interact with Americans while applying the techniques.

Ask your students how many times a day they have to repeat themselves and make of note of this as their What Factor. The goal is, of course, to get it down to zero.

Chapter 3: General Pronunciation

Here, you're diving straight into pronunciation, starting with an incredibly easy sound, **mmm**, which everyone can do. Have the student observe how and where the air comes out, the point of contact, and the vocality. This pre-answers a lot of questions that tend to come up, such as *What is a consonant?*, *What do you mean by voiced?*, *What's a nasal?* In Exercise 3-2, you'll have them take the baby step of adding the **ah** sound and some other bilabials, for a nice, clear **mah, pah, bah**. Repeat this several times, making sure that the **pah** and **bah** are sufficiently popped. You can have them hold their hand in front of their mouth to feel the air. Next, you're going to start combining pronunciation and rhythm with Exercise 3-3, using the physicality of snapping, slapping, or pulling. We'll delve more deeply into the different ways of making intonation in Chapter 4, page 26, but for the moment, just make sure they are using **pitch** and not **volume**. Encourage them to lengthen the vowel duration a bit when the second syllable is stressed.

In Exercise 3-4, you'll circle back for the third time to pure sound. The reason we approach this from so many directions is that students are *very* invested in maintaining the correlation between spelling and pronunciation. We've even heard people pronounce the **L** in **would** and **half**! Have the student read the three sentences and focus on pronouncing it exactly the way it's written. Quite often, they'll get very distracted trying to figure what the meaning is, but keep them laser focused on the sounds. In Exercise 3-5, they get to put it into regular English and in Exercise 3-6 to create the sounds while knowing what the meaning is. Your job is to make sure they maintain the **bä bläs diz jäb**, **skät tä də lät, dän bä də bäik** pronunciation.

Exercise 3-7 is a great reality check and students are amazed at what rhymes and what doesn't. Exercise 3-8 is a very soothing exercise, almost like chanting the sounds in sequence. The first column should be 95% easy, with just a few predictable hiccups on **rä** and **thä**. Based on the nationality, you'll also need to work on **bä/vä** (Spanish), **fä** (Japanese), **dä** (Spanish), **pä/bä** (Arabic), **lä/nä** (Southern China), **vä/wä** (India/Pakistan), **fä/vä/wä** (German), **sä/zä** (Spanish). Make sure that the vowel is clear and open, and you may need to have them double the vowel–**mä-ah**–to catch the musicality and the proper vowel duration.

The second column is a bit more problematic, both because **æ** doesn't exist in other languages and it's a rather unlovely sound. It's so distinctly American, though, that you need to have them get comfortable with it early on. The third column is as easy as **ä** because everyone has an **eh** sound. Other universal sounds are **eeh, ooh**, and the **long A** and **long I**. It's quite a task to get students to distinguish **ih / eeh** and **ü / ooh**. The latter pair can be illustrated with the chicken (**ü**) and the fish (**ooh**) in Chapter 20, *Tense & Lax Vowels*. Actually, **ih / ü** are very similar, as in **kick / cook**. The key is that should be no lip rounding with **ü**. The long vowels **A** and **I** are actually diphthongs and the task is to get students to produce both halves, **eh-ee** and **ah-ee**. This brings us to the neutral vowel, the schwa (**ə**), which students have a heck of a time distinguishing from **ä**. You need to contrast the two columns, side by side, **bä / bə, chä / chə, dah / duh**, etc.

Exercise 3-9 is important in that it helps with the lateral transfer of information. Rather than creating a sound from scratch, they can work from a nearby one in their own language. Chances are, when they read their character set, the vowels will be shorter than you want, so have them double them up. This is a good time to direct them to the Nationality Guides in the back of the book.

Exercise 3-10 is similar to Exercise 3-6 in that they will be transitioning from pure sound over to spelling again. Make sure to hold them strictly accountable for each sound, in particular **the**, as it's the most commonly used word in English. Exercise 3-10 will give you a head start on the **Th** (more detailed in Chapter 13). The main point is that although it's tempting to teach a breathy **Th**, it's actually popped in natural speech.

Chapter 4: American Intonation

You've already introduced intonation in Chapters 1 and 3, and now you're going to introduce the concept of musicality and tone shift that can be visually represented by the staircase. One of the most important things that students know intuitively in their own language is the importance of pitch change and the effect of shortening a word. For some reason, however, that information does not transfer in the second language. Students tend to shorten their words, which makes them sound *curt*, *clipped*, or *abrupt*. Literally, each of these words just means short, but figuratively (and that's what accent is all about) they sound rude.

Let the students know that they are to use this book and CD set on their own and that your role is to listen and give them feedback. They also need to know that they will not be losing their accent—they will be learning a new one. This is an important psychological point since people are nervous about the effects of such a change. As they learn the accent, they will make it their own, and their thinking won't change as a consequence; it's just a skill like a new dance step. It comforts students to hear that even among Americans there are misunderstandings due to intonation and meaning. Once a student can accurately hear and use the difference between a compound noun and a description, a large part of the intonation work is done.

Three Ways to Make Intonation

Once they have the sounds in place, you're ready to get more specific with the intonation. Demonstrate all three ways, and then have the student focus on **pitch**, rather than **volume**. Vowel duration is an extremely important component of intonation and it is covered throughout the text.

Nonsense Syllables

Exercise 4-1 is extremely important. Students can disassociate from grammar, content, meaning and vocabulary, and simply focus on the pure sound and rhythm of English. Some students are staccato, some heavy on volume, some monotone, some misplace the stress points, and some sound like they're singing rather than talking. You know what it should sound like—keep modifying until the student sounds like you. Female teachers should deepen their voices a bit with male students.

In Exercise 4-1, there are two groups—one of purely nonsense syllables and a second of the transition from nonsense to sense. In the first group, have the student read each row across (1-4) for the same pattern with different sounds, then down (A-D) for the same sound with different patterns. The main point here is to capture both the musicality and the vocal placement. If the student is able to sound American saying **duh-duh-duh,** everything else can follow from there.

In the second group, have the student read column A (1-4). Make sure that **duh-duh-duh** and **ABC**, **123**, **Dogs eat bones** all sound the same, in terms of voice placement, cadence and musicality. Then go on to columns B, C, and D.

Staircase Intonation

The staircase is simply a visual metaphor to help students understand pitch. It is the same as a stress point, the musical notes or an accent mark. The primary rule of stress in English is that, given no counter indicators, such as contrast, nouns are stressed. Have the student read Exercise 4-2, giving a slight lift to each noun. In Exercise 4-3, have the student read side to side, contrasting the noun stress with the verb stress. This makes the test in Exercise 4-4 extremely simple.

Shifting the Stress Points

Intonation is the mainstay of the American Accent Training method. It is the way that children learn their native language, and it is the main element that is usually missing when adults study a foreign language. Intonation is the pitch change pattern used by native speakers. Within a word, a phrase or a sentence, certain syllables are given more stress (accorded a higher pitch) than others. How this stress changes the meaning of a sentence, how it can move around in a sentence and how is can reflect the speakers intent or even personality is what you need to convey to your students.

Duh-Duh-Duh

One of the first steps in the transition from the printed word to the sound of spoken English is to have students start applying an unmistakable intonation to all sorts of different expressions. Even when you walk the student through the importance of the American up & down, people will still want to underemphasize.

To get around this, after the student reads the **New Information** sentence **It sounds like rain** and it sounds flat and unmusical, have them replace most of the words with **duh-duh-duh**. Stress **RAIN** very heavily. **duh-duh-duh RAIN**. If **rain** is stressed loudly but unmusically, have them put it on two tone levels: **ray-een**.

This tone shift will help students with the idea of the staircase. Have them read the four sentences, and every time they lose the intonation and start stressing each word (**It.Sounds.Like.Rain**), go back to **duh-duh-duh**. Every time they lose the musicality, break the key word into two parts, put it on a little stair step and make the pitch higher on the first step.

It sounds like **rain**.	duh-duh-duh **rain**
It **sounds** like rain.	duh-duh-duh **sounds** duh-duh-duh
He **likes** rain, but he **hates** snow.	duh-duh-duh **likes** duh-duh-duh,
	duh-duh-duh **hates** duh-duh-duh
The rain **didn't affect** his plans.	duh-duh-duh **didn't affect** duh-duh-duh

Translation

The next part of the intonation exercise is a translation. This again is twofold. In many English classes, native languages are implicitly or explicitly forbidden. Since language is such an integral part of an individual, it feels as if part of her or him is being denied or shut out. I think it is much preferable to use what you can of each language to show the student where his natural advantages lie. Most languages have a trilled **R**, which is instantly convertible to the American **T**. Let your students know what their strengths are, and you will have much more confident and teachable students.

Translation Summary

1. Translate the sentence.
2. Write it out on the board, phonetically or otherwise.
3. Students read them with their normal accents.
4. You read the sentences in an American accent.
5. Students imitate your accent.
6. Students read it in a native accent, emphasizing a word.
7. Other students guess which sound was stressed.
8. Explain the similarities or differences in intonations in different languages, such as the American staircase, the Indian upward glide, or the Swiss up-and-down.
9. Briefly discuss how this strong intonation feels to them.

Maybe in English, but in my dialect...

Have the students translate the sentence **I didn't say he stole the money** into their own language or dialect. Have them say it at a regular speed and intonation so you can hear how different it is from English. Then, jot down the translation, phonetically or by normal ABC's, and read it back with an average American accent. It's a hugely important exercise to have the student imitate you, saying their own language with an American accent. They should feel like they're talking and chewing gum. For them to speak their own language sounding like an American is funny and unnerving, but it definitely improves their American accent in English.

Next, have the student read the sentence with a natural, native accent, but jumping heavily on a stressed word while you identify which word stood out. It may take a couple of tries here, but it is important to get them to realize that it is only the sound you are looking for, not the meaning of the sound.

After they can move the intonation around freely in their own sentences, ask if this is it similar to his or her native language?; does it feel natural to do it?; how did it feel? You will get a wonderful variety of answers as they start thinking about how they actually do it. At this point, students realize that they do the same thing in their own language and it is just a question of applying concepts that they already know and use, to English.

Chapter 5: Syllable Stress

This is a dense and important section, where you'll be working on making sure that the student's pitch is appropriate, in terms of placement, pitch range and vowel duration. The one-syllable patterns contrast the single stairstep of the vowel in a word ending in a whispered consonant (unvoiced) with the double stairstep of a word ending in a voiced consonant. In the two-syllable patterns, you start to get into descriptions (stressing the second word—white house) and set phrases or compound nouns (stressing the first word (White House). Students often feel the need to have a set list of rules for syllable stress, but this is not typically a big problem. To assuage them, however, there is a Syllable Rules section on page 48. You will notice that Indians stress the first word in beginning and component, and the French like to stress the last syllable of just about everything, but this is minor compared with the rest of the intonation problems.

Chapter 6: Complex Intonation

This chapter starts getting to the heart of the rhythm patterns and you'll need to review it, both in exercises and in context while they are speaking. You'll notice that the sentences are fairly short in **Goldilocks**, and there are two reasons for this. The first is that they need to master the basics, and the second is that this will be contrasted with *sentence balance* later on.

Chapter 7: Phrasing

Phrasing is pretty straightforward in that punctuation is such a strong guide. Tag endings are included on page 63 because students tend to underuse them. They should practice with tags as both a query and an affirmation.

Chapter 8: The Miracle Technique

Reverse Phonetics

The purpose of this exercise is to get your students away from the impression that they can't do it—"it" being to produce native-sounding speech. Stated or not, conscious or not, students have resistance to changing their pronunciation either from their native accent or from how they think the spelling indicates. You need to hone their skill in hearing and reproducing pure sound, in or out of context, and they need to abandon the spelling crutch.

In Exercise 8-1, you're introducing the concepts of pure sound, of ignoring spelling, of using any phonetic system. Let them know that they are going to write backwards, but just two little sounds. Say **lie** and listen for the students to say back what they heard. They can write it **lie, ly, lye** or **läi**. Then, have them repeat it after you, making sure they get both the **ah** and the **eeh** sounds. When both sounds are in place, have them read it back themselves and decipher what it says: **I like it**. Read the sentence using the rubber band or tapping on the stressed word (**like**) until everyone sounds quick and fluent. After you've finished Exercises 8-2 and 8-3, have the students create their own sentences, broken up into pieces. They should give you the pieces, back to front, and you then decipher. Interestingly, in the beginning, as you read back, you'll have their accent. As they come to understand the rules, you'll sound more and more standard.

Chapter 9: Grammar in a Nutshell

Along with the Miracle Techique, this is a Desert Island exercise. If all you had was a sheet of paper with these two exercises, you could get a lot of English teaching done. It covers intonation, voice quality, linking, pronunciation, phrasing, and grammar. The only tricky part is when the students write their own sentences. To have as much linking as possible, follow the rules in Exercise 9-3.

Chapter 10: Reduced Sounds

This is part of intonation, but instead of focusing on the peaks, you'll be looking deep into those murky valleys. Students tend to over pronounce, so you have to be vigilant about not letting them get away with it. You may find yourself unsure about what "proper" speech is, but because this program is more descriptive than prescriptive, you'll need to focus on strong intonation, letting the schwas fall where they may.

Chapter 11: Word Connections

The point of this chapter is to get students away from sounding so staccato or robotic and into using the **wa-wa, nya-nya, woo-woo, bada-bada** sounds of spoken American English. The most important thing to stress is that, although students have learned to pronounce word by word, and, of course, that's how things are written, they have to regroup into sound groups rather than individual word groups. They have to listen for and hear whole phrases or they will miss the meaning. It's like when they say you can't see the forest for the trees—the students can't understand the meaning of the whole sentence because they are only listening for the meaning of each word.

They also have to stop intellectualizing every sound they hear—"[mēt]! What did that mean? Was it a noun (meat)? Was it a verb (meet)? An object? A subject?" By this time, the speaker has left the student in the conversational dust. The important thing to deal with is, of course, context. The identical sounds can be either logical or nonsensical: I'm meeting Bob or I'm eating Bob?

Have each student read the five sentences in Exercise 11-1. #3, **the D** will sound fine, but #4 will probably revert to **that he**. Bring this immediately to the students' attention and have each one concentrate on making #4 sound exactly like #3. Then, explain that certain sounds are just attracted to each other, like a magnet. There are four situations for connecting words listed just below Exercise 11-1. The first one is when a word ends in a consonant and the next one starts with a vowel—they automatically link up. Have the student read the three examples, preferably from the right-hand side.

Pronunciation

Chapter 12: Cat? Caught? Cut?

Exercise 12-3 takes a long time, but it lets students finally break through the spelling barrier of A's, O's and U's. There are 8 æ, 5 ä, more than 35 ə.

First, have students go through and ferret out the 8 æ sounds, writing the symbol over the words. It is better to do it first in pencil and then use a highlighter afterwards because any mistakes result in pink on top of blue on top of green. A student reading after each color facilitates correction because that way they are not targeting too many sounds at once. Then, look for the 5 ä words, first in pencil, then in color. Finally, ə. This takes quite a bit of time, and it's better to review them line by line, rather than trying to say all of them out.

Cat? (8)

The æ sound is relatively scarce, but is highly noticeable, and has such a distinctive sound that it is not difficult to train. It's just a combination of ä and ɛh. It sometimes helps to temporarily put in a small (y) before æ, such as **kee(y)æt** to make a huge exaggeration, which they can later relax into a regular æ. You should have them drop the jaw down (like ä) and then back (like ɛh) while pushing up the back of the tongue. Or have them say ɛh and leave the tongue in the same position while dropping the jaw.

Caught? (8)

The ä sound is easily cued to either *what you say to the doctor when he uses the tongue depressor* or the musical **lä-lä-lä**, so whenever they come to a word like **caught, thought, bought**, they can be cued with **kä-kä-kä, thä-thä-thä**, or **bä-bä-bä**, respectively. If a student is reluctant to fully pronounce this sound, have him put his hand under his chin to feel the jaw as it drops. The strong tendency will be to round the lips, because, after all, this is usually spelled with an **O**. Keep going back to the phonetics to break this habit.

Cut? (35+)

The schwa (a neutral vowel sound) is best done last since it is the most subtle and elusive of the three sounds, as well as the most common vowel sound in English. Because you eliminated the other two most likely candidates for confusion beforehand (æ and ä), the smoke screen is a little more readily penetrable. It is, in large part, due to the schwa that spelling is so difficult—the neutral vowel in **possible** and **passable** sounds identical, but needs to be spelled with appropriately different letters.

It is pronounced "uh," which is the sound that is produced when you press on your diaphragm and don't change your mouth position at all. If it's a group that has meshed well, I have them press on each other's diaphragm, so they can hear what a neutral, unforced sound it is. The point usually comes up of the difference between ə and ʌ (as in **a**bout and b**u**t) and ä and ɔ (as in **cot** and **caught**). For practical purposes, however, we will only use the first of each pair (ə and ä), the intent of the program being to get students to sound American, rather than phonetically "perfect," which, of course, Americans are not.

The schwa is the noise we make when we are thinking—**uh**, **um**—for Americans, it is an unconscious, but ever-present sound.

Read Down

After the paragraph has been completely worked for all three sounds, in order to get a flow going of a single sound, I have the students read each sound group, from 1–24 without stopping. Unless, of course, they fall back into the spelling trap and mispronounce, at which point we go back to basics with the original vowel sound, and then add on the new consonants around it. For example, ä, kä, **caught** or **uh**, k', **cut**.

Read Across

Once they can go through the entire list smoothly, basing pronunciation on the sound they know it to be from the category, rather than from what spelling would indicate, we read across the rows, incorporating all five sounds.

Random Reading

As a review, we come back to this exercise and they pick words out at random which I try to guess with no clues other than their pronunciation.

The æ, ä, ə Reading

There are three paragraphs in Exercises 12-4, 12-5, 12-6 for æ, ä, and ə, respectively. The targeted sounds are underlined to help students realize three things:

1. How many of that particular sound there are;
2. Where they are;
3. How the sound relates to spelling.

Chapter 13: Tee Aitch

If the tongue is too relaxed and protruding, not only does it not look good, it doesn't feel good or sound right. The tip of the tongue is tense and hardly protrudes as it darts quickly out and back. Contrast **th** with **s**, **z**, and **d**, using a mirror. For the voiced **th**, have a student practice on a word like **then**. Have him say **den** and then with the exact same feeling, say the **D** sound with his tongue slightly between his teeth. This should come out a good-voiced **then**.

For an unvoiced **TH**, do the same thing with **S**. Start with **sing**, move the tongue tip forward and say **thing**. They almost can't do it wrong. A good thing about highlighting all of the **th**'s is that a student can see how frequently used the sound is, thereby allowing him to realize that even that one small sound will leave him sounding accented if he neglects it. Bear in mind that, in every word count study, **the** is the most commonly used word in the English language, comprising 6% of all utterances. Hence, with this single word pronounced wrong, 6% of a student's speech is flawed.

If students have trouble with the **TH** paragraph, go to Exercise 17-2. Have them read A Surly Sargeant, replacing all of the [s]'s with [th]'s. They should sound like Daffy Duck on a good day.

When they go back to the regular **TH** paragraph, it's a lot easier. Another strange technique that works is to have students read the paragraph completely silently, but mouthing the words—and focusing on every **TH**. A mirror or a partner helps, too. Also, in Exercise 13-1, mark the 10 voiced and 2 unvoiced

[th]'s. Voiced sounds are easier than unvoiced sounds for English speakers to make, so the more common sounds tend to be voiced: *the, then, this*, etc.

Chapter 14: The American T

Beddy Ba Da Bida Bedder Budder This exercise leads students through the mysteries of what looks like a [t] but sounds like a [d], or worse yet, like nothing at all. The sound of each **T** is determined by its position on the staircase (you knew it would be—you can't escape intonation). Here are six rules of thumb.

Top of the Staircase

First, they go through and notice all of the **T**'s that are just **T**'s, which are explained in Exercise 14-3 on page 102 of the student text.

Middle of the Staircase

Then they pick out the nine **T**'s that are pronounced **D** (#4); this is easily explained using any language that uses an apical flap (trill) for an **R** (Spanish, Italian, Russian, Indian, Korean, Japanese, etc.) as what they use as the **R** sound in the various dialects. For example, if someone is having trouble with *ought*, to which Americans usually say in rapid conversation as *oughtta*, write **ara** on the board (or have them write it down, if you're on the phone) and ask them, with no coaching whatsoever, to pronounce it in their native language. Likewise with **bara**, *I bought a (bara) book*. Other pairs are: *bottom/baram; lot of/lara; ought to/ara; petal/per'l; could have/kura; caught a/kara*, etc. There are only a few exceptions to this rule: *politics, militant, crouton, futon*, etc.

Bottom of the Staircase

Last, they find the 7 **T**'s that aren't really pronounced at all, #5, #6, #7. One of the most difficult things for students to do is get used to not letting final **T**'s and **D**'s be plosive. Tell them not to pop their final consonants, just hold the tongue in position and don't let the air out. They are used to expelling the air after **T**'s, **D**'s, **P**'s, **B**'s, etc. Use matches in class and if the flame even wavers, they can see if they have gone too far. A less flammable way to test the **T** is for each student to hold his hand in front of his face to see if he can feel his breath. Remember to have them read the paragraph after each of the three selections to avoid overload.

The Held T before N

A difficult sound to produce is the **held T before an N**. The tongue goes to the **T** position, but the air is not released. Then, from the **T** position, an **N** sound is made. Not **-en**, just **nnn**. The sound rises quickly in pitch to the held **T** and then drops back down with the **N**. **Bitten** is pronounced **bi(t)n**. It is not pronounced **biTn** or **bi(t)ən**. On the other hand, the **D** sound before an **N** doesn't have the sharp pitch rise, contrasted in **written** and **ridden**. Commonly-used held-**T** words are *certain, gotten, forgotten, sentence, important*.

Silent T with N

In some commonly used words, the **T** just drops out completely since the **T** and the **N** are created so close together in the mouth (just behind the teeth). You'll hear this in *interview, advantage, percentage*, etc.

Held T with Glottal Consonants

Before a throat consonant or semi-vowels, **T** is held by the back of the tongue before W, R, K, G, Y.

Chapter 15: The American R

This is one of those high-value sounds and you are going to have to get your students to use the growly throat sound of the rhotic **R**, and not let the tongue touch any other part of the mouth, particularly the alveolar ridge. The hand trick on page 109 works really well. You can also have them put a spoon on their tongue while saying *race, berry*, and *car*. The spoon will impede the tongue tip from reaching up and forming a consonant, instead of the more liquid vowel-type sound that is the American **R**.

Chapter 16: The El

The El: A Diphthong Consonant

The **L** presents all kinds of interesting problems. It's hard to get students to appreciate what a big, round sound it is, with the back of the tongue dropped way down while the tip is firm and anchored to the top of the mouth behind the teeth. The American **L** is [ə] + **L**. Indians and Russians tend to make the **L** far too quick, but too heavy. Spanish speakers make it too quick and short. Chinese speakers just leave it off the end of words. Students need to put the **el** on the two-tone double stairstep, with the second half being əl.

Even when the **L** is silent, because it's a voiced consonant, it has the effect of lengthening the previous vowel. Here is a five-step technique that works well.

Final El

1. Have them talk without removing the tip of their tongue from the alveolar ridge.
2. Use a mirror to make sure that the bottom of the tongue is visible.
3. Hold the nose shut to make sure that the air doesn't escape through the nose, which results in an [n]-like sound.
4. Have them add a final, tiny schwa to finish off the **L** sound.
5. Connect the final **L** to a following vowel whenever possible (tell a story > te lə story).

Chapter 17: S or Z?

This is just getting used to [z]'s in **S**'s clothing. For a general rule, students can be told that the final consonant, voiced or unvoiced, of a word determines whether the plural **S** or third person singular **S** is voiced or unvoiced.

This topic is very important for Spanish speakers.

Chapter 18: More Reduced Sounds

Most students will pronounce *good*, **güd**, as **gūd** as in *smooth* (as well as *could*, *should*, *stood*, *look*, *took*, *book*, *cook*, *put*, *push*, *pull*, *wool*, etc.). In order to get rid of the pronounced lip movement in **ū**, work with **bic / bək / book** and **lick / lək / look** groups, which makes the throat work more than the lips. Read across **u / i / ü / ə / r**, feeling the difference between the first column words with strong, visible lip movement and the second and third column words with rear tongue and throat movement and almost no lip change whatsoever. **Ih** and **eeh** are usually paired as tense and lax vowels, but **ih**, **ü**, and **ə** are much closer, with just the tongue shifting back.

You'll have to explain to your students that it starts getting subjective here. Because **ü** is a soft, lax, or reduced vowel, it can very easily slip over into being a schwa. Therefore, some people may say either:

> There's a lot tü learn,
> There's a lot təlearn,

They're both correct, but a full **tū** sounds over-pronounced. It's a similar case before a vowel. To start out, it's probably better to have students make a [**ü**] and a glide before a vowel for clarity.

> ...that I'm easier tü(w)understand

When they are comfortable with the sound, the concept and their own intonation, they can later reduce it further.

> ...that I'm easier dənderstand

If you put *used to* in the middle of the sentence, it quickly reduces to *usta*. Not at the end of the sentence, however. It sounds abruptly Southern.

I ustə live in LA.
more than I used tū.

Chapter 19: "V" as in Victory

V Is just a Voiced F

Just as you repaired for the American **R**, it's a good idea to relieve students of a common misconception that **B** and **V** are related. At this point, review the pairs **f/v** and **p/b** and **w**. Indians reverse the two sounds.

For some reason, though, when pressed, students come up with an over-exaggerated **V** sound that involves biting their lips too far. I explain that native Americans don't put their teeth outside of the bottom lip, but rather draw the lip up and press the front teeth against the inside of the lip. Since most people have little difficulty with **f** (except the Japanese and Koreans), again we work from unvoiced to voiced, physically holding the lip in place against the teeth, if need be. The final surprise for them is the **v** of **of**.

Chapter 20: Tense and Lax Vowels

So far, you've been through most of the vowels with **Cæt? Cät? Cət? & How Much Wüd?**, including the tense/lax vowels **ū/ü**; **o/a/e** & **i** presented in Chapters 12 & 18.

Remember, tense vowels cause facial movement; lax vowels play up and down the throat and do not cause facial movement.

Part of the problem is that students don't double up on the sound, so when you come to any of these sounds, have the students put them on the little two-step staircase.

Chapter 21: The Ridge

This section groups all of the sounds that take place at the alveolar ridge, and it's a surprisingly large number. As you have the students contrast the sounds, they should notice that the main difference is how the air comes out: popped (ch, j, t, d); hissed or buzzed (s, z, sh, zh); or glided (n, l).

Chapter 22: Grammar in a Bigger Nutshell

This is an expansion of Chapter 9 and it's a good review for students, so they can realize how much progress they've made. They typically struggle with Chapter 9, but after going through this, when you take them back for a review, they see how easy it's become.

Chapter 23: Practical Application

This is to transition students to the real world. For some reason, they think they should stay with a textbook much longer than they really need. Explain that once they have the tools, they should start actively applying the techniques to materials that interest them, be it podcasts, audiobooks, or talk radio. They will want to use printed material, but orient them more toward audio.

Chapter 24: Nasal Consonants

Fortunately, this is an easy, self-explanatory chapter. There are three nasals—lips (m), tongue tip (n), and ng (glottal).

Chapter 25: Throaty Consonants

By the time you get here, you are reviewing sounds that have already been introduced, so like with **The Ridge**, you are getting them to focus on a particular area, while noticing vocality and air flow.

Index

CD Track Listing

CD Track Listing

Audio CD 3

1. Ex. 6-13: Description and Set Phrase Test
2. Ex. 6-14: Goldilocks
3. Phrasal Verbs
4. **Chapter 7—Phrasing**
5. Ex. 7-1: Phrasing
6. Ex. 7-2: Creating Word Groups
7. Ex. 7-3: Practicing Word Groups
8. Ex. 7-4: Punctuation & Phrasing
9. Ex. 7-5: Tag Endings
10. **Chapter 8—The Miracle Technique**
11. Ex. 8-1: Tell Me Wədäi Say
12. Ex. 8-2: Listening for Pure Sounds
13. Ex. 8-3: Extended Listening Practice
14. **Chapter 9—Grammar in a Nutshell**
15. Ex. 9-1: Noun Stress in Changing Tenses
16. Ex. 9-2: Pronoun Stress in Changing Tenses
17. Ex. 9-3: Writing Your Own Phonetics
18. Ex. 9-4: Supporting Words
19. Fixed Word Order
20. Ex. 9-5: Contrast Practice
21. Ex. 9-6: Building an Intonation Sentence
22. Ex. 9-7: Building Your Own Sentences
23. Breathing Exercises
24. **Chapter 10—Reduced Sounds**
25. Ex. 10-1: Reducing Articles
26. Reducing Sounds
27. Ex. 10-2: Reduced Sounds
28. Ex. 10-3: Intonation Pronunciation: "That"
29. Ex. 10-4: Crossing out Reduced Sounds
30. Ex. 10-5: Reading Reduced Sounds
31. **Chapter 11—Word Connections**
32. Ex. 11-1: Spelling and Pronunciation
33. Liaison Rule 1: Consonant / Vowel
34. Ex. 11-2: Word Connections
35. Ex. 11-3: Spelling and Number Connections
36. Ex. 11-4: Consonant / Vowel Practice
37. Liaison Rule 2: Consonant / Consonant
38. Ex. 11-5: Consonant / Consonant Liaisons
39. Ex. 11-6: Consonant / Consonant Liaisons
40. Ex. 11-7: Liaisons with TH Combination
41. Ex. 11-8: Consonant / Consonant Practice
42. Liaison Rule 3: Vowel / Vowel
43. Ex. 11-9: Vowel / Vowel Practice
44. Liaison Rule 4: T, D, S, or Z + Y
45. Ex. 11-10: T, D, S, or Z + Y Liaisons
46. Ex. 11-11: T, D, S, or Z + Y Liaison Practice
47. Ex. 11-12: Finding Liaisons and Glides
48. Ex. 11-13: Practicing Liaisons
49. Ex. 11-14: Additional Liaison Practice
50. Ex. 11-15: Colloquial Reductions & Liaisons
51. Spoon or Sboon?
52. **Chapter 12—Cat? Caught? Cut?**
53. Ex. 12-1: Word-by-Word and in a Sentence
54. Ex. 12-2: Finding æ, ä, and ə Sounds
55. Ex. 12-3: Vowel-Sound Differentiation
56. Ex. 12-4: The Tan Man
57. Ex. 12-5: A Lät of Läng, Hät Wälks
58. Ex. 12-6: What Must the Sun Above
59. **Chapter 13—Tee Aitch**
   Ex. 13-1: Targeting the Th Sound
60. Ex. 13-2: The Thuringian Thermometer
61. Ex. 13-3: Tongue Twisters

Audio CD 4

1. **Chapter 14—The American T**
2. Ex. 14-1: Stressed and Unstressed T
3. Ex. 14-2: Betty Bought a Bit of Better Butter
4. Ex. 14-3: Rule 1—Top of the Staircase
5. Ex. 14-4: Rule 1—Staircase Top Practice
6. Ex. 14-5: Rule 2—Middle of the Staircase
7. Ex. 14-6: Rule 3—Bottom of the Staircase
8. Ex. 14-7: Rule 4—"Held T" Before N
9. Ex. 14-8: Rule 5—The Silent T
10. Ex. 14-9: Rule 5—The Silent T
11. Ex. 14-10: Rule 6—"Held T" Before Glottals
12. Ex. 14-11: Karina's T Connections
13. Ex. 14-12: Combinations in Context
14. Ex. 14-13: Voiced & Unvoiced Sounds with T
15. Ex. 14-14: Finding American T Sounds
16. Voiced Consonants and Reduced Vowels
17. **Chapter 15—The American R**
18. Ex. 15-1: R Location Practice
19. Ex. 15-2: Double Vowel with R
20. Ex. 15-3: Pronounce Troublesome Rs
21. East Coast vs. West Coast
22. Ex. 15-4: Zbigniew's Epsilon List
23. Ex. 15-5: R Combinations
24. Ex. 15-6: The Mirror Store
25. Ex. 15-7: Finding the R Sound
26. **Chapter 16—The El**
27. L Compared with T, D, and N
28. Ex. 16-1: Sounds Comparing L with T, D, N
29. Ex. 16-2: Sounds Comparing L with T, D, N
30. What Are All Those Extra Sounds?
31. Ex. 16-3: Final El with Schwa
32. Ex. 16-4: Many Final Els
33. Ex. 16-5: Liaise the Ls
34. Ex. 16-6: Finding L Sounds
35. Ex. 16-7: Silent Ls
36. Focus on the Difficult Point
37. Ex. 16-8: Hold Your Tongue
38. Ex. 16-9: Little Lola
39. Consonant Clusters
40. Ex. 16-10: Dull versus -dle
41. Ex. 16-11: Final L Practice
42. Ex. 16-12: Thirty Little Turtles
43. Ex. 16-13: Speed-reading
44. Ex. 16-14: Tandem Reading
45. **Chapter 17—S or Z?**
46. Ex. 17-1: When S Becomes Z
47. Ex. 17-2: A Surly Sergeant
48. Ex. 17-3: Allz Well That Endz Well
49. Like with Like
50. Ex. 17-4: Voice and Unvoiced Endings
51. Ex. 17-5: Finding S and Z Sounds
52. Ex. 17-6: Application Steps with S & Z
53. Ex. 17-7: Your Own Steps with S & Z
54. Mid-Point Diagnostic Analysis
55. **Chapters 1–17—Review and Expansion**
56. Ex. 1: To have a friend, be a friend.
57. Ex. 2: To have a friend, be a friend.
58. Ex. 3: Get a Better Water Heater!
59. Ex. 4: Your Own Sentence
60. Are You Shy?
61. Ex. 5: Varying Emotions
62. Ex. 6: Really? Maybe!

Here's more expert help for students of English as a Second Language

501 English Verbs with CD-ROM, 3rd Ed.

Verbs are alphabetically arranged in table form, one per page, and conjugated in all tenses and forms. A bonus CD-ROM offers practice exercises in verb conjugation and a concise grammar review.

Paperback, ISBN 978-1-4380-7302-6, $18.99, *Can$21.99*

Handbook of Commonly Used American Idioms, 5th Ed.

This pocket-size dictionary defines approximately 2,500 American-English idiomatic words and expressions.

Paperback, ISBN 978-1-4380-0167-8, $8.99, *Can$9.99*

The Ultimate Phrasal Verb Book, 2nd Ed.

ESL and EFL students will find 400 common phrasal verbs and the ways they are used in everyday American English. Phrasal verbs are word groups that include a verb combined with a preposition or an adverb—for instance, "comedown," "breakup," and "showoff," among countless others.

Paperback, ISBN 978-0-7641-4120-1, $14.99, *Can$17.99*

Basic American Grammar and Usage
An ESL/EFL Handbook

This book explains different kinds of sentences—affirmative, negative, and interrogative, and follows up with focus on different parts of speech, describing their uses in verbal and written communication.

Paperback, ISBN 978-0-7641-3358-9, $16.99, *Can$19.99*

Painless English for Speakers of Other Languages, 2nd Ed.

This user-friendly book is especially useful for middle school and high school students in families where English is not the first language. A step-by-step approach covers all parts of speech, and is followed by advice for improving vocabulary, spelling, and American English pronunciation.

Paperback, ISBN 978-1-4380-0002-2, $9.99, *Can$11.50*

English for Foreign Language Speakers the Easy Way

Following a diagnostic pretest, the author guides students through the details of reading, writing, developing vocabulary and grammar, listening, speaking, and correct pronunciation of American style English. She devotes separate chapters to each of the parts of speech, as well as to sentence structure, punctuation, capitalization, word roots, homonyms and synonyms, idioms, rules for academic writing in English, and more.

Paperback, ISBN 978-0-7641-3736-5, $18.99, *Can$21.99*

The Ins and Outs of Prepositions, 2nd Ed.

Unlike most languages—which have relatively few prepositions to serve many different communication needs—English has dozens of them. But very few English prepositions follow a clear, consistent set of rules. This book offers practical guidelines for correct usage.

Paperback, ISBN 978-0-7641-4728-9, $12.99, *Can$14.99*

A Dictionary of American Idioms, 5th Ed.

More than 8,000 American idiomatic words and phrases are presented with definitions and sample sentences. Especially useful for ESL students, this book explains and clarifies many similes and metaphors that newcomers to American English find mystifying.

Paperback, ISBN 978-1-4380-0157-9, $16.99, *Can$19.50*

Prices subject to change without notice.

Barron's Educational Series, Inc.
250 Wireless Boulevard
Hauppauge, NY 11788
Order toll-free: 1-800-645-3476

In Canada:
Georgetown Book Warehouse
34 Armstrong Avenue
Georgetown, Ontario L7G 4R9
Canadian orders: 1-800-247-7160

Available at your local book store
or visit **www.barronseduc.com**

(#153) R4/13